THE
WOOLCRAFT
BOOK

THE WOOLCRAFT BOOK

Spinning, Dyeing and Weaving

Constance Jackson and Judith Plowman

CHARLES SCRIBNER'S SONS   NEW YORK

1 3 5 7 9 11 13 15 17 19 **I/C** 20 18 16 14 12 10 8 6 4 2

Printed in Hong Kong
Library of Congress Catalog Card Number 81-52244

ISBN 0-684-17419-7

Contents

Preface

WE LIVE AND WORK in New Zealand but have written this book for readers anywhere in the world who are beginners in the ancient handcrafts of spinning, dyeing and weaving. Craftworkers in other countries could be forgiven for gaining the impression that every New Zealand paddock is full of sheep and every New Zealand parlour full of spinning wheels. So many women (and some men) have become absorbed in spinning, weaving and woolcraft that an involvement in such crafts no longer occasions comment.

When the great revival of interest began about forty years ago, the spinners of New Zealand were virtually isolated from traditional European practices; the time-honoured equipment was not available and accurate information was hard to come by. Spinners were obliged to find their own way and, surrounded as they were by an abundance of the raw materials of their craft, they were led to re-examine ancient techniques in the light of their own circumstances, or to work in ignorance of them. This pragmatic amalgam of old and new has resulted in a very lively craft.

In writing this book we desired above all to present the reader with a reliable, comprehensive and practical course of instruction. So many of our pupils have stumbled at the same places, have asked the same questions, or have been baffled by the same mishaps, that we set out to write a book which could be used both as a self-teaching aid and as a work of reference. We have taken particular care to observe the problems encountered by the novice and to set down not only *how* to do it but also *why*, and *what* to do if something goes wrong. All crafts involve some difficulties, and we have not attempted to gloss these over.

The beginner who desires to learn the art of spinning from the pages of a book needs special consideration. In a class the teacher can ensure that essential skills are learned, but the author of a book has no control over what a reader will choose to read and learn, and what she will ignore.

Not one in a hundred spinners, in our experience, has attempted to learn to spin on a spindle; the attractions of the spinning wheel are evidently so compelling that the pupil has passed over the pages dealing with the spindle and has plunged straight into spinning on the wheel. In doing so she has failed to realise that essential information about drafting and the nature of spinning has been passed over at the same time, and that she has thus placed herself at a serious disadvantage. It is for this reason that we have taken the rather unusual step of touching on the spindle only briefly, and have related the tuition very closely to the Saxony spinning wheel.

The solo weaver also needs special consideration. If weaving is first learned on one of the small appliances, such as the frame or the inkle loom, the weaving is usually of the weft-faced or warp-faced variety, with which the method of laying in the weft and beating is different from that required for a balanced weave. Lacking the guidance of a teacher, the beginner is inclined to apply these early-acquired techniques indiscriminately to all types of weaving. In addition, matters which are perfectly obvious when demonstrated in a class can remain tantalisingly obscure to the learner who works alone. We have therefore confined the weaving section to learning to execute the basic weave structures on conventional looms, making the instructions as full and unambiguous as possible.

There are many books available on specialised aspects of weaving, and rather than cover the same well-trodden ground again we have concentrated on the use of wool, especially handspun wool.

The book deals primarily with wool because, although we have some acquaintance with other fibres, our main experience is with wool. The skills used in handling wool are fundamental to all fibres, and the craftworker who is in command of basic techniques can move on in whatever direction he or she chooses.

There are some variations in the types of fleece available from country to country, and these are covered in appendices relating to the sheep of Australia, Great Britain, the United States of America and South Africa.

Britain has a long and glorious history in the world of wool, and remains to this day Europe's most important producer. In the years of British colonial expansion, the hardy settlers who left those islands to populate the far corners of the earth took with them, as part of their survival kit, a selection of stock, including sheep. Very often these pioneers had astonishingly inaccurate expectations of their new lands, and the animals chosen were not always appropriate to the climate or geography encountered on remote shores. A period of trial and error followed, but in the long run it was the British sheep that met with triumphant success in New Zealand.

New Zealand owes a tremendous debt to the British sheep. Ninety-eight per cent of the entire flock is of British origin, and New Zealand has become, in consequence, the world's largest producer of British type wool, followed by the United Kingdom and Uruguay.

Although some of the breed names may differ, the New Zealand sheep is, therefore, irretrievably British. The differences between a New Zealand sheep and its British cousin are relatively minor, and will present no difficulty to the spinner in the British Isles. Because of the moderate climate, a New Zealand fleece is more even all over, requires less sorting and lends itself to several methods of preparation.

If, in the text, you encounter the name of an unfamiliar sheep breed, consult page 36 listing New Zealand breeds, note the characteristics and parentage given, and then refer to the British appendix for an equivalent. This appendix supplied by the British Wool Marketing Board and the National Sheep Association, lists fifty-three breeds, including Rare Breeds. The Merino is the only type mentioned in the text that does not have a British counterpart. It is not used for any of the projects, but is listed among the breeds because of its enormous commercial importance in wool-growing countries other than New Zealand and Britain.

Britain has a greater range of breeds in the 54's to 60's fineness range, and English spinners are indeed fortunate to be able to choose from such a variety. The Rare Breeds, with their subtle colouration, are viewed with envy by spinners elsewhere.

Because of the different marketing system you may not be able to buy fleece direct from the farm, and will rely instead upon the expert advice and service provided by the Wool Marketing Board. The address of the Board, and of numerous supplies of equipment and material, will also be found in the Appendix. The Wool Marketing Board produce an excellent leaflet for the guidance of the spinner listing the main types of wool and their most appropriate uses.

Spinning wheels, looms, and related items are very much the same the world over, and guidelines for buying and using them apply irrespective of brand name or country of origin. The little flick carder may be new to you, but because it is cheaper than traditional hand cards, and easier for a novice to use, you may like to try it out. Your choice of fleece, and your vision of the work in hand, will suggest the most suitable method of preparation and spinning. Each fleece has its own special qualities, and it does not matter whether the methods you choose are old or new, so long as those qualities are displayed to your satisfaction in the completed product.

We are grateful for the assistance of many individuals and organisations, including the makers of craft equipment, the Wool Department of Massey University for expert advice and information, Wiri Woolbrokers for the samples of fleece used in the photographs, the Australian Wool Corporation, the South Australian Department of Agriculture and Fisheries, the Wool Marketing Board (UK), the National Sheep Association (UK), the American Sheep Producers' Council, and the South African Wool Board.

Our thanks are also due to our many knowledgable friends in the New Zealand Spinning Weaving and Woolcrafts Society for helpful advice and discussion, and especially to Jenny Poore for her faithful support and encouragement.

C.J.
J.P.
Auckland

THE
WOOLCRAFT
BOOK

1 Spinning Wheels

BUYING A SPINNING WHEEL

THE PRESENT INTEREST IN HANDSPINNING has tempted so many woodworkers to try their hands at making spinning wheels that the would-be spinner is quite bewildered by the array from which a choice must be made. The beginner is often advised to postpone buying a spinning wheel until after learning to spin but, in most circumstances, it seems more sensible for the spinner to become accustomed to her own wheel right from the start. It should be the best that she can afford.

Although there are some very good wheels on the market the increase in quantity has, unfortunately, not always been accompanied by a similar advance in quality. How then does one make a sensible choice? A beautifully-crafted spinning wheel is a most attractive example of the woodturner's art but it is important to realise that whatever its aesthetic appeal it must also function properly or it will be of no practical use.

Listed on the following pages are some of the points to consider before a decision is made. It is a comprehensive list and it is hoped that it will be of use not only to the novice but also to anyone who may be considering buying a new spinning wheel. (The various parts of a spinning wheel are identified in fig 10 in the next section.)

Upright and Horizontal Wheels
The choice of an upright or horizontal wheel is entirely one of preference. Upright wheels occupy less floor space and are easier to pack into cars for transport to spinning meetings or classes. Horizontal wheels, on the other hand, usually have an orifice at a much more comfortable working height which makes the choice of a suitable spinning chair less difficult. In addition, they often have larger wheels which allow for faster spinning (figs 1a and 1b).

Double Band Wheels or
Wheels with a Scotch Tension Brake
A good wheel of either type will perform well and will cope with all types of spinning. For general everyday spinning or plying, a double band wheel is excellent — a spinner will enjoy the pleasantly regular rhythm between the rate of drafting and

the rate of winding on. With the Scotch tension wheel, because the spun yarn can be returned so quickly to the orifice with no further twisting taking place, fractionally more time can be allowed for drafting. Apart from the very temporary learning-to-spin stage — this action is of most benefit when bulky yarns are being spun and a large number of fibres must be handled and controlled. A well made double band wheel can usually be converted to the Scotch brake tensioning system should this be required — the reverse would rarely be true (fig 2).

Kitset or Assembled Wheels
Spinning wheels can be bought in either a kitset form (fig 3) or fully assembled. Kitset models are usually much cheaper. However, as many of these wheels have never been put together and tested for accurate fitting of essential moving parts, be careful to avoid those makes which have an habitually-bad reputation for sticking bobbins, noisy treadles, parts out of alignment, or unnecessary friction in places where they should run smoothly.

Assembled wheels naturally cost more, and you have the right to expect such wheels to function correctly, as supervision and care should have been given to their assembly. They should be a good buy, especially when they come from a small factory or workshop specialising in spinning wheels.

Spinning wheels that are only a moneymaking sideline from bigger factories depend upon the integrity of the people responsible for their production for the actual satisfaction they will give to a spinner.

Wheels produced individually by craftsmen should be a delight, *provided* the maker has studied all the necessary engineering problems, is proficient at woodwork, has all the necessary tools, and has learnt to spin so that he fully understands the spinners' requirements. However, be very wary of wheels made by the home handyman. These are frequently made from plans in magazines but have been designed by people with no knowledge of spinning and who think of their wheels more in the line of attractive working models. Their designers would be utterly astounded at the mileage we should expect to be able to put in on them.

Specific Points To Watch

Woodwork
Examine for good joints, no cracks, no knots, smooth finish, — note the quality of the finish on the bobbins.

Treadle
Test for ease of action, and whether it is heavy or light (this is most important). There should be neither too much movement nor too little. At its lowest position the treadle plate should be parallel with the floor or very slightly raised — never sloping backwards away from the spinner; and preferably it should be wide enough for two feet. Examine the pivoting system. Make sure your foot clears the platform or table on an upright wheel.

Moving parts — study these while treadling
Look for a smoothly running wheel with no wobble. Make sure the wheel is a true circle. The flyer should turn easily without jerking and there should be no unnecessary friction or noise anywhere. Study the wheel sideways as well as front on. Throw off all bands and brakes and treadle vigorously ten to twenty times. When your foot is removed the wheel should keep revolving on its own — forty times and above is excellent; above thirty is acceptable; below thirty, there is unnecessary friction somewhere. Flick the flyer. It too should revolve easily on its own. (Some allowance must be made for lack of oil in new wheels that have been standing in shops — but do not buy until you have seen them oiled and working.)

Check for alignment
The maidens and flyer must be at right angles to the drive wheel. The grooves on the bobbin and spindle pulley must be lined up with the drive wheel, otherwise the band is inclined to fall off — this alignment is adjustable in some wheels.

Orifice
A small orifice will accept only fine yarn, whereas a bigger one will accept fine, medium or bulky. An orifice of 1 cm - 1.25 cm ($\frac{3}{10}$ - $\frac{1}{2}$ in) is an acceptable size on an ordinary wheel. Take the little threading hook and try to pull some yarn through the orifice. One or two flyer designs make this simple operation infuriatingly difficult.

Flyer
There should be sufficient room between the maidens for all moving parts to run freely. The flyer arms should not be too close to the bobbin (figs 4a and 4b). (A full bobbin is barrel-shaped.) The width between the ends of the flyer arms should be about the same measurement as the length of the bobbin or a little wider. Hooks should be evenly distributed and smooth. The flyer must be balanced, so if there are hooks on one arm only, look for a balancing system — a heavier free arm etcetera (fig 5). Remove the flyer from its supports — is this an easy operation? Later test for ease of reassembly.

Bobbins
Measure the length of the bobbins. An inside measurement of 7.5 cm (3 in) is satisfactory, anything less is too small, 10 cm (4 in) is better, especially for bulkier yarn. (These measurements are for wool.) Three is the minimum number of bobbins required, but if it is to be your only spinning wheel you will need more, so enquire about extra bobbins.

Take all the bobbins being sold with the wheel and twirl them on the spindle shaft. They must revolve freely. Refuse them if they do not, for they will be useless.

Bearings
There will be bearings in the bobbins, on the maidens holding the spindle shaft, and in the drive wheel. Leather bearings are traditional and these are still acceptable, but the leather must be of good stiff quality. Many modern wheels have nylon or teflon bearings. Avoid buying a wheel with wooden bearings.

Wheel grooves
Examine the grooves on all the wheels. It is traditional for the spindle pulley to have at least two grooves. Each groove size has a purpose, and if they are not of differing diameters, the second groove is only decoration.

On double band wheels the groove in the bobbin (where the band must slip as well as drive), should be U-shaped and considerably deeper (smaller in diameter) than the spindle pulley grooves, which should be V-shaped.

A working demonstration is vital to test the efficiency of groove design and diameters. If they are incorrect the wool will not wind on, or will do so too slowly.

Reassemble the flyer
The spindle whorl is usually removable for bob-

Fig 1a. Upright spinning wheel (J. Beauchamp) ★

Fig 1b. 'Little Peggy' (J. Rappard) ★

Fig 2. 'Pipy' horizontal double band spinning wheel (Pipy Craft) ★

Fig 3. Ashford kitset spinning wheel (Ashford Handicrafts) ★

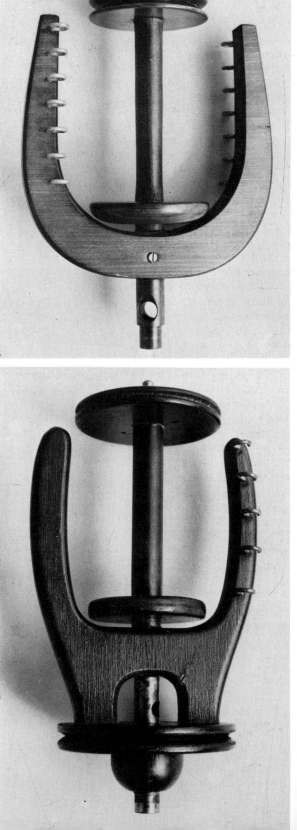

Figs 4a and 4b. Two well-designed flyers. Both have well-spaced arms which do not cramp the bobbins. The woodwork is smoothly finished and the hooks are arranged so that the bobbins will fill evenly

bin changing and, depending on the design, may be either a screw fit or a push fit. If it is a screw fit make sure that it screws back on with a left hand (anti-clockwise) thread and that it does not unscrew when the wheel is running in the opposite direction. (Take care not to screw in the wrong direction or you may strip the thread.)

If the maidens were turned aside for the removal of the flyer assembly check that they are now back in alignment, and — more important — that they will stay in position (a weak point with many wheels).

Tensioners

Turn the tensioners, and make sure that they not only move easily but will also hold well in any position. On a double band wheel there is one tensioner. On a Scotch brake wheel there are two and they must both work easily. The peg tensioning the brake is the one you will use while spinning, whereas the main tensioner on this type of wheel is set before spinning is begun. With both

Fig 5. A flyer with hooks on one arm only. The free arm is heavier so that the flyer remains balanced

types of wheel it is usual and desirable to be able to adjust the spinning tension quickly with one hand.

Extras

A threading hook is a necessity. It should have a permanent anchorage and a safety tie as well. Spikes for carrying at least two extra bobbins are a desirable feature, as are caps on the spikes to stop the bobbins falling off when the wheel is being transported (figs 6a and 6b).

Many spinning wheel makers now offer separate spindle pulleys in a variety of sizes, for spinning yarns of different thicknesses. Most are large-sized and suitable for spinning chunky wool. These are an additional attraction only if the orifice, hooks and bobbin will accommodate thick wool. (These large-sized pulleys can occasionally be a help to the elderly or disabled, for they slow down the speed of the flyer and, on a double band wheel, increase the draw-in of the spun wool on to the bobbin — thus helping to avoid over-spun wool for the not-so-nimble fingered.)

On a few wheels with the Scotch brake tensioning system, the groove in the bobbin whorl is of greater diameter than the groove in the spindle whorl and this is acceptable. One or two makers of this type of wheel offer *bobbins* with grooves of different diameters but, in doing so, they have not fully understood the object of the exercise, which is to alter the drive-ratio between the spindle pulley and the big wheel. This can only be done with different sized *spindle* pulleys.

A bobbin whorl with a larger diameter than the spindle whorl is not acceptable on a double band wheel because slippage would occur first on the smaller spindle whorl instead of on the bobbin where it is wanted.

Practical Demonstration

This may prove difficult because you will need the help of a good spinner who enjoys trying wheels other than those to which she is accustomed. However, make the effort to find someone, because you should never buy a wheel without having had a working demonstration of its capabilities. Warn your spinning demonstrator beforehand what you are going to ask her to do, as she may wish to take some prepared wool with her.

Request to have demonstrated — for at least five minutes — spinning of each of the following:

> a medium thickness yarn
> a yarn as fine as sewing thread
> a thick soft yarn
> some plying and some fancy yarns.

Do not buy a wheel if it fails any of these tests. If it does, it is not working properly and it will fail in other directions too. There are other spinning wheels on the market that will pass with flying colours. Save your money and spend it on one of these.

To sum up, never buy a wheel that:

1. Has unnecessary friction in any moving part.
2. Has bobbins that will not twirl freely on the spindle.
3. Has incorrect wheel ratios on double band wheels.
4. Has anything out of alignment.

Comfort is very important. There will be many days when you will want to spend four or five hours spinning steadily. Arms which ache from being held at too high an orifice, and ankle and leg muscles stiff from a wrong treadle action, are very different from a few minutes' vague discomfort at the time of purchase.

Take your time and choose well. Read the sections on How Your Spinning Wheel Works and Care of Your Spinning Wheel. You may then better understand some special points about spinning wheels that will help you with your final choice (fig 7 and 8).

Fig 6a. Nagy wheel (I. Nagy)★   Fig 6b. Carlisle wheel (E. A. Wildy)★   Fig 7. Princess Indian Spinner
(Both wheels in 6a and 6b carry five bobbins.)   (Sleeping Beauty Craft Products)★

Fig 8. Polywheel (Pipy Craft)★

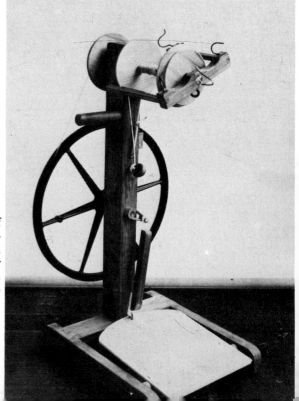

The Indian spinner is for spinning large quantities of very bulky yarn. The wheel differs from others illustrated in that it has the drive band on the bobbin and the brake on the flyer. The Polywheel is a designer wheel for spinning a variety of yarns from fine to bulky. The drive ratio can be altered and there is an attachment for production spinning

HOW A SPINNING WHEEL WORKS

For centuries all spinning was done with spindles. The spinner twirled the spindle with the fingers and as it revolved it twisted the fibres she drew out with her hand. As soon as a short length of yarn was spun the spinner had to stop and wind it around the shaft. The spindle was a useful implement that was easily transportable but the spinning process was slow (fig 9).

The spinning wheels in use today allow a yarn to be spun and wound on in one continuous process. The spinning wheel still uses a spindle but now it is supported horizontally between two posts (called the maidens). The pressure of a foot on the treadle drives the big wheel which, in turn, twirls the smaller spindle whorl by means of the drive band. Because the spindle whorl is much smaller, it will revolve several times to every single turn of the big wheel.

The front end of the spindle is a hollow tube. The yarn passes through this tube, emerges through a hole bored at right angles across the spindle, and is then transported towards the central shaft by hooks on the prongs of a wishbone-shaped fork. The spindle and fork assembly is called the flyer (figs 10a to 10f).

Fig 9. Two hand spindles

Fig 10a. Parts of a spinning wheel
1 Drive wheel
2 Leather tag
3 Cord footman
4 Treadle
5 Stock
6 Tensioner
7 Mother-of-all
8 Maiden
9 Spindle whorl
10 Bobbin and flyer
11 Drive band
12 Crank

Fig 10b. Side view of an upright wheel giving a clear view of the flyer, treadle, footman and crank

Fig 10c. A close-up view of the spinning unit on a double band wheel. The round disc and the horizontal bar above it, which together form the 'mother-of-all', support the upright 'maidens', which in turn support the flyer. The screw and slot in the centre of the horizontal bar are for moving the spinning unit backwards and forwards so that the multiple grooved spindle whorl can be lined up with the drive wheel. The tensioner slides the whole spinning unit up and down the stock to tension the drive band. The orifice and eye through which the spun wool passes can be seen at the front of the flyer — see also figs 12 and 50

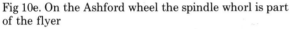

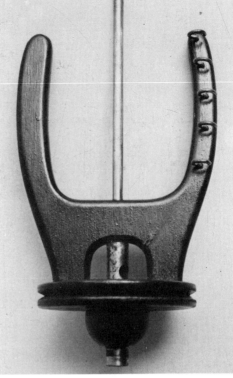

Fig 10d. Spindle and flyer, with various bobbins and spindle whorls. The bobbin which slips on to this flyer is just beside it. The whorl that screws on after the bobbin is at left centre of the photograph. The grooved end of the bobbin fits next to the grooved spindle whorl. (see fig 12)

Fig 10e. On the Ashford wheel the spindle whorl is part of the flyer

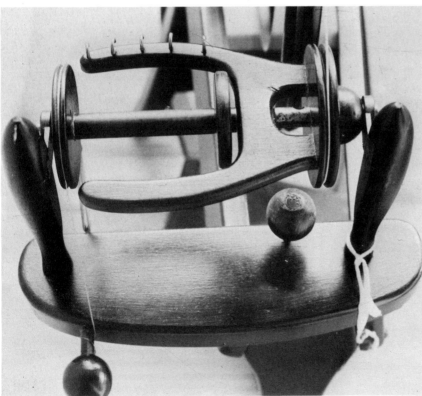

Fig 10f. The bobbin is slipped on to the spindle in the usual way, but this results in the two grooved whorls being separated. The bobbin is a little further away from the spinner, but this design makes for speedy bobbin changing

On a spinning wheel the yarn is not wound directly on to the spindle. A bobbin is slipped over the shaft. Besides holding the yarn the bobbin has yet another purpose: one end is grooved so that it will carry either a drive belt or a brake cord, and it then acts as a third wheel. Because it is either a different size (double band wheels) or braked (Scotch tension wheels) — the bobbin will revolve at a different rate from the spindle-pulley and flyer, and thus cause the yarn to be wound on.

Double Band Spinning Wheels

The term 'double band wheel' is rather a misnomer as the wheel really has one long band which has first been crossed like a figure of eight and then folded over so it looks like two bands. This band drives all three wheels (the drive wheel, the spindle whorl and the bobbin whorl), and therefore the different whorl or pulley sizes and their ratios one to another are of vital importance. The diameter of the spindle pulley determines the number of revolutions it makes to one turn of the drive wheel. The resulting ratio is one of the factors that controls the number of twists per 3 cm (1 in) that can be comfortably put in your yarn.

The diameter of the spindle pulley, relative to the diameter of the bobbin, controls the efficiency of the drawing-in and winding-on process and is another determining factor in the amount of twist in spun yarn. On a double band wheel the diameter of the bobbin whorl should always be smaller than the diameter of the spindle whorl. It follows that the bobbin will turn more *quickly* than the spindle and flyer (fig 11).

Fig 11. The flyer, bobbin and spindle whorl of a double band wheel. Compare the deep U-shaped groove in the bobbin with the shallower grooves in the spindle whorl

Scotch Tension Wheel

A Scotch tension wheel has a single drive band around the big wheel and the spindle pulley, and the ratio of these two wheels is again important. A second, completely separate cord, attached to a tension peg, runs over the bobbin and, when pressure is applied, it acts as a brake and so *retards* the speed of the bobbin (fig 12). With this type of wheel the relative size of the spindle pulley diameter to the bobbin groove diameter is not critical. However, the larger the circumference of the bobbin groove, the greater will be the surface on which the brake cord is able to exert pressure, and the less the tension that will be needed for efficient and sensitive braking.

Fig 12. Scotch brake tensioning system. The single drive band connects the drive wheel and the spindle whorl. This band is made of twisted black cotton tape and is bulky enough to touch the sides of the spindle whorl groove. Traction is excellent. A very low tension can be used, which in turn makes for easier treadling. Should the band stretch slightly and become slack, the large round knob can be loosened to slide the spinning unit further to one side.

The fine white cotton brake cord can be seen running from the peg near the front maiden, along under a small hook in line with the bobbin groove, whence it travels straight up over the bobbin, and connects by a small spring back to the hook again. Turning the brake peg tightens or slackens the pressure of the brake

The Drive Band and Brake Systems

The drive band functions slightly differently in the two spinning-wheel systems.

The Scotch tension wheel

On a wheel with Scotch tension the function of the drive band is to connect the big wheel and spindle pulley and so turn the spindle and flyer. To act efficiently the band requires maximum traction through bulk, and should fit as snugly as the grooves allow.

The Scotch brake, which controls the adjustment of the twist to the winding ratio, should be made of finer, softer cord so that the bobbin will slip when the demands of the spinner so require. Bobbins with U-shaped grooves may require a slightly heavier brake cord than would be necessary for V-shaped grooves.

The double band wheel

The double band wheel has one long band and it must be suitable not only for the driving action required but also it must allow for slippage by the bobbin. As, obviously, the band cannot be altered for its different functions, the grooves in the wheels and pulleys must be specially designed so that the one band can perform differently in the separate grooves. The spindle pulley groove should therefore be V-shaped to gain full traction and the bobbin groove should be U-shaped to allow for slippage.

The Tensioning System

The purpose of the tensioning system is to provide an adjustable control which will:

1. Keep the driving and brake band sufficiently taut to allow the different wheels and pulleys to fulfil their correct functions.
2. At the same time, it should keep the balance between the wind-on rate and the amount of twist being inserted as the bobbin fills and its core diameter increases.

The double band wheel

The double band wheel has one tensioner that moves the whole spinning unit closer to, or further away from, the driving wheel. This adjustment tightens or loosens the one long band and therefore both the traction and the wind-on rate are affected.

The Scotch tension wheel

The Scotch tension wheel has two tensioners. The first moves the spinning unit closer to or further away from the driving wheel to tighten or loosen the main driving band, and is set before spinning starts. The second takes the form of a tension peg which controls the brake band which, in turn, controls the wind-on rate to the bobbin. This peg tensioner is used during spinning.

CARE OF YOUR SPINNING WHEEL

Basically, the mechanical parts must be kept running smoothly and the other parts looked after according to their function and the materials from which they are made.

The mechanical parts which will need attention are:

1. The spindle shaft and flyer.
2. Bearings at both ends of the bobbin.
3. Bearings on the maidens holding the spindle shaft.
4. The shaft for the big wheel — fore and aft.
5. The bearings on the big wheel.
6. The footman at the top and, possibly, at the bottom.
7. Treadle hinges or pivoting pins.

Cleanliness

It is most important to keep mechanical parts clean, and free from grit and dirt, both of which will cause wear. It may also be necessary to apply a lubricant to assist smooth running and to prevent unnecessary wear. Unfortunately most lubricants attract dirt and grit, or are themselves dirty to use. Some are easier to apply than others, and some seem to suit particular squeaks and groans better than others.

Suitable Lubricants

Sewing-machine oil
Readily available, attracts dirt and is also dirty to use. Nozzle on oilcan is useful for less accessible spots.

Vaseline
Readily available, attracts dirt but is clean to handle. Transportable; can act as a cushion for worn bobbins on old wheels.

Graphite
Available from garage or hardware shop; does not attract dirt or grit but is filthy to use. Particularly good where wood runs on metal.

Lube stick
Available from garages, attracts some dirt but is reasonably clean to handle. Transportable; good where wood runs on metal.

Neatsfoot oil
Available from hardware shops. Suitable for all leatherwork.

The Spindle Shaft

The smooth and cleaner you keep the spindle shaft the better — some enthusiasts polish it with silver cleaner. Cleanliness may be all that the shaft requires, but most wheels also require a little lubricant. Clean thoroughly with soft paper towels before you reapply any lubricant.

Bobbins

At each end of the bobbin (where it touches the spindle) is a bearing. It may be leather, it may be teflon or nylon. Teflon and nylon, in theory, should not need a lubricant; in practice, a little does help sometimes. The inside of the bobbin shaft should be cleaned out regularly.

Leather Bearings

Leather bearings on the bobbins, maidens, drive wheel and footman require sufficient oil to keep them supple — too much will make them soft and soggy. New leather will need more attention than old (unless the old leather has been allowed to dry out and harden). Neatsfoot oil is the special oil for leather. Vaseline or lube stick will not do any harm if you are caught without a can of neatsfoot, but take care not to clog up your bobbins.

Woodwork

Most of your spinning wheel is made of wood and it is important it should not be allowed to warp, so keep the wheel out of hot sun and away from heaters. Dust it frequently, so it never collects a heavy coating of dirt and grit which can be scattered on to the mechanical parts.

Wood finishes

Polyurethane finish: a general cleaning should be sufficient.

Oil finish: an oil finish soaks into the wood and actually helps to prevent warping; however, it must be reapplied regularly. A new wheel will need the wood oiled about every six weeks. Later, every six months should be sufficient. Try to keep the oil away from the grooves where the band runs. Use raw linseed oil and apply with a soft cloth.

Warning: Never leave cloths containing linseed oil lying about.
They should be disposed of in an incinerator on the completion of the oiling operation. They must not on any account by wrapped in paper and put into a waste-paper basket or tin. **Linseed oil rags are self-combustible and can cause fire!**

Grooves

Every so often, examine the grooves where the belt has been travelling. It is difficult to keep the belt absolutely clean when you are changing bobbins and spinning, but the collected dirt then rubs off the belt into the grooves, particularly the groove on the spindle pulley. Clean this out with a sharp knife if the lumps are hard, but take great care to scratch gently so that the wood will not be damaged.

Flyer

The flyer is one of the first parts of the spinning wheel to show bad signs of wear and you may need to have the damage repaired professionally. If the wool catches frequently, examine the hooks and make sure they are screwed right down into the timber. If they are ordinary round hooks made of soft steel, grooves may have formed where the yarn has been carried. If this has happened the hooks will need replacing.

Depending on the shape of the flyer, the spun thread may have cut a groove at the place where the yarn travels across it from the spindle eye to the hooks. This can be most annoying if the thread being spun is not the same size as the groove. Repair work is called for, and generally it seems more satisfactory to enlarge the groove rather than to try filling it.

After any repair work on the flyer, you must test it for balance. It is not a bad idea to test it anyway, as it is not unknown for a new wheel to have an unbalanced flyer. Lift the flyer right out, remove the bobbin and spindle whorl, and rest the tips of the spindle on the rim of a cooking pot with a diameter slightly smaller than the length of the spindle. The saucepan rim and base must be absolutely even and the surface on which it is standing should be quite level. If the flyer persists in flopping in one direction it is unbalanced.

Generally, it is easier to add weight to the lighter side than it is to whittle pieces off the heavy side and run the risk of ruining both the woodwork and the shape of the flyer. If your wheel is new you would be justified in complaining to the maker, as even twisting of the wool is quite impossible if an unbalanced flyer causes the yarn to wind on in jerks.

Treadle

It is traditional for spinning wheels to have the footman tied to the treadle with leather or cord. Some adjustment can be made to this tie to suit the individual spinner. However, because there is so much movement in so many directions at this point the tie can stretch or become loose quite quickly. As it is behind the wheel the spinner does not always notice something is wrong, especially if it is a new wheel.

When re-tied, the treadle plate should be flat and parallel to the floor (or even a little above this position) when the crank is at its lowest. If the treadle plate slopes backwards it is tiring to use and will not be good for your own joints. Take care to make the tie so that the footman does not knock against the treadle plate when it is moving.

If the wooden footman breaks it can be replaced (temporarily or permanently) with a strong cord reaching from a leather tag on the crank to the hole in the treadle plate. At least one wheel on the market is manufactured in this way. The action feels slightly different, especially if you are accustomed to a wooden footman, but there is a responding springiness which can be less tiring for ageing ankle joints or for long hours of spinning. When the connecting cord is new it stretches a little and may need adjusting once or twice to keep the treadle plate in the correct position.

Driving Bands

All spinning wheels need their driving bands replaced when they wear out and break or — an often neglected point — when they become so dirty with dust or grease picked up from the wheel and the wool that they cannot function as they should.

Function of driving bands

On a double band wheel the band should be rough enough to drive well, but not so rough or hard that it will damage the wheel grooves. It must have enough bulk to fit snugly in the spindle whorl yet be fine enough to slip in the bobbin groove. On a wheel with Scotch brake tensioning, two bands are needed — a driving band, which must fit snugly in the spindle whorl, and a brake band, which can be finer and smoother.

The perfect spinning band has yet to be found. In the past, when little else was available, spinners made their own woollen bands by using tightly twisted thread which was plied by doubling it over on itself. Many spinners still prefer this woollen band, but others heartily dislike it. Some spinners use linen or seaming twine. These wear rather smooth but last well and do not stretch. However, it is this complete lack of elasticity that makes them so unsympathetic to work with.

Cotton cords are ideal but it is often difficult to find one of the right diameter, of sufficient roughness without being hard, and not so prone to stretching as to render it useless. Cotton tape 9 mm ($^3/_8$ in) or a little wider, twisted into a band, is fairly satisfactory. It is sufficiently bulky, rough yet still soft, and wears well. However, it does stretch, particularly when new, and then it must be cut, tightened and sewn again. (Boiling the tape before use helps somewhat.)

Nylon and polypropylene cords are also possibilities. They are about the right diameter and both have some degree of elasticity and roughness. Once they are run in they do not seem to stretch unduly, and they have the advantage of being able to be joined by a flame from a match, into a practically seamless band. It takes a little practice to perfect the art of joining and it is wisest to do so away from the spinning wheel.

Cut the cord cleanly with sharp scissors and turn on the cold water tap. Put the two blunt ends of the cord in the flame, holding them upright and parallel. When the ends have melted, gradually lower the cords until they are flat and butt on to each other. Hold in this position for a few seconds, then run your fingers under cold water and quickly roll the hot joint until it is smooth.

On no account use the cord on your spinning wheel if it has a hard sharp lump at the join. A little lump you may be able to melt down, but anything larger should be discarded and you must start again. The polypropylene cord is softer, and could probably be joined by sewing; however, if you can master the art of the heated joint it is quicker and easier, and also pleasant to use.

Scotch Tension Brake Cord

For the brake you will need a much finer and smoother cord. Smooth cotton cord or string is suitable. Never use nylon fishing line as it will cut into the bobbin grooves, however light the tension.

To Put on a New Drive Band
Double Band Wheel

You will need a length of cord probably somewhere between 3 - 4 metres (measure the old band). Use the tension adjuster and move the mother-of-all as close as possible to the big wheel, if you are putting on a cotton band, which is liable to stretch, or to about the halfway position if you are using nylon or polypropylene.

This one long cord will wind around the main wheel twice, passing over the spindle whorl on the first circuit (use the larger groove if you have more than one) and over the bobbin groove on the second circuit. The two ends are then joined at a comfortable but not taut tension, either by lapping them over each other and stitching, or by heat as already discussed.

When the band is put on in this way the ends should be crossed correctly before being joined. This crossing-over occurs in a position more or less below the main wheel. The band from the rear groove in the big wheel comes forward and around the bobbin whorl, and the band from the front groove in the big wheel goes back and around the spindle whorl. Make sure the portion of the band going to the bobbin whorl lies *above* the portion going to the (larger) spindle whorl — otherwise there will be continual friction on the cord at the cross (figs 13a and 13b).

The cross in this (lower) position will suit most of your spinning as the wheel is normally used clockwise. If you use the wheel anticlockwise (as in plying for example) the cross automatically transfers itself to an upper position. That is, it always comes from the big wheel and feeds toward the bobbin. Unfortunately, when the cross is in the upper position the band rubs against itself and friction occurs. You cannot make the band in a way that will suit both positions, so if you are going to spend some days spinning anticlockwise you would be wise to make a second belt. (On upright wheels the cross is to the left of the main wheel when it is used clockwise, and to the right when it is used anticlockwise.)

Scotch Tension Wheel
On a Scotch tension wheel the band is single and

Fig 13a. The drive band on a double band wheel, viewed from the front. The crossing of the band near the underside of the main wheel is difficult to see from this angle, but both loops travel quite freely around the bobbin or spindle whorl without rubbing against each other

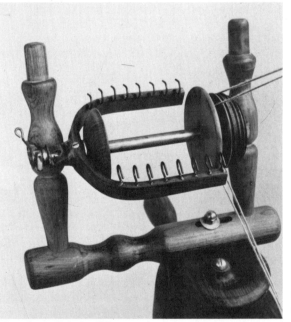

Fig 13b. A slightly different view, showing how the band passes around the bobbin whorl and the spindle whorl. The actual crossing of the band can be glimpsed in the lower right corner

passes around the drive wheel and the spindle whorl in one continuous circuit. The tension required is light. Lap or join the band as described before.

Servicing

When your wheel has had several years of hard use it may require an overhaul. Spinning wheels do not last for ever and early replacement of small worn parts can prevent larger faults developing. Servicing also allows the maker to see how his wheels are standing up to hard wear. Frequently, he will have made some improvements to his wheels over the years and similar adjustments can often be made on an earlier model during servicing.

Special Problems

Driving Bands on Double Band Wheels

On some spinning wheels (particularly antique wheels) the groove in the bobbin is not U-shaped and consequently a bulky drive band will not allow the bobbin to slip. A finer drive band will be necessary. Some traction will be lost but at least the wheel will spin.

Driving Bands on Scotch Tension Wheels

The drive band on some Scotch tension wheels may require retensioning during spinning — particularly when the bobbins are full and therefore heavier. With two wheels heavily tensioned and the third one braked, the going can be rather hard. If the grooves on the wheels are deep enough, try using a heavier drive band to get better traction without heavy tension.

Upright Wheels with Rear Maiden Tensioner

Upright wheels sometimes have a rear maiden that screws up and down for tensioning. This is a traditional way of tensioning upright wheels but it suffers from a design weakness — only the back of the flyer is raised.

The system works best with a single drive band (which seldom needs adjusting) and a separate Scotch brake.

When a double drive band is used on a wheel of this type, the amount of tension required is inclined to tip the whole flyer forward so that it becomes considerably higher at the back than at the front, and a stretched drive band will aggravate the problem. In this position not only will there be undue wear on the bearings but also it will be virtually impossible to obtain the extremes of tension required for spinning very fine or very thick wool (fig 14).

A small number of wheels have another adjuster on the front maiden to keep the flyer and bobbin at right angles to the wheel and parallel to the floor. If your wheel lacks this second adjuster, you would do better to convert it to the Scotch tensioning system and to avoid working with a stretched driving band.

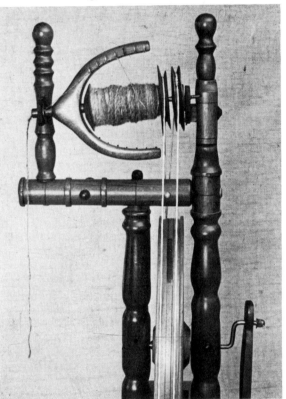

Fig 14. An upright wheel with a rear maiden that screws up and down to tension the double drive band. No adjustment of the front maiden is possible to return the flyer to its correct horizontal position. The drive band on the wheel illustrated was so badly stretched that the bobbin could barely turn. The wheel would be more satisfactory with a single drive band (which needs little or no tensioning) and a separate brake tension on the bobbin

OTHER EQUIPMENT NEEDED
FOR SPINNING

The following items are required for immediate
use:

1. A flick carder and a 30 cm (12 in) square
   of vinyl or leather. The flick carder should
   have fine teeth and a long handle (fig 15).
   or
   A dog comb (fig 16).
2. A niddy-noddy for winding and measuring
   skeins of wool (figs 17a and 17b). This job
   can be done on improvised equipment, but
   a niddy-noddy is not very expensive and
   its usefulness far outweighs the cost.
3. A lazy-Kate or bobbin rack (fig 18).

Further equipment which can be purchased as
needed:

A swift for holding skeins when ball-winding
(fig 19).
A pair of hand carders (fig 20).
A drum carder (fig 21).

This last item is not necessary for people who
spin for knitting, as the wool they use is frequently too fine for a drum carder. However, for
weavers it is a most useful piece of equipment.

Hand Carders

A pair of hand carders is the traditional equipment for preparing fleece for spinning, and for a
true woollen spin they are essential. A well-made
pair is fairly expensive, but on no account waste
money on carders of inferior quality as they are
useless.

Fig 15. Flick carder and a folded square of vinyl. Note
the long handle and fine teeth — 84 to 2.5cm^2 (1 inch
square)

Fig 16. A comb. This dog comb with its comfortable
handle is very suitable for wool combing

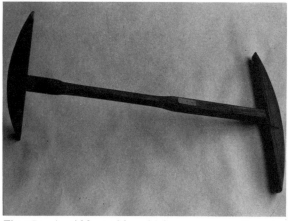

Fig 17a. A niddy-noddy which measures a 2 metre
(6-foot) skein

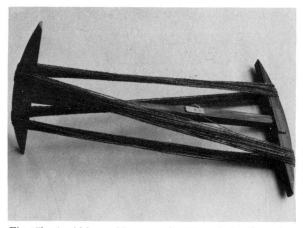

Fig 17b. A niddy-noddy wound with a skein of wool

Good carders usually have curved surfaces. Sometimes the whole wooden back of the carder is curved; sometimes only the face is curved and the back is left flat. The leather or rubber surface which covers the face is embedded with fine wire teeth, and these should be tested by running your thumb over them in the direction they are bent — they should feel quite flexible. When the palm of your hand is run over the carder the surface should feel rough, but you should not be able to feel individual hooks digging in.

The handles should be rounded and comfortable to hold. If the backing material is rubber, the carders can be washed. Thorough and careful drying is very necessary, of course. However, if the backing material is leather the carders should not be washed and they are better kept for use with washed wool. Carders should always be kept scrupulously clean. Greasy or waxy wools make them sticky and reduce their efficiency.

Traditionally, new carders are always marked 'left' and 'right'. It is a good idea to mark them on the face so that you can check that the correct one is in each hand while you are using them. The reason for this practice is that the hooks wear in a certain way and the carders may be ruined if you chop and change from hand to hand. All other such claims mentioned in this book have undergone thorough testing but, with the price of a pair of carders today, the writer, for one, is willing to bow to traditional practice!

Drum Carder

The drum carder is probably the most misunderstood piece of equipment on the market. This is not always the user's fault as one seldom finds instructions for its use issued with the implement. Properly used, the drum carder is an article that is well worth possessing, but it is rather expensive, so take care over the purchase. Carry your own prepared fleece and ask for a working demonstration of any model you are considering buying.

Here are some points to look for:

1. The two cylinders must be parallel.
2. The hooks should not be as fine as those on hand carders or it will be difficult to lift the wool off the drum.
3. Where the carding cloth is joined (on the larger cylinder) there should be a gap of about 2 cm (¾ in) free from teeth so that there is a space to push a steel skewer through to lift off the batt of wool.
4. The distance between the two cylinders should be adjustable. Usually the drums are set so that a piece of paper can be slipped between them, but sometimes, with particular fleeces, a setting fractionally closer than this (or farther apart) is more efficient.
5. The setting of the front cylinder in relation to the feeding tray is also important. This varies slightly in different makes, but generally you should not be able to get your fingers under the front cylinder. The best position is usually where the teeth are just touching, but not scraping, the tray. The feeding tray should extend right under the front cylinder, otherwise the wool can miss being picked up by the teeth and can fall through on to the debris underneath.
6. There should be full instructions for maintenance supplied with the carder showing where it needs oiling, how to adjust the controls for the correct setting, and how to take it apart for a general cleaning.
7. A steel needle should be supplied with the machine but, if it is not, a No 8 (4 mm) steel knitting needle works well.

Care of the Drum Carder

General maintenance and observance of the following rules should keep a drum carder in good running order:

1. It should be used only with washed wool. (The carder will work with greasy wool but the grease can rot the carding cloth in which the teeth are imbedded.) The wire teeth also pick up the grease and transfer a grey film back on to the wool, and this is not always easy to wash out.
2. Only thoroughly prepared wool should be used on the carder — great stout locks of unprepared fleece will create tangles which will pull the teeth out.
3. Keep a stiff little brush with the machine for cleaning the drums at the end of every carding session.

Fig 18. A lazy Kate or bobbin rack for use when plying

Fig 19. A swift which expands or contracts according to the length of the skein it is required to hold. Swifts are often made to clamp to a table, but this one has a heavy wooden base. It stands on the floor and twirls around while the skein it holds is wound into a ball.

Fig 20. Handcarders. Note the fine teeth, the curved face and the very comfortable handles. The backing in which the teeth are set is rubber — the carders can therefore be washed

Fig 21. A drum carder. The teeth are coarser and more widely spaced than on hand carders. The feeding tray runs right under the front roller so that the wool cannot drop through. The distance between the drums is adjustable.

2 The World of Wool

THE QUALITY OF HANDSPINNING depends as much on the excellence of the wool from the sheep as it does on the competence and skills of the particular spinner, but while the techniques of the spinner and the problems she will encounter are universal ones, the wool she must use will vary according to the locality in which she lives. Within the context of this book it is quite impossible to name and discuss every sheep breed throughout the world. Necessarily they have been restricted to the breeds of New Zealand with which we are familiar.

There are many complex factors which determine the number and type of sheep breed each country possesses. Climatic conditions and topographical features are always major considerations; historical and sometimes political factors have also played their part. A country's geographical situation is of great importance, particularly for places like New Zealand where the size and isolation of the country must have greatly influenced the selection of the original breeds.

Historically, the story of our sheep relates less to centuries of wars, political intrigues and motivated gifts, and more to the settlement of the country and the opening up and development of farming land. Merinos were introduced in the early days and did particularly well on the tussock grasslands of the South Island. Lincoln and English Leicester, with their stronger wools, were found to be more suitable in the North Island where the forests were freshly cleared and both rougher and wetter conditions prevailed.

The emphasis on sheep produced almost exclusively for their wool changed to more dual-purpose breeds with the advent of refrigeration and the consequent export of mutton. In the South Island, Merinos were crossed with longwool breeds to give meatier carcasses (Corriedale were established about this time) but the British breeds were more generally used in the North Island. Fat-lamb production gained in importance with expansion of the meat trade, and for this industry the sires of Down breeds were crossed with the ewe flocks of the country. As more land was opened up and developed, Romney became the established breed in the North Island, while in the South Island Merinos continued in importance, but more particularly in the high country. The fine-wool breeds, Halfbreds, Corriedale and Three-quarter breds (all of Merino-longwool origins) became predominant where conditions were suitable, with Romney used elsewhere.

As in all woolgrowing countries, breeding programmes continue to improve both the quality and the quantity of what has already proved worthwhile.

The wool section of this book opens with a chapter for the beginner, 'Choosing Your First Fleece'. No matter where you live, the principles involved are the same whatever breed of sheep the wool must come from. Romney has been mentioned as suitable but there is nothing compulsory in the suggestion. Common sense must prevail: no craft can survive, grow and flourish where stringent rules take precedence over practical considerations.

'Wool For Spinning' deals with the technical aspects of wool as understood in the wool trade. All countries have some system for classifying and grading wool which is to be sold. The standards may vary slightly and may also be changed when their usefulness has been outlived. What is a suitable system at one time becomes outmoded in another age. These particular grading standards have been included because there is much to be learnt from them when one is a spinner and a buyer of wool.

The pages on sheepbreeds relate more directly to the needs of the spinner. The breeds are grouped according to the relative similarity and end-use of the wool. This group classification is usual, but does vary from country to country according to their specific breeds as well as their numerical strengths. Many New Zealand sheepbreeds will have familiar names to spinners and weavers living elsewhere — Merino, Suffolk, Southdown, Cheviot, Romney, Leicester, Lincoln, to name but some. Others, such as Polwarth, Halfbreds, Corriedale, Perendale and Coopworth, will be better known in some places than they are in others. Mention of them should present few problems to anyone familiar with handling wool as they are all the result of crossbreeding programmes and their original parentage is fully explained.

The sheep breeds of Australia, the United Kingdom, South Africa, and the United

States of America are listed in Appendix A at the back of this book. It is hoped this information will be of use to all spinners and not only those living in the countries concerned.

Note. Where fleece breeds are mentioned in the text but are not available in your area, consult the Appendix and select the nearest equivalent.

CHOOSING YOUR FIRST FLEECE

By far the highest proportion of sheep in New Zealand are Romneys, and because of this most New Zealanders will find a Romney fleece is the one most easily obtainable for their first spinning wool.

Romney, of course, is not the only breed of sheep that has wool suitable for handspinning. It should be understood that each sheep breed has wool that is more suitable for some purposes than others. A fleece should always be chosen for the particular project for which it will be used, and when it is required for learning to spin, Romney is an excellent choice. However, whereas all Romney wool can be used by the wool trade, a much smaller proportion is suitable for the handspinner.

The following are the particular qualities your first spinning fleece should have.

The Fleece Should Be Sound (fig 22)

Wool growth is indicative of sheep health. Lack of food, the stress of lambing, sickness or shock are all factors that can contribute to a thinning of wool fibres. Prolonged animal suffering will result in wool that is 'tender' or lacking in tensile strength for much of its staple length. Sudden and/or severe stress may cause a temporary cessation of all fibre growth, and this will result in a localised weak spot called a 'break'.

Sound wool should have staples — that *ping* when held taut and flicked with the ring finger.

A tender staple will pull apart with a tearing sound which you can *hear*. A break is nearly always obvious to the eye. A general thinning of the staple can be seen and the regular pattern of the crimps will be interrupted. (Hold the staple up to the light.) Your first fleeces should be free from these faults.

(However, with experience it becomes possible to cope with some degree of tenderness. If the fleece has other special characters and can be prepared easily with a minimum of waste — as some tender fleeces can — it may not always be necessary to reject it.)

Make sure the fleece is not 'cotted' or matted. The locks should be free one from another, that is, not felted together. In a badly cotted fleece the individual staples will not pull apart at all.

The Fleece Should Be a Good Colour and Not Stained

Greasy fleece varies in colour from pale gold to dirty white, depending on the breed: when washed it will vary from deep cream to bright white. However, it can sometimes have stains that will not wash out. Some of these can be from vegetation but a common fault is canary stain, which is induced by the climatic conditions of heavy rainfall, heat and humidity. As the name suggests, the colour is quite distinct on the fleece. If you know your fleece has come from an area with this type of climate, be on the watch for this stain as it is unscourable.

The Fleece Should Be Relatively Clean

All raw fleece contains some dirt, but it should be dirt that is easily removed either by washing or in the preparation of the fleece for spinning.

Types of Dirt

Dust

All fleece has dust and dirt in the tips of the staples where it has been exposed to the environment. This is normal. However, depending on the breed of sheep or the area from which it comes, dust may well have penetrated much further into the fleece. It is usually easily removed by washing and teasing. Avoid black dust from land that has been burnt off — it isn't worth the trouble of trying to get rid of it when cleaner fleeces are available.

Vegetation

The odd seed, bit of twig, or gorse prickle is to be expected, but the fewer the better. A heavy infestation of seed can cause hours of wasted worktime, particularly if the seed has prickles or burrs which become thoroughly entangled in the wool.

Fig 22. Faults in fleece *Top, left to right*:

a. Log stain from burnt land.
b. Seeds in neck wool.
c. Moit i.e. twigs and sticks.
d. Canary stain visible in washed staples.
   Both b and c are acquired during grazing.

Lower, left to right:

f, g and h are tender wool.

f. The most miserable staple from the most miserable sheep. It is short, it is tender throughout its length, and has a localised weak spot or 'break' as well.
g. The crimp pattern is uneven throughout the staple length. The staple formation is not well defined and the wool has an obvious break.

Rimu, kahikatea and macrocarpa twigs are other forms of vegetation which should be avoided for the same reason.

Skirtings

A handspinner requires a well-skirted fleece. Skirtings should have been removed from the edge of the fleece in the wool-shed, but how well this has been done varies considerably. (Skirtings are wool which differs from the main body of the fleece — e.g. necks and pieces. They may be dirty and comparatively heavy.) Don't pay for what you can never use as a handspinner.

h. A very severe break. The upper parts of the staples are coming adrift of their own accord.
i. 'Tippy' wool.
j. A portion of a badly cotted canary-stained fleece. It was quite impossible to separate a smaller portion for the photograph.

Middle left:

e. A not-so-obvious break in an otherwise beautiful fleece. Testing proved its presence, however. An experienced spinner used this fleece — it was hand-carded and woollen spun.
   None of the fleece on the bottom line would be worth spending time on ★

The Quality Number of Count System — Fineness or Coarseness (fig 23)

Some fleeces have finer fibre than others. This is a factor which varies from breed to breed, but there can also be a big variation of fleece type within one particular breed. For instance some wool is coarse and suitable for rugs while some is fine and suitable for knitting.

When you read the pages 'Wool For Spinning', you will see that in the wool trade fleeces are systematically graded by numbers according to the relative fineness of their fibres. You can buy a fleece of a particular fineness by its number, and a

Fig 23. Two staples of wool showing crimp formation.
The staple with the finer or more closely packed crimps
comes from a fleece suitable for spinning into knitting
wool. The other staple, also from a good fleece, would
be suitable for a much bulkier or less elastic yarn,
possibly for a weaving project

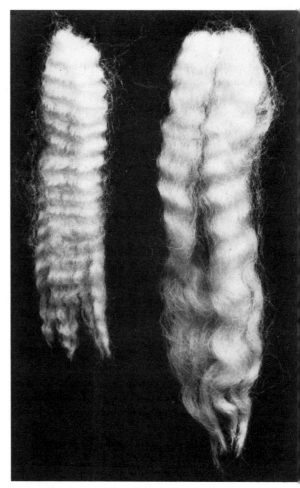

repeat order will give you a fleece of a similar
fineness or coarseness. As you become more
familiar with handling wool you will learn to tell,
with reasonable accuracy, the quality number, or
count, of any fleece.

This is not as difficult as it sounds. Generally
speaking, there is a strong relationship between
the crimps or wave patterns in the staples and the
diameters of the fibres. Fine wools have tightly
packed little waves or crimps while coarser wools
have more widely-spaced waves or crimps. Wool
sold for spinning generally ranges from 48's to 52's
and it is from within this range that you too would
be wise to select your first fleece. If you are a
knitter, buy towards the finer end of the scale — or
the 52's quality number. If you are a weaver you
can lean towards the coarser wool or the 48's. Do
not limit yourself to these quality numbers for
ever. It is, however, a good range from which to
choose wool for your first efforts.

Staple Length
A good staple length for spinning is about 10-13
cm (4-5 in). Both longer and shorter fibre can be
used, of course, but it usually requires different
spinning techniques and is more difficult for a
beginner.

Other Qualities You Should Look For
The crimps should be well defined and evenly
spaced for the whole staple length. The size of the
crimps should be reasonably consistent over the
whole fleece. A big variation points to a poorer
type fleece.

The staple tips should not be excessively long —
or 'tippy', as this fault is called. Long tips will not
have been sufficiently compacted to protect them
from over-exposure to the weather, and parts of
the staple tip may have broken away unevenly —
more still will break off during spinning
preparation.

The fleece should not be hairy or full of 'kemps'.
These fibres show up quite distinctly, particularly
in coloured fleece. (They have a different compo-
sition from a wool fibre and do not dye readily.)
Sometimes they are used as a feature, particularly

in tweeds, but you are better without them in your
first fleece.

Try to cultivate an awareness of the feel, or the
'handle' of your wool. Some fleeces will feel silky
and soft — some will feel much crisper. Some will
remain rather flat when pressed by a hand, while
others will have more 'loft' or fullness.

Choosing a Coloured Fleece
A coloured fleece should be chosen with the same,
if not even more care than a white one. The standard of coloured fleeces on the market is mer-
cifully improving but, unfortunately, in the past
much of this wool has come from people keeping
one or two pet sheep. They have little knowledge
of animal health and less of wool, but have heard
they will always get a good price for a coloured
fleece from a handspinner.

Coloured fleeces suffer from all the faults to
which the white ones are prone. Some of these
faults show up more, some are less apparent at
first glance. Test for them all. Of course you will
fall for a beautiful colour — we all do — but

remember fleece wool is comparatively expensive these days. We purchase it because we want to make use of it, not just so that we can admire its hue.

To sum up, you will require a fleece that is:
1. Sound.
2. Clean.
3. Of good colour with no unscourable stains.
4. In the 48's to 52's quality number range.
5. With a staple length of 10-13 cm (4-5 in).
6. With the staples evenly crimped and not hairy, cotted or tippy. A Romney fleece would be a suitable (but not the only) choice.

Note also that this fleece will not be the cheapest one you can buy. It may well be the most expensive. However, with a good fleece you will enjoy the many hours you spend with it, whereas with a poor one you will struggle with every staple of it until you finish it.

The quality of the products you possess at the end of all this time will reflect the care you took over the choice of your fleece in the first place.

Where To Buy a Fleece
Wool stores – especially those that select special fleeces for spinners.

Handcraft supply shops – which specialise in spinning and weaving equipment and where the proprietors are themselves spinners and weavers who will have some knowledge of your requirements.

A friendly sheepfarmer – especially if his wife is a spinner, or if you can tell him *exactly* what you want. Remember too, that some areas have better wool than others.

It is better not to buy commercially prepared wool when you first begin to spin. Learn to prepare your own wool and then you will be able to judge for yourself whether the prepared wool is a good buy. Some is reasonably good for some purposes, but some is very poor. Examine it carefully, feel it, and hold it up to the light before purchasing.

WOOL FOR SPINNING

The wool industry has a certain number of technical terms peculiar to itself. A knowledge of these terms will be of benefit to handspinners when they are dealing with trade people and making known their requirements for fleeces.

Fineness Grading
Traditionally the relative fineness of wool has always been described by a number system.

Originally the 'count' of wool was related to the spinning industry: an estimate was made of how many hanks of yarn each 560 yards long could be spun from 1 pound of raw wool. The word 'count' has remained as a manufacturing term for describing yarn.

The relative fineness of wool is described by 'quality number'. However, with improvements in science and technology there is now a trend towards quoting the average fibre diameter in microns – units of one millionth of a metre.

(In farming circles the word 'count' is still commonly used for what is really 'quality number' and here we accept the terms as being synonymous [fig 24]).

The wool most spinners use falls between 48's and 52's. It is easily spun with good soft results and the fleeces are readily available. However wool up to 56's should not be overlooked, as it is not difficult to manage and is softer still.

Higher than 56's the fibres tend to be shorter; more time, patience and skill are required for spinning, but it is from within this range that we find the Merinos and Halfbred fleeces from which are produced luxury garments possessing super softness, lightness and warmth.

Wools stronger than 48's are usually chosen for products that must withstand hard wear or when a longer stapled fleece with high lustre is required.

Style Grading
This heading refers to what would normally be understood as 'quality', but in the wool trade that word had already been used to indicate relative fineness, so the word 'style' was adopted instead.

It is the term used to differentiate between fleeces that are free from faults and those that suffer from them.

A grading system is used to indicate the

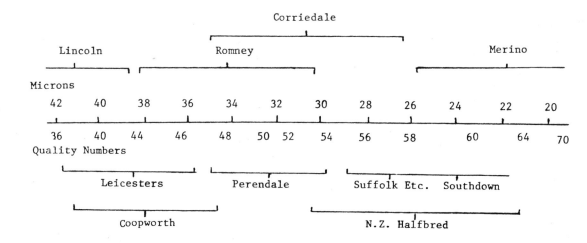

Fig 24. This chart shows the quality numbers, their micron equivalents, and where the various breeds fit on the scale

Fig 25. Style grading, indicating approximate proportion of each grade in the New Zealand clip. The proportion may vary from season to season

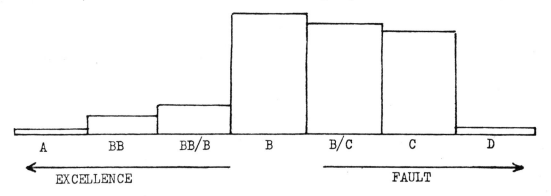

seriousness and/or number of faults — the grades are based on both a lettering and a descriptive system, either of which may be used. The letters run from A to D with, for some obscure reason, a BB (called 'double B') included. Intermediate grades are used as well, e.g. BB/B ('double B bar B') (fig 25).

Grades

A or Super

To qualify for this grade wool *must* be: of good colour, white or practically white, well grown, even in quality and length, with clearly defined staple and crimp formation. It must be sound, well skirted, free from hair; completely free of seed or moit.

'A' style wools are perfect, or nearly perfect, and the only allowable faults are those slight enough to be of no economic importance and which are removed in normal processing e.g. very light dust in tips.

BB Good to Super

To qualify for this grade wool *must* be: of good colour (allowing for medium natural grease and/or a little dust), well grown, even in quality and length, with well defined staple and crimp, that is, good character. It must also be well skirted, free from hair, free, or practically free, from seed. There may be slight tenderness.

BB/B Good

This wool falls just short of BB style. It is of good colour but lacking in character. It is well bred but too dusty or heavy in condition to be styled BB.

Colour and character are suitable for BB style but the wool is a little too tender.

B Good to Average

This wool lack points of excellence — but has no serious faults. The wool should be: of fair to good colour, skirted, and free from hair. It may be tender, plain, slightly cotty, and contain slight seed but must have no unscourable stains.

B/C

For wools that fall short of B style. The wools may be of a good colour but are either unskirted, or poorly skirted, or dusty enough to conceal some possible stain. They may be of reasonable colour but contain some hair, or, mainly a good colour but with some permanent stains.

C Average

Quite faulty wools. They *must* be at least fair in colour but may be unskirted, tender or contain break; seedy, hairy, somewhat cotty, quite dusty or stained.

D Inferior

Very inferior — poor colour, heavily stained, very seedy and showing any other faults found in wool.

The grade probably used most generally by handspinners would be BB/B because of its availability. It is sound enough and of sufficiently good colour for a top-grade product.

Grades A, BB or BB/B all indicate suitable spinning wool. However, with careful selection some suitable fleeces could also be found in B grade or even B/C although they would contain more waste. C grade fleeces are frequently stained and their suitability for spinning would depend upon the project for which they were intended.

Yield

Yield is the term used to describe the weight of clean usable wool that can be expected from a fleece after it has been scoured.

All fleeces carry extraneous matter such as grease, dust and dirt. This waste has weight, and too much of it in the fleece can mean a poor buy. A fleece with a yield of 80 per cent would lose 20 per cent of its weight when cleaned, but a fleece with a yield of 60 per cent would lose 40 per cent of its weight. This is naturally of concern not only to spinners but to the whole wool trade, so much so that wool prices have always been based on clean fleece.

A fleece with a poor yield is not only poor value for money but can also be difficult to handle. Excess grease can not only be very sticky but may also be hiding stain.

For handspinning you require medium to high yield wool. Wool style-graded as above B grade would automatically be in this category.

Some Further Wool Terms

Lambs Wool
Fleece from a lamb shorn at six months old or less. It falls apart in individual staples rather than holding together as a fleece. The staples have a characteristic small curly tip.

Shorn Hogget Fleece
The fleece from a young sheep shorn at about fifteen months of age and previously shorn as a lamb. Usually the most attractive fleece the animal will produce.

Woolly Hogget Fleece
The fleece from a hogget that was not shorn as a lamb. Usually about fifteen months' growth and therefore it is very long and still has the lamb's tip.

Mature Fleece
The fleece from a mature sheep (two years and older).

Full Fleece
Twelve months' growth of wool.

Early Shear
Spring shear — about six months' growth of wool.

Second Shear
Autumn shear — about six months' growth of wool.

Pre-lamb Shear
Twelve months' wool. Shorn before lambing. This may be any time between early winter and spring, depending on locality and management practices.

Strong
Coarse i.e. thick-fibred (do not confuse with 'sound').

Fine
Relatively thin fibred (opposite of 'strong').

Kemps
Brittle hairy fibres — short and straight. They are invariably shed after growing a short time.

Sound

Wool of sufficient tensile strength throughout its length. Wools which are tender or show a break can be referred to as 'unsound'.

Tender

Wool deficient in tensile strength for much of its length.

Break

A localised weak place in the staple due to the sudden thinning of fibres and invariably caused by severe stress to the sheep e.g. lambing-break.

Stylish

Evenly grown — well charactered (crimped).

Plain

Straight-fibred wool — lacking the crimp which is characteristic of the breed concerned.

Blocky

Indicates evenness of fibre diameter and length in staple — opposite of tippy.

Tippy

Wool with a superabundance of tip. Usually indicates a large variation in both fibre length and diameter in the staple.

Mushy

Wool which is dry, open, lacking character, and will give much waste when combed, e.g. back wool which has been badly weathered.

Webby

Usually poorly grown wool deficient in tensile strength and in the early stage of cotting.

Cotty or Cotted

A fleece in poor condition which has shed fibres into itself which, with moisture and movement, have become matted and felted.

Stain

An unscourable stain which lowers the value of the wool. Stains can be caused by management practices and/or nature e.g. drenching stain, log stain, canary stain.

Moit

Refers to foreign vegetable matter present in wool other than burr or seed, e.g. twigs, hay, leaves etc.

Seed

Seeds and burrs which have become firmly attached to wool by means of barbs or hooks (bidi-bidi, clover burr, horehound). Removal is difficult and expensive.

Yolk or Grease

A combination of wool wax and suint. It is scourable.

Wool Wax

A product of the sebaceous or fat gland. It protects the skin and the wool fibres. Merinos and fine-wool breeds produce far more wax than long-wool breeds. (Lanoline is purified wax.)

Suint

A product of the sweat glands which is cold-water soluble. It also contains some yellow colouring matter. It is hygroscopic and is responsible for the tacky feeling a greasy fleece has in humid weather. Long-wool breeds produce more suint than the fine-wool breeds.

SHEEP BREEDS

The wool from New Zealand sheep breeds can be classified into three groups:
    Fine wools.
    Down wools.
    Crossbred wools (Longwools).
Both genetic and environmental factors contribute to the physical characteristics which distinguish one group from another. The end-use of the wool from any breed depends more on its placement within this group classification than it does on the specific characteristics of each individual breed.

This is a point worth bearing in mind when ordering fleeces from wool stores. There is a limit to the number of top quality fleeces, and demand can exceed supply, particularly in those breeds that are numerically small. You could be offered better spinning wool if, instead of insisting on a

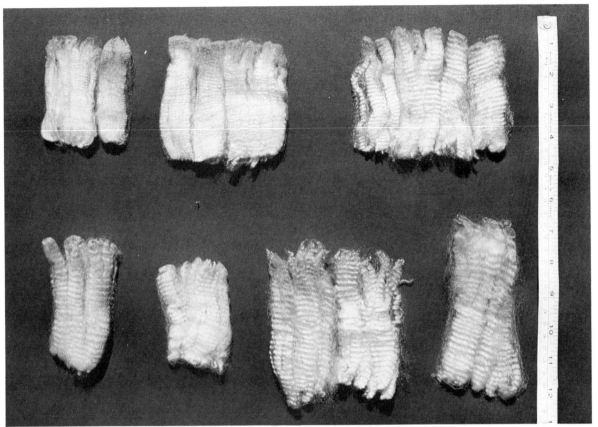

Fig 26. Fine wools
Top, left to right:
a and b Merino (a is finer than b).
c. Polwarth

Lower, left to right:
d. Corriedale.
e, f, and g. Halfbred wools (e has been washed) ★

specific breed, you asked simply for a Fine, Down, or Crossbred fleece — giving other relevant details so that it could meet all your requirements.

Fine Wools (fig 26)

These wools come from sheep that are bred primarily for their wool. They include wool from the high-country Merino as well as from the hill-country breeds.

These fine bright wools are extremely soft. The fleeces are densely packed with firm staples that are well crimped but with a characteristic waxiness and a tendency towards dusty tips. Because of this the fleece may need washing before it is spun, although sometimes warmth will soften the wax sufficiently. The spinner's ability should be better than average to make the most of the special qualities these wools possess.

Uses

Finest and softest wearing apparel — both knitted and woven, and fine worsteds. Also for evening-wear stoles, shawls, lace weaves and baby wear.

Merino is more suitable for top fashion, luxury garments òr articles that do not need constant washing. For example — heirloom baby shawls rather than everyday baby-wear.

Fine-Wool Breeds

Merino

Quality No: 60's to 70's, occasionally as fine as 90's (average 64's-70's). Staple length: 5-10 cm (2-4 in). A very soft bright wool. The waxy staple is firm with a blunt tip which is inclined to be dusty. A good fleece should not be too waxy and greasy and not too hard. It seems to demand being spun very finely and requires more twist than one would expect — even for a fine thread. It has a tendency to shrink when washed.

Polwarth (stabilised cross of ¾ Merino and ¼ Lincoln)

Quality No: 58's to 64's (average 60's). Staple length: 7.5-12.5 cm (3-5 in).
Polwarth has a good staple length for its fineness. It is soft and bright but silkier and creamier than

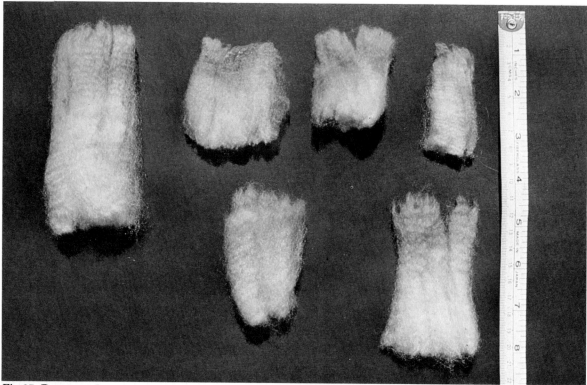

Fig 27. Down wools
Top, left to right:
a. Suffolk
b. Southdown
c. South Hampshire.

d. Dorset Horn
Lower, left to right:
e. Polled Dorset.
f. Cheviot (a Down type). ★

Merino and is a free-flowing fleece which is easier to prepare. It also requires careful laundering.

NZ Halfbred (cross between a Merino and a long-wool breed)

Quality No: 54's to 60's. Staple length: 7.5-12.5 cm (3-5 in) (woolly hoggets longer).

The staple length is longer than that of Merino and the wool is creamier but still very soft and bright. It is easier to spin, as the staples are free and it does not contain as much wax. However, it requires spinning finely as the finished thread puffs up and expands more than one would expect.

Corriedale (stabilised cross between Merino and Lincoln or English Leicester)

Quality No: 50's to 58's (average 52's to 54's). Staple length: 10-12.5 cm (4-5 in). Woolly Hogget 12.5-17 cm (5-7 in).

Corriedale has an intermediate length staple which is characterised by its rectangular shape and blunt tip. There is some character variation between fleeces. It is creamier than Merino and is

useful for a fine wool when little lustre is required.

Down Wools (fig 27)

These wools come from sheep bred mainly for meat although traditionally their wool has always been regarded as high quality hosiery wool.

The fleeces are spongy and full handling. The fibres have a crispness although the degree of this varies and the wool has a flat chalky appearance as opposed to the lustre of some other breeds. The normal staple length is rather short, but woolly hogget, if obtainable, is longer. Staple crimp is seldom apparent, but individual fibres are crimped.

Uses

These wools are too often overlooked by spinners because of the shortness of staple, but they are ideal for spinning a true woollen yarn.

Down wools are used for springy knitwear with excellent shape retention. They give soft full yarns for soft full fabrics that are light but warm. They are also suitable for travel rugs, blankets, woollen cloth etc.

Fig 28. Crossbred Wools
Top, left to right:
a and b. Perendale.
c and d. fine Romney.
e. medium Romney
f and g. strong Romney.

Lower, left to right:
h and i. Coopworth.
j. Border Leicester.
k. English Leicester — an unusually short staple but enough to show the very pronounced crimp and flatter staple formation than in the Border Leicester.
l. Drysdale (six months' growth) used in the carpet industry ★

Down Breeds

Southdown
Quality No: 58's to 64's. Staple 2.5-6.5 cm (1-2½ in). Free of black kemps.

Suffolk
Shropshire
Dorset Down
Hampshire
Quality No: 54's to 58's. Staple 6.5-9 cm (2½-3½ in.). Some black kemps.

Ryeland
Dorset Horn
Quality No: 54's to 58's.
Staple 7.5-12.5 cm (3-5 in). No black kemps.

Cheviot
Quality No: 50's to 56's. Staple length 7.5-12.5 cm (3-5 in). White kemps.

While Cheviot is not strictly a Down breed it has a Down type wool. It has been used traditionally for high class tweeds.

Crossbred or Longwools (fig 28)
These wools come from sheep that are bred for both their meat and their wool. In the New Zealand wool trade they are commonly referred to as 'Crossbreds'.

Their fleeces are long-stapled, lustrous and have wavy crimps. Some variations occur between the different breeds and, particularly in Romney, there is wide variation within the breed. They should require little preparation, are easy to spin, and the fleeces are readily available.

However, remembering that these sheep are bred for a dual purpose, this availability can be a mixed blessing. Some of the districts in which the sheep are bred are not the good wool-growing areas but are the very places where unscourable stains and other faults are most likely to develop because of climatic conditions. Spinners in these areas must be very selective when choosing their fleeces.

Uses

Crossbred wools are mostly used for products that must stand up to hard wear. However, as their quality numbers suggest, Romney and Perendale both have wool suitable for a much wider range of goods. Romney hogget is probably the favourite spinning wool of many spinners. It is excellent for all knitwear, whether for babies or adults. Perendale has better fulling qualities for woollen cloth but it is also good for knitwear and is lighter in weight than Romney. Stronger Crossbreds are excellent for hardwearing outdoor garments, upholstery materials, floor rugs and wall hangings.

Crossbred or Longwool Breeds

Perendale (a stabilised cross of Romney and Cheviot)

Quality No: 48's to 54's. Staple length 10-15 cm (4-6 in).

A low-lustre springy wool. It is not as silky as other Crossbred wools and is therefore more manageable for beginner spinners. There is some variation in fleeces within the breed and also within individual fleeces. A good fleece should have no kemps.

Romney

Quality No: 44's to 52's. Staple length: 12.5-17.5 cm (5-7 in). Hogget: 10-15 cm (4-6 in). Woolly hogget: up to 25cm (10 in).

Romney is the general-purpose sheep of New Zealand — roughly two thirds of the sheep population belongs to this breed. The wool is lustrous, often silky, with an even wavy crimp and is cream in colour. It has little fulling character. It is easy to spin, requiring only minimum preparation. (There must be many New Zealand spinners who have never spun wool from any other breed.) Fine and lighter hogget wool is used for fine knitwear and weaving, medium Romney for bulkier spinning wools and articles, and strong Romney Crossbreds for floor rugs, upholstery and wallhangings.

Coopworth (stabilised cross of Romney and Border Leicester)

Quality No: 40's to 48's. Staple length 12.5-15 cm (5-6 in).

A fairly lustrous silky wool — intermediate between Romney and Border Leicester. It is suitable for medium to bulky yarn.

Border Leicester

Quality No: 40's to 48's. Staple length 15-20 cm (6-8 in).

A butter-coloured silky fleece with a very high sheen. It has free, loose, independent staples with a corkscrew curl at the tip. It fluffs like mohair rather than pilling or matting. A bulkier spin enhances the best characteristics of this breed.

English Leicester

Quality No: 36's to 44's. Staple length 15-20 cm (6-8 in).

A fairly rare sheep with highly lustrous, silky, but coarse wool.

Lincoln

Quality No: 36's and coarser. Staple length 18-25 cm (7-10 in).

A rare, coarse-woolled sheep. The fleece is long stapled and lustrous. The staple has a compressed crimp pattern with a large curl at the tip.

SORTING A FLEECE

Put a protective covering on the floor and spread out the whole fleece with the tips upward, and the cut ends to the floor. Examine it carefully and notice how the wool grows in staples, or bundles of fibres tapering to one tip. Note also that these staples are arranged in rows. When dividing the fleece for sorting, washing or spinning, make use of nature's dividing lines to avoid wastage from tangled fibres.

Press one side of the division flat with your free hand.

Select the wool you want to pull, grasp it firmly in the middle of the staples and then pull away sharply.

Discard any skirtings which have not already been removed.

Make a separate pile of any sound but coarse wool that is out of character with the rest of the fleece. (This can often be washed and used for other projects, such as stuffing cushions, etc.).

Remove any other wool that is not worthy of having spinning time spent on it, such as very short pieces from second cuts, or parts thick with seed.

Now separate the main part of the fleece into bundles of 250-500 g (½lb-1lb) for washing, or into bundles of two or three staples for spinning.

A coloured fleece which has wide variations in colour is often more useful if, at this stage, it is sorted into colour batches.

Whether you wish to spin your fleece in the grease, or wash it before it is spun, will determine your next step.

Fig 29. Sorting a fleece. Discard any dirty or otherwise unusable wool from around the edges. A really good fleece from a wellbred sheep seldom requires much sorting into different grades. However, the diagram should make it plain where the trouble spots are most likely to occur. The back of a sheep is always exposed to the weather, be it wind, sun or rain, so watch for dry, brittle or tender wool. The throat, neck, and head come in contact with seed and other forms of vegetation while the sheep is grazing and feeding. The lowest parts of the animal are nearest to wet pastures, mud and dirt. Rump or britch wool can be flattened, and, in some breeds, hairy. The best wool is most likely to come from the shoulder, followed by the upper sides

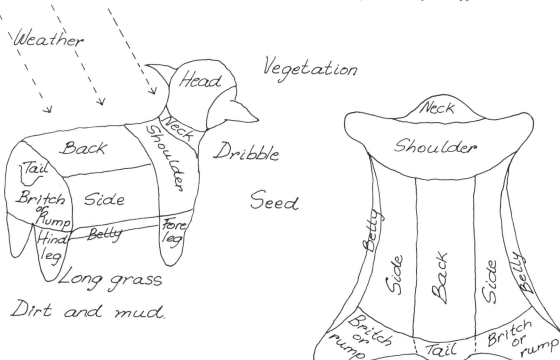

3 Washing and Storing Wool

TO WASH OR NOT TO WASH – BEFORE SPINNING

COMPETENT SPINNERS can produce superb hand-spun yarn from good fleeces whether the fleeces are still in the grease, or have been washed and re-oiled, or have been washed only. The results of spinning competitions bear this out.

In many countries it is traditional for wool to be washed before it is spun, partly for reasons of hygiene, but also because stock are often wintered in confined quarters (even indoors in some countries) and in this environment their coats naturally become matted with dirt and impregnated with seed.

Spinners who enjoy spinning greasy wool will know full well the feel of a freshly shorn fleece between their fingers; warm greasy fibres, free-flowing, and in need of only the minimum of preparation, seem to move in harmony with the hands. Greasy fleece will usually stay in this spinnable condition for at least a year, sometimes longer, depending on how well the wool has been stored. Often a little warmth from the sun or the fire at preparation time is all that is needed to bring it back to life.

Many spinning publications insist that it is much easier to wash dirt from fleece before it is twisted into thread; but when a good fleece has been used, washing and drying two or three greasy skeins of yarn cannot be compared with the slog of washing pound after pound of raw wool.

Nevertheless, even relatively clean wool is sometimes better washed before it is spun. Odd individual fleeces seem more manageable and, of course, fleece that has been stored for a long time will be usable only after the grease, that has set hard, has been removed. Fleece that is to be dyed must be washed, and so too should fleece that is to be drum carded. When hand carders are to be used for preparing the wool, the necessity for scouring the fleece should, in theory, depend upon whether the hand carders themselves can be washed; but in practice it will be found that many greasy wools so reduce the efficiency of carders that it is better to card scoured wool.

Only some fleeces can be spun in the grease, but all fleeces can be spun washed. A gentle washing with soap removes the most objectionable smells but still leaves sufficient grease to make spinning a pleasure. Heavier washing with detergent or soda could mean the fleece will require re-oiling – though not necessarily so.

It is usually easier to wash and dry fleece wool in the warm summer months. It is a slow, time-consuming job, but once the task is completed the fleece is ready for immediate use, be it drum carding, dyeing or spinning. Any moth eggs will have been drowned, and with the dirt and smell removed there will be little problem with storage. White fleeces seem to stay whiter if they are stored clean.

Surprisingly, the wastage during spinning is about the same whether the spinner uses greasy or washed wool – the exception being handcarded greasy wool, for which both preparation and spinning waste are higher. Spinning-time is always shortened by any form of preparation, and this includes washing. It is nearly always easier to control yarn regularity with clean wool, as most greasy fleeces have a certain amount of stickiness – some worse than others – and some parts of the fleece are more tiresome than others. Stopping to pick at these parts of the fleece does not make for good continuity while spinning.

Selling Greasy Wool

Nearly every spinner at some time gets a request for greasy knitting wool to make garments for trampers, mountaineers or sailors. Spun greasy wool does not mean wool with the urine, dags and their associated smell still in the fleece: to sell wool like this would be inconsiderate and thoughtless. A cold water rinse, then a cool wash with the minimum amount of soap, will not only remove all the offensive matter but will also make the wool softer and much more comfortable to wear. Enough grease will be left in the wool to keep any sailor happy!

WASHING AND DRYING WOOL

Beware And Take Care:

Too much soap causes the wool to felt.

Hot water and movement, combined, cause wool to felt.

Swiftly running hot or cold water also causes felting.

Wool needs time and room to absorb water thoroughly.

Wool should not be allowed to support its own weight when saturated. When its properties of elasticity are abused, it can stretch to the point of no return.

So:

Limit the amount of wool you try to wash at one time.

Be sparing with the soap.

Keep the temperature of the washing and rinsing waters as even as possible.

Run the taps into an empty bucket.

Put the wool in the water when the temperature has been adjusted and when the taps are firmly turned off.

Refrain from stirring and churning the wool while it is wet.

Accept that time and gentle soaking will remove the dirt.

Support the wool between rinses in a colander or some other utensil that will allow it to drain.

Drying

All wool must be thoroughly dry before it is stored, whether it is fleece or spun yarn. Damp wool attracts mould and bacteria which may discolour it.

STANDARD WASH FOR FLEECE

Restrict the amount you try to wash at one time to about 250-500 g (½lb to 1lb) unless you have special facilities that can cope with larger quantities.

Dissolve a small amount of pure soap or Lux flakes in hot water, then cool the bath with cold water until it is pleasantly warm.

Immerse the wool and give it a short initial soak for about two hours.

Remove the wool and drain for ten to twenty minutes.

Rinse in lukewarm water twice.

Prepare a second warm soapy bath but this time give a long soak — overnight if possible.

Rinse thoroughly three or four times or until every trace of soap has been removed.

Drain for about twenty minutes.

Put the wool in a thin cotton bag and spin-dry in the washing machine. Spin-drying does not harm the wool. By removing the excess water it makes drying quicker, which in turn, keeps the wool softer.

Dry the wool thoroughly in the open air in a gentle draught.

Note. Many spinners prefer to give the fleece an initial soak in cold water. This may be a good idea, especially with some white fleece. Try it if you

wish, then proceed as directed above.)

Practical Tips

Rinsing and draining

A plastic colander with flanges that will sit astride a bucket is ideal for rinsing and draining. It is also possible to buy plastic seed trays which fit modern washtubs. They can be used lengthwise on the bottom for washing, then lifted and placed across the tub for draining.

Protecting your plumbing

The plughole needs some protection to prevent bits of wool from blocking the drainage system. Strainers to fit are hard to find, but an old plug-chain coiled in the plug hole makes a good substitute. If the normal plug will not fit on top of this, use the broad flat type that sits on top of the hole and is kept in place by the weight of the water.

Drying

A wire netting rack or hammock, which allows air to circulate right through the fleece, is ideal for drying. During inclement weather caravan drying-racks are also useful. These can be slung from doors or windows, under the eaves, or from cup hooks on an inside wall. With a space heater or stove and a caravan-rack to hang above it, wool can be washed and dried the whole year round.

A tumbler dryer is not suitable for drying wool. The heat and movement combined cause felting.

Soaps

In areas with good water, pure soap leaves the wool softest. Wool that is to be dyed (particularly plant-dyed) will require every trace of grease removed. Washing soda is the traditional additive for difficult dirt and grease, but limit the amount you use — 15 ml (1 tbsp) in a 9-litre (2-gal) bucket of soapy water is plenty.

In areas with hard water you have a choice between adding a water softener or using a detergent. Detergents certainly remove every trace of grease, but they make the wool feel very dry.

WASHING MERINO, HALFBRED, OR OTHER WAXY WOOLS

Washing soda is a commodity that is not always on the shelves of modern homes, but it is very necessary for removing the wax in these wools as neither soaps nor detergents alone do the job efficiently. Use as directed above. A little vinegar can be added to one of the rinsing waters to counteract the alkalinity of the soda, if desired.

If Merino wools are being washed as fleece, take bundles of staples and secure them loosely with ties (otherwise the fleece wool is inclined to lose its form and fluff up like cotton wool). As an added precaution place the bundles of staples in a mesh bag while they are washed.

WASHING SPUN WOOL

All skeins of wool ready for washing should be secured at regular intervals with ties, to prevent tangling. Four ties are desirable in a 2-metre skein and they should be loosely made so that the soapy water can penetrate the wool beneath them (fig. 30).

Skeins of spun plied greasy wool

Wash as for fleece. However, if there are only one or two skeins they may not need soaking for quite so long.

If the skeins of wool are to be used for knitting they should be subjected to one of the pre-shrink softening processes (described later in this chapter) before they are spun-dried.

Then hold the skeins at one end and give them a vigorous swish before tying them to the clothes-line with individual tapes. Turn them from time to time while they are drying, and give them a shake — this should be sufficient to keep the threads free.

However, if the threads have a bad tendency to cling to each other, remove the skein from the line

Fig 30. A skein with ties at regular intervals, ready for washing

before it is quite dry — put your hands through it (as if you were holding it for winding) and pull your arms apart quite sharply two or three times.

To retain the smooth appearance associated

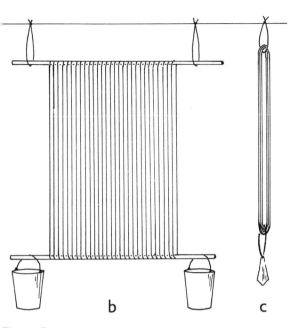

Fig 31. Drying skeins of wool
From left to right:
a. A woollen spun skein of knitting wool, without weights.
b. Spun singles wound evenly on two parallel rods. The top rod is tied to the clothes line and the bottom rod is weighted to keep the wool taut.
c. A skein of worsted knitting wool tied with a tape to the line and weighted at the bottom

with worsted yarn it is usual to weight the lower ends of the skeins while they are drying. Care should be taken not to overweight them or the wool may be over-stretched.

Skeins of woollen spun yarn are better not weighted.

Skeins of spun singles
Wash by soaking as for fleece. However, when drying time comes, a slightly different treatment is required. Spread the threads out evenly around two parallel rods — one at the top and one at the bottom. Be careful to keep the threads from piling one on top of the other, as this can cause them to dry at an uneven tension (fig 31). Tie the top rod to the line and weight the bottom rod at each end. (Fishing sinkers or plastic buckets with water in them make suitable weights, but make sure they are balanced.) If singles are not dried under tension they curl into kinks when dry and are impossibly difficulty to deal with.

Be careful not to overstretch the skeins — experience alone can guide you. Firmly-spun singles for warps can stand considerably more tension than plump, thick, softly spun, or textured weft threads.

Skeins spun from pre-washed fleece
It is just as important for these skeins to be washed as it is for those spun from unwashed fleece. A light wash should set the twist and remove any signs of grubbiness. Soak for half an hour in warm soapy water and rinse well. If the wool was oiled, a second soak may be required.

PRE-SHRINK AND SOFTENING PROCESSES FOR KNITTING WOOL

Most of us like to give one further treatment to our knitting wool before putting it to use. A little harsh treatment at this stage will later make for garments that will not only wear well but will also keep their shape. There are two favourite processes and, as with most things in spinning, both have their adherents. Both are good — but stick to one method for each separate project.

Process I
Fill a tub with really cold water and fill a bucket with the hottest possible water straight from the tap. Dip the wet skeins into the hot water and leave there for a few minutes until they have thoroughly absorbed the heat. Scoop them out and drop them straight into the icy cold water. They will gasp with indignation at this treatment and puff up in protest. This is exactly why we use it!

Process II
Put the clean skeins of wool into a pot of cold water and bring them very slowly just to boiling point then simmer for only a few minutes. This process, although less dramatic, also encourages the spun fibres to swell. It is a particularly useful treatment for wool which has been spun from a

fleece that has been kept for a long time, un-washed. Sometimes the yolk has set hard and is not quite removed by ordinary washing. The spun wool feels hard to handle. This treatment softens it beautifully.

When the wool has dried thoroughly it may be used immediately or put into storage. Either way, it is wise to get into the habit of re-winding the skeins on a niddy-noddy to measure their length, then weighing them, and recording the results on tags attached to the skeins. Variations occur between breeds, but loss of length and weight after washing can be fairly dramatic, especially if the wool was spun in the grease. Calculations for any project are useless unless measurements of length and weight are accurate.

STORING FLEECE

Stored wool needs protection from moths, and by far the easiest way to store it is to keep it in un-bleached calico bags. One metre makes a good-sized, general-purpose bag that will store both small and large fleeces without compressing them. Tie tape tightly around the neck of the bag — white tape for white wool, black tape for coloured. Attach a luggage label to the tape with all the particulars of the fleece, including the date and place of purchase.

Keep wool away from cardboard cartons and paper bags — they have too many crevices, and moths seem to take a perverse delight in proving that such containers are not impregnable. Boxes can be sealed — but what a performance when you want to select a fleece for a special project! Plastic bags are bad for the wool as it sweats inside them — anyway, no keen moth was ever deterred by the taste of a bit of plastic (fig 32).

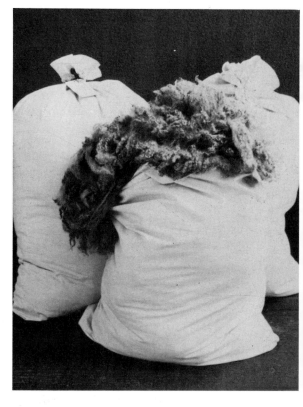

Fig 32. Calico bags are excellent for storing wool and for keeping out moth. The early colonists stored blankets and woollen clothes in new unbleached calico bags, claiming that moths disliked the dressing. Washed bags, tied tightly at the neck, are also suitable.

**Take care there are no moth eggs in the wool
before you store it!**

4 Preparation of Wool for Spinning

IT IS WISE to prepare a reasonable quantity of wool so that you can enjoy an uninterrupted spinning session. The preparation of fleece is by far the dirtiest part of the spinning process, so take care to cover your clothes.

Various methods of preparation are given. If you are a beginner, start with combing or flick-carding and progress gradually to the more complicated methods.

Whatever method you use, make a thorough job of it, as once you have mastered the basic skill of spinning your success will largely depend upon the choice of fleeces and the care you take over their preparation.

TEASING
(suitable for washed or greasy wool)

Teasing is opening up the wool fibres with the fingers. Hold the locks firmly with one hand and with the other hand pull small amounts sharply sideways. Any loose foreign matter, such as seeds or dust, will fall out, but anything hooked into the wool (such as thorns or prickly vegetation) will have to be removed separately. A well teased fleece looks like a fluffy cloud. It can be spun in this state though with doubtful results, as teasing is chiefly used as a preparatory process for carding.

A washed fleece may be re-oiled at this stage if desired. Spray the mixture on, then roll up the wool in a towel for some hours before carding but, as the oil will turn rancid, do not leave the wool unspun for too long.

Oil Mixture

Olive oil and water — equal quantities shaken together. Or, neatsfoot oil and water — equal quantities shaken together. One to two 15 ml spoons (1-2 tbsp) of each oil and water should be ample for 250 g (½lb) wool. Any good vegetable oil may be substituted for those mentioned but test first on a small portion to make sure that it is readily removed by ordinary washing.

COMBING
(suitable for washed or greasy wool)

The most suitable comb for this operation is a coarse dog comb with a handle.

Hold two or three staples in one hand, with the tips pointing away from you, then gently open up the tips of the staples with the comb — thus freeing the fibres and removing the dirt. Comb the underside too (fig 33).

Now turn the staple in your hand so the butt end (i.e. the end where it was cut from the sheep) is facing away from you, and open up the fibres at this end. The butt end should also be turned over so the underneath can be combed. For some projects this will be the end from which you spin,

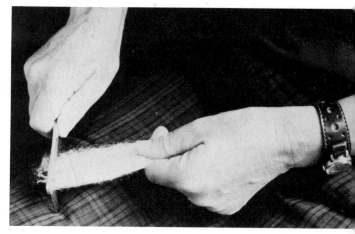

Fig 33. Combing the tips of the staple

Fig 34. Combing the butt end. The operation is almost finished and the fan is forming. Make sure all the fibres are completely free one from another and that there are no parts of the staple which have missed the comb. As you spin, the separated fibres, one after the other, will be drawn into the thread very quickly. Any parts of the staple tips left clinging together will be drawn into the spun thread and form a lump

so make sure all the fibres are quite free. At this stage the wool in your hand should look rather like a small fan (fig 34).

The combing operation can be heavy or light. If the comb is dragged through the staple, all the short fibres will be removed — these are the fibres in wool that fluff up, entrap the air and so keep us warm. A heavy combing therefore removes some of the most highly desirable properties of wool.

Place the opened-up wool in a box or basket with all the tips facing one way and the butt ends the other. Beginners will need to mark their baskets, but experienced spinners soon recognise which end is which.

Combed fleece may be spun with no further preparation. It may also be used on the drum carder.

FLICK CARDING
(suitable for washed or greasy wool)

A flicker-carder is a reasonably priced little implement that is ideal for opening up wool for spinning. It is especially suitable for opening up the finer wools. A piece of leather or vinyl about 30 cm² (1 sq ft) is also needed to cover your lap.

The handle on flick carders is deliberately made fairly long. This extra length is necessary to balance the bouncing action you must cultivate with your wrist (fig 35).

Grasp the handle lightly — right at the free end. Hold the locks firmly in one hand with the tips placed down on the leather.

With the other hand *bounce* the carder lightly up and down on the *tips*.

This way the little flicking action should come automatically. When beginners are told to flick (rather than bounce) they are inclined to drag the carder through the wool like a comb — this is incorrect. There should be very little waste — just some dirt and a tiny piece of fluff. A great deal of waste means you are being too heavy-handed with the flicking action.

Turn the locks over and flick the underside of the tips — just the tip, not the whole staple.

Then do the butt end — both sides.

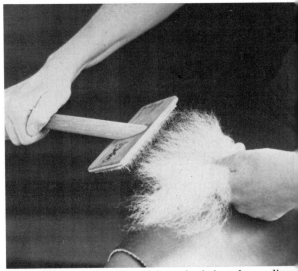

Fig 35. Flick carding. The flick carder is just descending to the wool. Note the position of the thumb on top of the carder. Working over the edge of the leg avoids the risk of carding the fingers holding the wool

The staple ends should be free from dirt and the fibres completely separated from one another. Again, they will look like a fan. Store the prepared fleece in the same way as combed fleece. Flick-carded fleece may be spun without further preparation or, like combed wool, it may be further prepared on the drum carder.

It will be noted that in both these processes, (combing and flick-carding) the tip of the staple is treated first. This is to encourage the dirt to fall out freely — nature made wool staples in such a way that the dirt works its way *down* the locks.

Flick carders are not a traditional implement for preparing wool and in some places they are not well known. In countries where the craft has grown, they have become so popular that they are now regarded as an essential part of spinning equipment.

HAND CARDING

There is no great mystique about hand carding although written instructions perhaps give rise to this impression.

Carding, simplified, is brushing the tangles out of the wool so it can be spun. Because the wool is held on a solid surface, it must be turned over at some stage, so that the tangles on the underside are brushed as thoroughly as those on top. One carder holds the wool while the other one acts as the brusher. Halfway through the process, their functions and positions are reversed.

Holding the Carders

The carders must be held firmly, but the particular grip you use will not greatly affect the quality of the carding. However, the traditional hand positions do contribute to economy of movement and consequently save time. When several hundred rolags are required, time and energy both begin to matter.

When acquiring any new skill it is usually better to learn the accepted and proven method, as correcting bad habits can sometimes be more troublesome than starting again.

Hand positions

The underneath carder is always the wool holder.
Put your hand out as if to accept some shopping change.
Put the carder handle across your palm and grip firmly.
Carder teeth upwards.
Palm upward.
Thumb facing away from you.
The top carder is always the brusher.
Pick it up as if it was a hairbrush and grip firmly.
Carder teeth downwards.

Palm downwards.
Thumb facing away from you.

Note. An underhand grip is used for the bottom carder.
An overhand grip is used for the top carder.
Both thumbs point away from you.

The only times your hands change their grip are:

1. Halfway through carding, — when their functions and positions change.
   (a) The former top brushing carder becomes the underneath one, holding the wool, so now requires the underhand grip.
   (b) The former bottom carder now becomes the top one and so the brusher, and requires an overhand grip.
2. At the end of carding, — when the wool must be stripped completely off both carders. Both carders will then require an underhand grip.

The carders can be held in the air if you so desire. Again, this will not affect the quality of carding — it is just a waste of energy. It is more comfortable if, when the *left* carder is the bottom one holding the wool — it rests on your *left* knee. Then when the *right* carder is the bottom one, rest it on your *right* knee.

Preparing Wool for Carding

The staples of wool should be no longer than the depth of the carders. Before it is carded the wool should be thoroughly teased, or opened up with the fingers. It may be still in the grease, or washed and dried then re-oiled several hours previously, or just washed and dried.

(Note. If the wool is clean make sure your carders are clean.)

Putting the Wool on the Carder

Place the left-hand carder on your knee, ready for use.

Hold the staple of wool in the right hand.

Press the butt end of the wool into the teeth at least 1 cm (½ in) from the top of the carder.

Hold it down with the left hand while the right hand draws away, anchoring the rest of the staple in the teeth down the carder face. (It needs your two hands to do the job quickly.) (fig 36)

Continue across the carder face until it is filled.

If the wool is very short e.g. perhaps a Down fleece — make two or more rows of wool. Put the bottom row on first, one third to halfway up the carder face and the next layer above and overlapping the first.

Fig 36. Putting the wool on to the carder

Carding Instructions

Place left carder (holding the wool) on your knee.

The right carder brushes about six times, swiftly, but gently (figs 37a and 37b).

The result will be that each carder will have about half the wool on it, partially straightened out, and with a fringe hanging over the bottom edge. Most of the wool embedded in the teeth of the bottom carder will now stay there, and will be the underneath layer, which will be carded later. But the upper layer must be brushed again, so it must be transferred back to the bottom carder.

Figs 37a and b. Starting to brush. It is usually more comfortable and efficient if the carders are on a slight angle so that the brushing carder is drawn back towards you. Because of its rounded face it will lift slightly upwards as it is used

Fig 38. Transferring. The left carder is upright and starting to be drawn very quickly upwards. Observe how the end of the fringe has been flicked up so that it will catch naturally in the teeth of the upright carder

Fig 39. The wool has been transferred back to the left carder so that it can be brushed again

Fig 40. The second half of carding. The right carder is now on the right knee and the left carder is doing the brushing

Transferring

Lift the left or bottom carder into an upright position on your knee.

Put the toe of the right carder against the heel of the left with the teeth facing and the carders almost at right angles (fig 38).

Suddenly scoop swiftly up with the left carder (fig 39). (The wool should now be back on the left carder, but it will not be so firmly embedded — so take care.)

The left carder is placed back on your knee.

The right carder — again brushes half a dozen times. (Start with the bottom fibres and work up — you are less likely to create tangles.)

When no more fibres are coming off:

Transfer the wool back to the left carder to be brushed again.

The right carder then brushes for the third time — this will probably be enough.

Do not transfer

Halfway. Now the underneath layer must be treated.

Change Grips and Change Knees

(Right carder on knee — underhand grip.

Left carder on top — overhand grip) (fig 40).

The second part of carding cannot start with brushing as half the wool is still on each carder. You must therefore begin by transferring all the wool to the bottom carder. The action is the same as before but, of course, the opposite carders are used.

Transfer

Hold the *right* carder upright on your knee.

Put the toe of the left carder against the heel of the right.

Scoop swiftly up with the right carder.

Brush — with the top left carder half a dozen times.

Transfer — the wool back to the bottom carder.

Brush — with the left carder again.

Transfer — the wool back to the bottom carder.

Brush for the third and last time.

Do not transfer

Stripping

Now the wool must be removed from both carders.

Change grips — both underhand.

Hold the carders — both upright in an open V-
   position with the teeth facing (fig 41)

Quickly but lightly:

Pull up with one carder, then

Pull up with the other (figs 42a and 42b).

— and repeat.

Fig 41. Stripping. The wool is now carded and must be removed from both carders

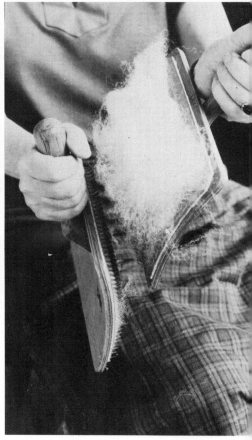

Figs 42a and b. Be careful not to double the fringe over. Pull up quickly, with each carder alternately, until all the wool lies loosely on one carder

Making the Rolag

All the wool should now be sitting loosely on the top of one carder face. Starting at the bottom, either push it into a roll with the other carder, or try the easier way and use your two hands to roll the wool up the teeth into an airy but *firm* sausage (called a rolag) (fig 43). The wool fibres should be lying at right angles to the column of air in the middle of the rolag.

Mixing Colours on Hand Carders

Hand carders can also be used for mixing colours for multicoloured yarns. Put staples of different-coloured wools on the carders, alternating them side by side; or put one layer above the other. Experiment with small amounts until the arrangement produces the exact effect desired, then keep the same arrangement on the carder for every rolag.

Fig 43. Roll the carded wool up the face of the carder into a firm rolag. Give it an extra roll with the palms of your hands if it looks at all shaggy

PROBLEMS WITH CARDING

Unwanted solid tips and pieces in the rolag

The wool was not prepared sufficiently — hard tips need a thorough opening or teasing, sometimes even removing. Butt ends need opening and any second-cut pieces need removing. The amount of preparation required will depend upon the fleece.

If during carding you see anything on the carders which was missed during preparation, pick it out with your fingers. If it is allowed to remain, it will get into the rolag and subsequently spoil your yarn.

Fibres folding over and becoming entangled

This trouble plagues some people. At some stage the fringe has got caught — it usually happens when brushing. The fringe must be flicked up in the air to keep it free while the brush is coming down again to make contact with the wool-holding carder. It can also happen when transferring and stripping, although this is less common. Make sure the wool is kept at least 1 cm (½ in) away from the top of the carders.

If you find yourself troubled by this problem, examine your carders at every step, to find exactly when it is occurring.

Exhaustion!

You are brushing too slowly and too hard. Brushing is a relatively swift action, but it should be gentle, as though you were brushing a baby's head. There should be a gentle rustling, not a grating or rasping sound.

Do try to keep the wool-holding carder on your knee. Learners are inclined to work up to a position more appropriate for playing the cymbals. No wonder they get exhausted!

DRUM CARDING

Step 1 — Preparation

Note. Drum carders are not suitable for fleece finer than a 56's, and any fleece finer than a 52's should be treated with caution and given a test run to make sure the fibres will not be torn and become more tangled.

The fleece must be washed and thoroughly dry.

It must then be prepared for use by the carder, either by:

thorough and careful teasing,

or combing,

or flick-carding

The success of your drum carding will depend upon the thoroughness of the preparation and the quality of the fleece you are using.

Step 2 — First carding

Start turning the handle of the carder, place the wool on the tray and *feed it into the machine*. Do *not* hang on to the wool and hold it back on the tray. This common practice serves no other purpose than to deliberately encourage the carder to tear the wool. It also causes the wool to wind around the front roller, thus obstructing the teeth, which should be doing the job of carding. The front cylinder, properly set and properly used, should stay almost permanently clean except for a stray fibre of two and, perhaps, the odd bit of teasing rubbish, which has inadvertently fallen in with your fleece (fig 44).

Be careful not to feed in too much wool: 28 g (1 oz) of wool will make three batts; two batts would be the limit for good spinning.

A useful guide for how much wool to use is to make sure you can see the carding cloth through the wool during the entire operation.

As soon as the last of the wool that has been fed into the carder has settled on the large cylinder, stop turning the handle as no useful purpose is served by continued revolving.

Step 3 — Removing the batt

Stand *behind* the carder and move the handle until the seam of the cloth is on top of the big cylinder. Slide a steel needle under the wool right across the carder and lift up the needle until the batt breaks (fig 45). Reverse the turning of the drum (keeping the needle behind the batt and near the teeth); gently lift the wool off backwards.

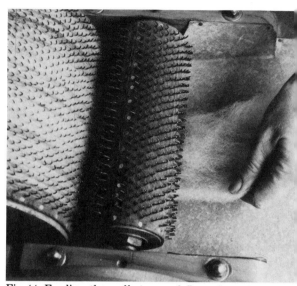

Fig 44. Feeding the well-prepared fleece into the drum carder. There is almost sufficient wool on the drum for one batt. Note how little fluff has gathered on the front roller

Fig 45. Removing the batt. The steel needle has been slid under the wool at the place where there is a seam in the carding cloth. The needle is being pulled up and in a moment the batt will break. (This photograph clearly illustrates the uneven distribution of the wool after only one carding.)

It may have to be assisted occasionally by putting the needle carefully through a row of teeth (fig 46).

Do not force any tangles off. They are better left behind and picked off separately afterwards, when they can usually be thrown away as they will rarely card satisfactorily.

Hold the batt up to the light. Inspect it for any lumps, and tease these gently with your fingers. If they will not separate, pull them out and discard them. Against the light it may be seen that the wool has been reasonably well carded but it is unevenly distributed throughout the batt. This will make spinning difficult so a second carding will be necessary to remove this fault.

Step 4 – Second carding
For the second carding you have a choice of three procedures:
1. Take handfulls of carded wool and feed them in as you did in the first carding. This probably works better when there is a motor on the carder and you have two free hands. Or –
2. Tear the batt down the middle lengthwise and draw out the halves to make long thin strips. Feed these strips into the carding machine, guiding them from side to side on the tray with one finger so that the big cylinder will be covered evenly. This works beautifully but is rather time-consuming. Or –
3. Tear the batt into thinner strips and put them through as they are.

Step 5 – Remove the batt
Step 6 – Inspect it against the light again
The wool fibres should be well carded and evenly distributed throughout the batt – there should not be a fibre out of place. If there is, card again.

The batts can be left flat or rolled up. The easiest way to use them is to tear them into strips and then spin from them lengthwise. However, a fluffier spin results from using them rolled up like hand-carded rolags. Break the batt in half and make two rolags, as they are more manageable this size.

Mixing Colours on a Drum Carder
A drum carder is the ideal instrument for mixing coloured wools. However, it fulfils two entirely different functions in this respect:
1. It can mix several different colours or several shades of one colour together, until the fibres are so intermingled they appear as one colour only.

Fig 46. The batt is held and lifted backwards off the drum while still being given some support from the needle. The drum will have to be further rotated in reverse so that the rest of the batt can be removed

2. It can partially mix colours, and so produce a multicoloured batt for spinning a multicoloured thread.

It has a tendency to work quickly towards the first result, so if you are aiming for the second, take care.

Thorough mixing
The first carding is done the same way as before. For the second carding, mix portions of the batts together – put half of batt A with half of batt B or C.

A third carding is often necessary, repeating the mixing. Make sure you mix the batts on the top of the pile with those from the middle and bottom. It is extraordinary how often stray shades of colour are found in one portion of the pile.

Limited mixing
For the first carding – card each of the colours separately.

For the second carding – mix the colours by carding a handful of A, then a handful of B, then a handful of C – or, two of A to one of B and one of C.

Keep to the same proportions for each batt. This gives a good multicoloured thread.

Or, each batt can be torn in halves or thirds. Either layer A over B over C, and let the three layers go through as one; or put them through separately, but so that they will lie one on top of the other on the big cylinder. This method is particularly suitable for making a thread of one colour blended from different shades — perhaps a blue thread combining: green-blue, blue and purple-blue. The resulting thread has a sparkle and life that a one-tone thread does not possess.

Or, long strips can be made of the separate colours, and put through the carder one after the other. By controlling the snakelike movements with your guiding finger on the tray, interesting colour effects can be produced.

Experiment until you can produce a batt from which you can spin a thread with the colour arrangement you require.

PUTTING AN ELECTRIC MOTOR ON A DRUM CARDER

The chief advantage of driving the carder by a motor is that both hands are left free to manage the wool. A motor of quarter horse-power rating is needed — an old washing-machine motor is suitable. The speed at which the motor turns the carder must be reduced by a system of V-belts and pulleys until the larger cylinder rotates at somewhere between 60 and 120 revolutions per minute. THE MOTORISED CARDER IS, OF COURSE, A POTENTIALLY DANGEROUS PIECE OF EQUIPMENT and is not desirable in a house where there are children. For your own safety there should be a cut-off switch readily accessible on the machine and safety guards to protect you and your clothes from the motor, belts and wheels.

Always disconnect the machine from the source of power at the end of a work session so that it cannot be accidentally switched on again.

5 Spinning
Part I: Learning to Spin

LEARNING TO SPIN from a book is not easy, as spinning is a practical subject. It is as difficult to describe in words the coordinated movements and the rhythm involved in spinning as it is to describe the actual sound of a sonata or a song.

These days it is fairly easy to get spinning lessons, but there are always those few people who, for one reason or another, find regular attendance at classes difficult, and for them the whole procedure has been written out in full.

However, bear in mind that even a few lessons will not only make many things so much clearer but will also provide the opportunity to have individual difficulties discussed, so do take advantage of any tuition when available.

The following is a list of skills which must be mastered. In a practical course they may all be taught together, but with written instructions they must be fairly sharply defined.

1. Drafting.
2. Treadling.
3. Controlling tension.
4. Treadling, drafting, controlling tension, twisting, joining and winding on.

It makes no difference whether you learn to draft or to treadle first. In some ways drafting is easier at the wheel because the drag from the bobbin gives you something to pull against. Unfortunately, learning to draft at the spinning wheel requires coping simultaneously with all the other skills necessary for spinning. Similarly, if you are working absolutely on your own, conquer treadling before you begin working with wool at the wheel.

Before starting on the course, study your own spinning wheel carefully. Take the bobbin off and put it back on. Study the drive band. Turn the main tension knob and the brake tension peg, if you have one. Give the wheel a good clean and an oiling, particularly if it is new.

DRAFTING

Drafting is the process by which the prepared fleece is elongated and evenly thinned so that any consistent number of fibres can be presented to be twisted into a thread.

Most people spin with the right hand working in front near the spinning wheel and the left hand drafting (or pulling back the wool) slightly to their left side. It does not really matter which hand you prefer in front and which at the back — in most methods of spinning one way is as comfortable as the other.

It is important to understand however that the rear hand will be controlling the drafting and doing most of the moving. The front hand remains fairly stationary about 15-22 cm (6-9 in) from the orifice, but the forefinger and thumb of this hand work hard, constantly guarding the twist and doing any other refining work.

Drafting practice
Take a small bundle of flick-carded or combed wool with the butt (or shorn) end facing away from you and the tips nearest the body. Pull forward, or slightly loosen a few fibres from the butt end.

Hand positions
Front hand. Put the front hand out as if you were going to shake hands. Relax, curl the fingers a little and rest the hand on your knee. Hold the loosened fibres with the ball of the thumb exerting a gentle pressure just above the middle joint on the forefinger.

Rear hand. Place the rear hand on the wool mass in the same way (but approach from the opposite direction). Now turn the rear hand a little so that the two thumbs make a 'T' where they meet (fig 47).

1. Tighten the pressure of the back thumb a little and pull the wool back for 5-8 cm (2-3 in). The pressure of the front thumb must be light enough to allow the bulk of the fibres to be pulled back, but firm enough to hold some of them (fig 48).

Fig 47. Hand position for drafting, thumbs in T-shape.

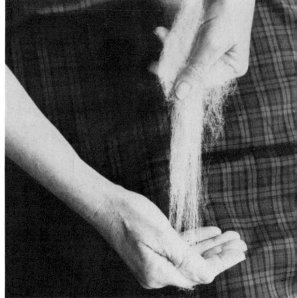

Fig 48. Drafting back — the front hand stays in position holding a few fibres; the rear hand draws back the main fibre mass.

2. With the front hand grip the wool where the thinned fibres cease and the main fibre mass starts again. Pull back with the rear hand again (fig 49a & b). Repeat five or six times until you have a long airy-looking worm of wool. (If you wish, you can put this sliver of wool on your thigh and rub the palm of your hand over it — like a rolling pin, rolling in one direction only — away from you. This will twist the wool slightly and consolidate it a little, so that you can wind it into tiny balls to be spun up later.)

Repeat the drafting exercise with the front hand *anchored on your knee throughout.* When you work with the wheel it will exert a pull and will drag the wool forward. In the meantime you will have to draft back, then flick the wool forward yourself.

Repeat these exercises several times.

Note. The length of the staples controls the length of the draft, e.g. with a 18 cm (7 in) staple length you can draft back 13 cm (5 in) comfortably. But with a 10-13 cm (4-5 in) staple length, a draft of 13 cm (5 in) would cause the fibres to part company in the middle.

Fig 49a. The front hand grips the wool where the thinned fibres cease

Fig 49b. The rear hand drafts back again

TREADLING

When a spinning wheel is treadled the big drive wheel will turn happily in either direction. When it revolves clockwise the thread you are making will have the twist sloping up to the right. When the wheel revolves anticlockwise, the thread will also twist in the reverse direction. Thus it will be obvious the wheel must be kept turning in one direction only for total length of the thread you are spinning. On paper it sounds simple but, in practice, gaining control of the wheel may require some perseverance.

Treadling practice

Put your fingers on the spokes (avoid handling the rim) and turn the wheel by hand. At the back of the wheel shaft is a crank which is usually L-shaped but is occasionally curved. This crank is attached to the connecting rod or cord (called the footman) which is tied to the treadle. Watch the movement of this crank — it too turns in a circle.

When the crank is at its highest position, the treadle will also be at its highest. When the crank is at its lowest position, the treadle too will be at its lowest. In either of these positions, no leverage is possible with the treadle, and the wheel will have to be started with a hand on the spokes. This is not easy when your hands are full of wool, so one of the arts of treadling is preventing the wheel from stopping in either of these positions.

Turn the wheel with your hand until the crank is between the 1 o'clock and 2 o'clock positions. Press downwards on the treadle and the wheel will turn clockwise. (This is the direction it will turn for most of your spinning.) Now turn the wheel, by hand, until the crank is between the 10 o'clock and 11 o'clock positions. Press on the treadle again. The wheel will revolve just as easily but in the reverse direction. (This is the direction it will turn for most of your plying.)

On old sewing machines the treadle was pivoted in the middle and to keep the wheel revolving, equal pressure was applied first with the toes, then with the heel. However, on spinning wheels, as the treadle is nearly always pivoted or hinged at the front, the downward pressure with the toes must be strong enough to force the wheel to complete the whole turn. (Some wheels are counter-balanced or have weights in their rims to assist with this.)

A *strong* downward push is particularly important when first starting the wheel. Once it is revolving the wheel gathers sufficient momentum to help you keep it going. (Beginners are inclined to give a tentative first push. The crank only reaches its 11 o'clock position and then, of course, the wheel promptly reverses on the second push.)

Remember the first push is *strong*.

Practise treadling and stopping, treadling and stopping, until you can make the wheel go clockwise or anticlockwise at will.

Make sure your toes are kept on the treadle plate all the time you are treadling. Wheels with a cord footman or a long tie at the base of the footman will shudder if your foot is lifted. If you do acquire this bad habit you will always be restricted in the choice of a wheel.

DRIVE RATIO

Tie a short length of coloured wool on to one arm of the flyer. Put the crank at its highest position and turn the big drive wheel very slowly by hand for one complete revolution. Keep your eyes on the decorated arm of the flyer and count the number of revolutions it makes to the one turn of the drive wheel. (On most wheels the number is most likely to fall between five and eight.)

Remember this number, because it means every time the treadle is pressed and the drive wheel goes around once, the flyer is going around 'x' times and is putting that number of twists into your wool. This is known as the drive ratio of a spinning wheel and is expressed as follows 5:1, 11:1, or whatever it is.

THE LEADER AND TENSIONING

The leader

Cut a length of machine-spun wool at least 2-3 m (6-9 ft) long. (The rougher or hairier the wool the better — carpet wool is ideal.) Tie it very firmly around the shaft of the bobbin on the wheel, twisting it two or three times to make sure it has a firm grip.

Bring the long end of the wool from the bobbin shaft across to the nearest hook on the flyer. It must then travel outside that hook and all the other hooks nearer the orifice. Push the threading hook through from the front of the orifice, out through the eye, and pull the wool through (fig 50). This length of wool is known as the leader. It will stay on the bobbin until it is so old that it needs replacing. All your other bobbins will require a leader too. The wool to be spun is twisted or tied on to this leader, which will then guide the spun wool back through the orifice, around the hooks and on to the bobbin.

Never work with a short leader. It should always be long enough for testing the tension on the wheel and getting it correctly adjusted before you begin to spin.

Tensioning

Double band wheel. Slacken the tension until the driving belt is just driving all three wheels — the drive wheel, the spindle pulley and the bobbin.
Scotch tension wheel. The drive belt must have just enough tension to drive the spindle pulley and flyer. Set this before you begin to spin and then leave it alone.

Now the brake band must also be placed in position. It should wind around the tension peg once or twice before going under a hook directly in line with the bobbin groove. It will then travel over the bobbin groove and connect by a spring or elastic band to a hook on the other side, or come back to the first hook. (The path alters slightly with different makes of wheels.)

Make sure the tension peg is firmly in its hole, then turn it until the brake is resting gently in the bobbin groove. This is a very sensitive tensioning system and the tiniest turn will alter it dramatically. If the brake is tightened too much, neither the bobbin nor the flyer will rotate.

Sit on a chair and make sure that your wheel is positioned comfortably in front of you.

Take hold of the leader about 15 cm (6 in) away from where it protrudes from the orifice. Hold

Fig 50. The leader has been tied on the bobbin, threaded through the orifice, then allowed to wind on to the bobbin while the spinning wheel is treadled and the tension adjusted

your hands as if you were drafting wool. Start treadling.

One of three things may happen:
1. The leader will slide gracefully through your hands into the orifice and start winding on to the bobbin.
2. It will twist and snarl in the length between your front hand and the orifice but refuse to wind on.
3. It will be swept out of your hands at a rate that leaves you gasping.

The first alternative is the correct one and you must turn your tensioner gently until this is exactly what happens. If the leader refuses to wind on, check that it is gripping the bobbin shaft — tighten the tie if necessary. Sometimes turning slippery bobbins once or twice by hand helps to get things moving.

Do not attempt to spin with your fleece wool until you are quite sure you have the feel of the tensioning system. Loosen it, tighten it, and experiment generally. Practise drafting-movements with your hands while you are experimenting.

SPINNING A CONTINUOUS THREAD

Have ready a basket of prepared wool and cover your lap with a protective cloth of a contrasting colour.

1. Treadle the spinning wheel clockwise until about 25 cm (10 in) of leader is left hanging out of the orifice.
2. Pick up some wool and hold it in your rear hand with the cut ends towards the spinning wheel (as for drafting practice).
3. Pull out two or three fibres in front.
4. With the front forefinger and thumb hold these fibres firmly against the leader about 15 cm (6 in) from its end (fig 51).
5. Start treadling.
6. The minute the fibres start to twist and catch around the leader — quickly —
7. Draft back with the rear hand.
8. Now relax the pressure on the front forefinger and thumb just enough, so that when you —
9. Bring the rear hand forward, the drafted fibres will slide through to be twisted and wound on.
10. Quickly pinch the twisted thread when you come to the end of the drafted fibres and hold while you —
11. Draft back again.
12. Relax the pressure of the front forefinger and thumb,
13. Bring the rear hand forward and let the drafted fibres slide through.

With a revolving spinning wheel in front of you it will be impossible to follow these instructions step by step. Read them carefully until you have thoroughly absorbed them, then as you start to spin use an abbreviated version to murmur as you work:

1. *Pinch*   (front hand)
2. *Draft back*   (rear hand) (fig 52)
3. *Relax* and   (front hand) (fig 53)
    slide through (rear hand moving forward)

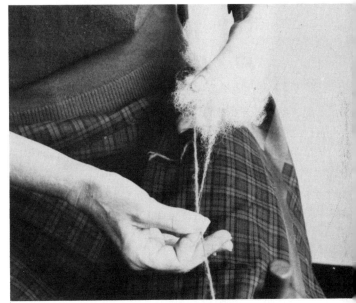

Fig 51. Attaching the wool to the leader. Two or three fibres are held against the leader about 15cm (6in) from its end. Treadle, and, when these fibres are caught by the twist, draft quickly back. Then slide forward, but hold the twisting fibres alongside the leader until all are caught in

For the sake of clarity the technique has been written as three movements, but when the action is carried out, it is more like two — there is only a fraction of a second between pinching and drafting:

Pinch and *draft back*.
Relax and *slide through*.

The front hand should be held in the same position as it was when you were practising drafting. However, now the drafted fibres will lie in a fan shape between the two hands, and there will be twisted thread between your front hand and the orifice. You will need to work with your front thumb pressing and relaxing over the thread on

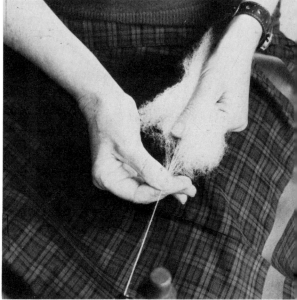

Fig 52. Pinching with the front fingers while drafting back with the rear hand. Note the fan shape of the drafted fibres

Fig 53. The front hand is still in the same position but the pressure of the thumb on the forefinger has been relaxed so that the drafted fibres can slide through to be twisted while the rear hand moves forward

the first joint of your forefinger. This thumb and finger will also be providing a smoothing action when the fibres slide through them.

Be careful to pinch quickly and firmly before the spin runs into the main fibre mass. Once those fibres get twist in them they have in fact become a thick thread and it will be impossible to draft from them. If they will go through the orifice let them do so, although it is probably better to break off and start again as they will very likely get caught on the hooks.

If the thread is not winding on, tighten the tension — *a little*, and try again. If it is winding on at a pace you cannot cope with, slacken it off.

At this stage do not worry about spinning a perfect thread.

Your aim is to keep going: *treadling, drafting, twisting, winding on* and *joining*.

Just as you must learn to keep afloat before you learn to swim, you must now learn to keep everything going together before you learn to spin. Perfection of style in both activities can be acquired only after you have conquered the basic skill.

When you get to the end of the unspun wool, pick up another prepared piece. Pull out two or three fibres — hold them about 15 cm (6 in) from

the end of your spun thread, treadle, and, as you feel the twist gathering under your forefinger and thumb, draft quickly with the rear hand — just as you did when you were joining your wool on to the leader.

When starting with the new wool, change also to the next hook on the flyer, if you have not already done so. It is very important for the bobbin to fill evenly for its entire length.

As the bobbin fills, the core becomes heavier and fatter and the wool has farther to travel as it winds on. Consequently the tension must be tightened to pull the wool on more quickly, so that it can travel the greater distance in the same time.

With experience you will *sense* when the tension needs altering.

When learning, tighten the tension a little each time you fill an entire length of the bobbin. On the return journey up the bobbin use each hook in the reverse order.

Relaxing

Spinning is a relaxed occupation.
The tension on your wheel should be as loose as you can possibly work with.
Your foot should be treadling effortlessly.
You should be comfortable on your chair —

support your back with cushions if you need them.

Your arms should be at a comfortable height, with your hands and fingers relaxed and not clutching at the wool.

If you are straining anywhere, *work out why.*

Do you need a different chair?

Could your spinning wheel be turned slightly so that it is at a more comfortable angle?

Is your wool prepared properly so that it will spin easily?

Perhaps you need to go back and practise treadling?

Don't struggle to get going for hours on end — you will only become more and more tense. Have a rest and find a different occupation for a while.

Remember — like swimming again — there's that moment when you can't — and that wonderful moment when suddenly you can!

PROBLEMS AND POSSIBLE SOLUTIONS

Twist

Undertwisting and winding on too rapidly: loosen your tension.

Overtwisting and winding on too slowly: tighten your tension.

Overtwisting alone:

1. Draft back much farther. You can draft back about 3 cm (1 in) less than your staple length with complete safety, or
2. Draft more quickly — if you cannot do this to begin with, slow down your treadling to a suitable rate for your hand movements.

These things affect the amount of twist in yarn:

The ratio of the drive wheel to the spindle pulley (page 57). This is a built-in feature of your wheel and no matter how slowly or how quickly you treadle, you will not be able to alter it.

However, the rate of treadling must be related to

1. The rate and length of drafting and
2. The rate of winding on — according to the diameter of the thread being spun.

All these things the spinner has the freedom to adjust.

How to judge twist

To a certain extent judging twist comes with experience. However, there are one or two little tests that may help.

1. The best test is to stop treadling, then continue to hold the yarn taut but transfer the task of pinching to the forefinger and thumb of your drafting hand.

With your free hand, hold up the yarn about halfway between the orifice and the wool-holding hand. Gently relax the tension by moving the rear hand with the wool forward, towards the orifice. The wool should double over where you were

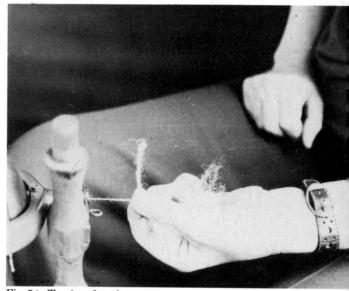

Fig 54. Testing for the correct twist by allowing the spun thread to ply back on itself

holding it up and twist around on itself. If it looks like light airy plied wool it's fine (fig 54). Allow for the difference between greasy or washed wool, and remember it will puff up still more when washed. If it forms little kinks all the way up the thread, the yarn has too much twist in it.

2. Feel the wool on your bobbin. There is an old saying — 'A soft bobbin means soft yarn'. However, treat this remark with some caution; a soft bobbin can also mean inefficient filling of the bobbin.

Joining

If the spun thread breaks — and it is bound to, several times, until you get control — break off the twisted threads protruding from the fibre mass and rejoin with completely unspun fibres. It also helps if the thread hanging from the orifice is not too tightly spun. Let it unwind a little while you are picking up the new wool and join unspun fibres to unspun fibres.

Try to remember which hook you are working from. A broken end can wrap itself around the bobbin with alarming rapidity and completely disappear. If you know which part of the bobbin you are filling you will have some idea of where to start looking for it. Occasionally reverse treadling aids recovery but sometimes nothing helps. It remains lost!

If there is a lump where every join is made you are trying to join with too many fibres. One, two or three fibres are sufficient.

A good join will require: a sufficient length of spun thread — 15 cm (6 in), a few new fibres, and quick drafting.

A poor join will result from an insufficient length of spun thread 2.5-5 cm (1-2 in), a bundle of unspun fibres, and slow drafting.

Loose fibres protruding from the join can be avoided by using your finger and thumb to aid the twisting provided by the spinning wheel.

Drafting

The tension on the wheel must not be so strong that it pulls the wool forward and does the work of drafting for you. If this is allowed to happen you will have no control over the number of twists you are putting into a given length of yarn, and also the resulting yarn is likely to be very hairy.

Occasionally there is a problem with fibres sticking out sideways from the wool mass and not being drawn into the draft. Remember the wrist of your drafting hand does not have to work as if it had a splint on it. Revolve your wrist, twist it and make use of your fingers too.

Some spinners grip their fibre mass too tightly. This tends to flatten it and leaves you with a handful of tangled fibres which have to be discarded.

Beginners working with flick-carded wool may find drafting easier if the prepared wool is folded over and then drafted from the fold — this is quite acceptable. The resulting yarn will be slightly different, so at some stage you should learn both ways of holding the wool (fig 55).

Evenness of yarn

When concentrating on an even yarn the place to watch is the drafting zone between the two hands.

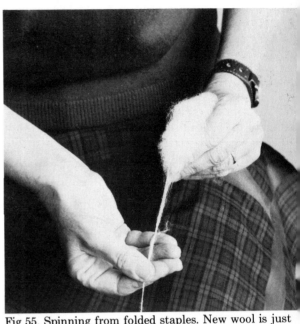

Fig 55. Spinning from folded staples. New wool is just being joined on to the spun thread. The staples have been flick carded, then folded butt to tip. The fold is held upwards and drafting runs from the bend in the fibres. When a fluffier spin is required this is a good way of handling staples which are too long for hand carding

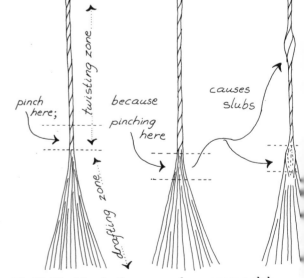

Fig 56. Pinching in the wrong place causes a slub

ry to keep the same number of fibres in the rafting zone, and present the same length of fibre o be twisted each time. This will give you a yarn f even diameter with the same number of twists er 2.5 cm (1 in) for its entire length. Beginners are aclined to watch the spun yarn, but once the bres are twisted it is too late to rectify any faults.

Some spinners' threads are a series of small lubs. This is the result of pinching on unspun ibres instead of at the end of the spun thread fig 56).

Make sure you have prepared enough wool for a omplete spinning session. Cultivating a sense of ouch is very important and this cannot be achieved without a certain amount of continuity. Preparing two or three staples, spinning them and then stopping again to prepare more wool, just as you are getting the feel of things, is not a good way to work.

Treadling and wheel troubles

Wheel reversing — the old trouble. The *first* push on the treadle must be *strong*.

Wheel sliding away from you — you may be sitting in a chair which is too low and then pushing outwards instead of downwards when you treadle. Sometimes the floor really is too slippery, and you will need a non-skid mat under the wheel.

6 Plying for Plain Knitting Wool

HANDSPUN WOOL IS USUALLY PLIED with only two strands, occasionally three. Bulkier wools are generally spun thicker in the first place rather than by adding extra threads at the time of plying (as is the usual commercial practice). There is certainly no rule about this however, it is more a matter of the time involved. When you are more proficient you may please yourself. In the meantime while you are learning it would be wise if you restricted yourself to plying with just two strands.

The two bobbins of spun singles are put on a bobbin rack, called a lazy-Kate. (If you do not possess one, two knitting needles poked through a box work just as well.) Some wheels have built-in lazy-Kates but generally these are more suitable for storing full bobbins than they are for plying, although they can be useful in an emergency. However, do not use a built-in lazy-Kate for your first efforts.

As the wool must be free to run smoothly from both bobbins at the same rate there should be an equal quantity of yarn on each one, — not one bobbin full and heavy and the other only half full. Smooth running is also helped if the lazy-Kate is raised up off the floor on to a low table beside you. This prevents the yarns reversing and winding around the pins when there is any relaxation in tension.

Sit back comfortably in your chair. The hands will work one in front of the other, as they do when spinning. The yarns coming from the lazy-Kate should be on the same side as the hand you previously used for drafting.

Tie the two single yarns on to the leader with an overhand knot. (Most spinners start plying by letting the wool twist on to the leader, as in spinning, but at this learning stage it is safer to use a knot even though it may require some assistance through the orifice and around the hooks.)

When wool is being plied it is important for it to be held so that it can run in a direct line straight into the orifice. With the rear hand, hold the single yarns against your body directly opposite the orifice and *hold them there for the entire operation.* Keep one or two fingers between them to stop any tangles or kinks running into the plying area (fig 57).

Treadling must now turn the wheel in the **reverse direction** from that in which the yarns

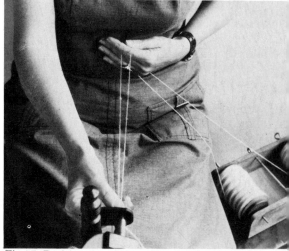

Fig 57. Position for plying. The rear hand stays in this position throughout

were spun. Begin treadling and by using the long leader get the tension adjusted before you start with the threads that are to be plied. This is very important, and the tension should be as loose as you can work with.

The front hand should lightly accompany the twist down the thread. It is not used with a heavy smoothing action, but acts more in the nature of a guardian, with the forefinger and thumb ready to pinch the yarn quickly if you have to stop for any reason.

Now start plying.
Treadle — one, two, three, four, five, six times.
Allow the twist to run up the entire length of the yarn (which must be constantly held taut between the orifice and your body, if you are to get an even twist) (fig 58).
Pinch the plied yarn quickly, with your front fingers — and then —
Shoot the thread forward into the orifice (refer to fig 57 again).
This action automatically unwinds fresh yarn from the lazy-Kate and you are now ready to continue:
Treadle — one, two, three, four, five, six times while the twist runs up.
Pinch — and shoot the thread forward into the orifice.

Now stop and examine the yarn where it winds off the hooks on to the bobbin.

Does it *look* right? It will have twisted, certainly — but has it twisted the right amount? Your eyes are the best guide of all, both while you are treadling and when you examine the yarn near the bobbin. If it is not correctly plied, something must be adjusted.

1. Tension adjustment. If the wool is winding on at a comfortable rate (as it should be if you used the leader for tensioning before starting), leave it alone. If it is not — adjust the tension now.

2. Treadling adjustment. This is probably where the adjustment will be needed. The distance from the orifice to the place where you are holding the yarn against your body is probably somewhere between 38-45 cm (15-18 in). This distance will remain the same for the entire time you are plying.

In this plying zone you are going to need: more twists if your plied wool looks sleazy; or fewer twists if your plied wool is like a hard twisted cord.

For more twists — give one more treadle: treadle — one, two, three, four, five, six, seven — while the twist runs up, then pinch and shoot forward.

This treadling adjustment puts a definite number of extra twists into the yarn. It may be only six or seven, but even this small number, going into the constant length of your plying zone, may be enough to make the difference between well-plied wool and poorly-plied wool.

For less twist — give one fewer treadle and take out a definite number of twists. Treadle one, two, three, four, five times.

Keep the treadling absolutely regular, even when you are shooting the plied thread forward — this may take half to one treadle with a Scotch tension wheel and, perhaps, two treadles with a double band wheel. The extra treadlings are still putting twist into the yarn, of course, and this is why the final examination must take place at the bobbin, and not at the orifice.

Remember to change hooks frequently, as otherwise the wool will pile up rapidly on one place on the bobbin. Plied yarn is more than twice the thickness of the single strands being doubled, because plying not only twists the two strands together in the reverse direction, but also it removes about half the original twist, so that the singles themselves soften, puff up and become bulkier in the process.

Keep examining the yarn at regular intervals even when you are sure it is twisting correctly. Pay particular attention to it when you make a slight tension adjustment.

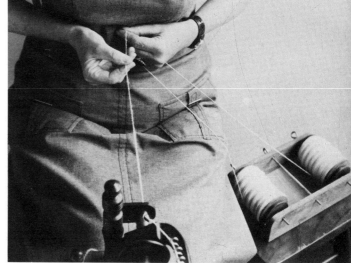

Fig 58. The front hand has moved back as it accompanied the twist running up the threads. It will pinch off the twist, then will move quickly forward with the plied yarn as it winds on to the bobbin

Another acceptable method of plying is to let the tension of the wheel pull the plied yarns steadily through the orifice with no deliberate holding back or shooting forward. The singles are run through the separating fingers of the front hand while the rear hand is used for feeding the yarn forward from the lazy-Kate.

There are some disadvantages to this method, especially for beginners. The tension must be tightened considerably right from the start, which means working with a heavy tension all the time you are plying. The treadling is faster, there is a less obvious viewing area, and no constant length over which the spinner can exercise control.

If you are interrupted while plying, on no account leave the yarns dangling from the spinning wheel. The twist, with snarls included, will run right up to the lazy-Kate. It will be almost impossible to unwind this mess and to accurately reproduce what you were previously doing with the wheel.

If you do have to stop, pinch in the correct place, pull some yarn out from the bobbin if need be, and quickly wind it around some knob on the spinning wheel to hold it under tension. You can then pick up again where you left off.

Two things set the twist in spun wool: one is leaving it undisturbed on the bobbin; the other is washing. If there is any reason for doubting the evenness of the twist throughout the yarn that has just been plied, remove it from the bobbin as soon as you have finished. (This is actually a good procedure to follow at all times. [fig 59].)

Put the spinning wheel about 3 metres (10 ft) away from you and skein off the yarn, keeping it under a light, but sufficient tension for the small irregularities to move and even out. Tie the skein in at least four places and wash it immediately. Use one of the final shrinking and softening processes before hanging the wool on the line to dry.

Leave the wool in the skein until you are ready to use it.

Note. Some spinners prefer to leave the wool on the bobbin before skeining and washing. They maintain the yarn is smoother if treated this way, and the wool needs to rest. The yarn certainly appears smoother when it is first reeled from the bobbin, but after many test batches of skeins had been washed, no difference could be detected with either the naked eye or with a very strong magnifying glass. Only the timing of the resting period is altered if you reel off straight away.

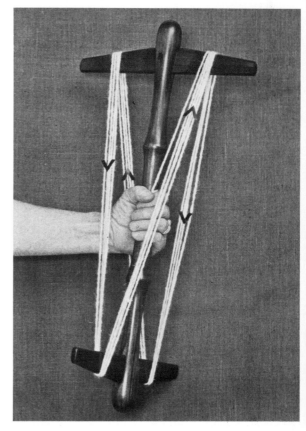

Fig 59. Winding the spun yarn on to a niddy-noddy so that it can be measured and washed. (See also 17b.)

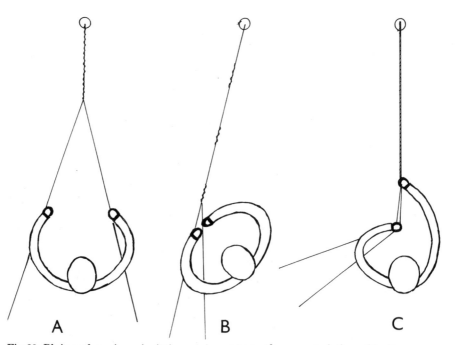

Fig 60. Plying: the spinner's sitting position and the angle at which she feeds the separate yarns into the orifice contribute to the even twisting of both yarns. A, Incorrect, except for fancy yarns. B, Risky. C, Correct position

PROBLEMS WITH PLYING

The two main problems are bound to be: judging the correct amount of twist; and, getting an even twist.

Judging the correct amount of twist
Your *eyes* are the best guide; this cannot be stressed too often. While spinning, judging the twist with your eyes is difficult. While plying, judging the twist with your eyes is not only easy — it is a necessity.

For 2-ply knitting wool a suitable number of twists per 2.5 cm (1 in) would be the same number as were in the original singles — e.g. six twists per 2.5 cm (1 in) in the singles yarn will require six twists per 2.5 cm (1 in) in the plied yarn.

Singles — 2-ply

$$\frac{6 + 6}{2}$$ = 6 when plied in reverse direction with six twists.

(half the twist removed when plied)

It follows that singles spun for plying with three strands (3-ply wool) must be more softly spun in the first place to get a similar twist result in the ply.

Singles — 3-ply

$$\frac{4 + 4 + 4}{2}$$ = 6 when plied in reverse direction with six twists.

(half the twist removed when plied)

Of course three singles with six twists per 2.5 cm (1 in) can be plied together, but they will require nine twists per 2.5 cm (1 in) in the plying, which may not be what you want. The angle of the plied twist will be very steep and this does not always look very attractive in 3-ply knitting yarns.

Note. The *actual* number of twists required will depend upon the diameter of the yarn. Thin yarns require more twist than thick yarns, both in the spinning and the plying.

When the skein has been reeled, hold it up by one end. If the twist in the spinning and plying balance each other, it will hang straight like a necklace. If there is insufficient twist in the ply, the skein will continue to twist itself in the direction that it was plied. If there is too much twist it will try to unwind itself by twisting in the opposite direction.

Remember this is a test for *balance* between the spinning and the plying, and that it is possible for the spinning and not the plying to be at fault. If the appearance of the yarn indicates there is sufficient ply but the twisting of the skein suggests otherwise, then obviously the original spinning must be the cause of the trouble and the singles yarn must have been overspun.

It is very important for this balance to be correct because, if it is not, there can be problems later. If a faulty yarn is used for knitting stocking stitch the stitches will slant sideways instead of lying straight up and down. (If this does occur, knit instead with a rib stitch.)

Getting an even twist
When two evenly-spun yarns are plied according to the directions given, they should twist evenly. However, if the yarns are not evenly spun but are a series of thick lumps and thin places, they may be better left as singles. If they are plied, the twist will tend to accumulate in all the thin spots and skip the fatter bulkier places, and there is little that can be done about it. A beginner's first spinning may well fall into this category.

The cause of one thread coiling around the other, rather than both threads twisting evenly, can again be uneven spinning. It can also be the result of the spinner working at a poor angle to the wheel — the yarns may be feeding into the orifice at an unequal tension (fig 60).

For plain knitting yarn, *never* try to ply holding one yarn in the left hand and one in the right hand. Anything from a telephone bell to a sneeze can cause your hands to quiver independently, and the even tension will then be upset.

Joining threads when plying is not recommended. It can be done, by thinning out the ends of the two threads to be joined, overlapping them, pinching above the join to hold back the twist, then relaxing the pinch and letting the twist run up quickly. Care must be taken with the thinning process, and even when this is done the yarns are inclined to revert to unspun fibres, rather than becoming thinner twisted threads.

It is usually wiser in the long run to make a knot. Mark it with a coloured thread so it can be avoided later when the yarn is being knitted.

When plying very thick softly-spun yarn, loose

or fluffy fibres can catch on the hooks of the flyer. Any unevenness in the spinning will make this problem worse. If this does happen, use one hook at a time and let the wool make a direct journey from this hook to the spindle eye.

On some Scotch tension wheels with very large bobbins, you may find that when they are nearly full (and therefore heavy) it is necessary to tighten the main tensioning system as well as the brake. (See Care of Your Spinning Wheel.)

EXAMINING YOUR KNITTING WOOL

Hold a length of plied wool up to the light. The thread should have definition but it should appear light and airy and have no solid-looking areas. If the general effect is solid, it is overspun and has too much twist in it.

The remedies are either to treadle more slowly to suit the movements of your hands; or to draft back further and present a greater length of fibre to be twisted. Patchy solid areas obviously call for more even drafting.

2. Examine your wool by feeling it. It should feel soft to handle, and as a hank it should have a certain amount of loft or springiness. When a skein is held between two outstretched hands its elastic properties should be apparent. It should also be obvious that the individual threads are free and are not sticking to each other.

If the wool feels hard, flat or lifeless it could be overspun, overplied, or both. A more common cause is the choice of a poor fleece in the first place.

If you are sure the faults are caused by none of these things, it is possible that you may have spun a yarn that is unsuitable, or out of character, for the particular fleece you are using. A fine yarn for baby clothes spun from a coarse fleece more suitable for rug-making is an exaggerated example of this type of fault. Remember, fine yarn needs fine fleece.

3. Look at your skeins of wool. Have you produced the type of yarn you intended to produce? If you meant the yarn to be even, are both the spinning and the plying even, or are there a series of thick bumps and thin hard places? Poor drafting, poor joins, or pinching on unspun instead of spun fibres can all cause this trouble. Poor preparation of wool is another frequent cause of unattractive spinning.

If the spun wool you are examining is white, is it evenly white or does it have yellow patches that will show as streaks when it is used in knitting? If this is so, take more care over the selection of the fleece next time.

If the spun wool is coloured, is the colour variation distributed evenly, or is each skein a distinctive colour that will be the cause of unattractive stripes when knitted? When a coloured fleece is to be used for knitting, it is sometimes wiser to tease the whole fleece and mix it thoroughly, before carding or spinning begins.

Put a sheet on the floor, spread out the teased wool, then toss it in handfuls, high in the air. Keep on tossing and turning it over very gently until all the colours are evenly mixed. This job can take two to three hours to get an even colour from a variegated fleece. A drum-carder is a great help, but if the fleece is too fine for this treatment, mixing by tossing must be very thorough.

In one batch of wool, do all the different skeins have threads of a similar thickness? When a quantity of wool is required it is necessary to have some guide to work from. Keep a sample of your spinning wound firmly around one of the maidens on your wheel or leave a length of singles on the bobbins after plying, to act as a guide when you start spinning again.

Spinners with a plentiful supply of bobbins often spin sufficient wool for an entire project before they start plying. They then ply, by mixing the wool from different bobbins. (To do this of course you will need to have had sufficient experience to be able to judge how much yarn you are producing [fig 61].)

Fig 61. A basket of knitting wools and wooden knitting needles ★

7 Knitting with Handspun Wool

KNITTING WITH HANDSPUN WOOL requires a little more care during the planning and preparation stages than is necessary when using millspun wool and a commercial pattern.

All the wool set aside for knitting should have been washed, pre-shrunk and dried. At this stage it should still be in skeins with the length and weight of each one recorded on a tag. A few quick calculations will give the number of metres in every 25 grams (or the number of yards in an ounce), and will complete the information required.

Some knowledge of the relationship between the length and weight of millspun wool is very useful for the handspinner, when selecting knitting needles, choosing patterns, or when calculating the weight of wool which will be required for a project.

Many spinners calculate the quantity of wool that will be needed by length, rather than by weight. They find that similar projects in plain knitting require a comparable length of yarn. This system works well when there is not a great variation in the diameters of yarns used for knitting. Some caution is needed however when the threads are either extremely fine or extremely chunky.

You will find it useful to keep records of both the length and weight of the wool used for each garment, as well as samples of the fleece, your singles, and your plied yarn.

The following chart for millspun wool is useful as a guide. Different brands of wool vary slightly and current fashion dictates the length of a jersey and thus affects the amount of wool required. The metric chart is not an exact conversion of the imperial chart. New yarns have appeared on the market, and where these are in more regular supply than the older yarns, appropriate metric lengths have been given.

Conversion of your own handspun yarn to metrics is fairly simple. The number of metres in 25 grams is about four fifths the number of yards in 1 oz. For example 100 yd to 1 oz, would be the equivalent of 80 metres to 25 g.

COMPARISON OF YARN SIZES

Metric

25 g	Length of skeins	No. of 25 g balls Jersey 91 cm chest	Total length for jersey	Conventional needle size
2-ply	150-200 m	9	= 1350-1800 m	2.5 mm
3-ply	100-120 m	12	= 1200-1440 m	3 – 3.25 mm
4-ply	75-100 m	14	= 1050-1400 m	3.5 mm
Double knitting	50- 60 m	18	= 900-1080 m	4 mm
Triple knitting	30- 40 m	24	= 720- 960 m	5 mm
Chunky	25- 30 m	28	= 700- 840 m	6 mm

Imperial

1 oz	Length of skeins	No. of 1 oz balls Jersey 36" chest	Total yardage for jersey	Conventional needle size English	American
2-ply	200-250 yd	8	= 1600-2000 yd	12-13	1-0
3-ply	130-150 yd	10	= 1300-1500 yd	10-11	3-2
4-ply	100-125 yd	12	= 1200-1500 yd	9-10	4-3
Double knitting	60- 75 yd	16	= 960-1200 yd	8	5
Triple knitting	40- 50 yd	20	= 800-1000 yd	6	7
Chunky	30- 40 yd	24	= 720- 960 yd	4	9

Preliminary Skein Sorting for a Knitted Jersey

Spread the skeins out on a table and examine them carefully. Put aside any that are out of character, that is, are slightly thicker or more uneven, or have twist in the ply that is not quite up to standard. These are best used for the ribbed bands of the garment.

Choose sufficient wool for the sleeves. These skeins should be very evenly spun so that you can be confident both sleeves will knit up the same size. Choose a good average skein for your sampling tests.

Finally, cast a very critical eye over all the skeins and assess whether they are really suitable for a plain jersey in stocking stitch, if this is what you have in mind. Remember, stocking stitch exposes every fault in spinning and your wool might look more attractive knitted in a rib stitch.

KNITTING NEEDLES

Handspun wool needs plenty of room to make the most of its special qualities of softness and fullness, and for this reason knitting needles can be one size larger than would be used with comparable millspun yarn. Ribbed bands however, should always be firm, therefore the needles used for these should be two or even three sizes smaller than those used for the main part of the garment.

Well made wooden knitting needles are delightful to use with handspun wool. They have not been easy to come by, but a few craftspeople are now making them again and they are worth hunting for.

For producing an even tension the best shaped needles have sharp tips and a short taper.

TENSION SAMPLING

The making of tension samples is an essential part of knitting with handspun wool. Consult the chart for millspun wool then select the needles you think will be the most suitable, and sample as well with one size smaller and one size larger. Cast on twenty to thirty stitches and knit in stocking stitch for 5-10 cm (2-4 in). Cast off, then wash, press and dry each sample thoroughly.

Take your time over choosing your best piece. Test for 'feel'. Remember too, although you are not aiming for the flat compressed appearance which is typical of most commercial knitting, neither will you want a garment that is so loosely knitted it will not spring back into shape; so test carefully for both softness and elasticity.

Finally, on the chosen sample use pins and a measuring tape to count both the stitches and the number of rows over 5 cm (2 in). Double check if possible over 10 cm (4 in).

KNITTING PATTERNS

Knitting patterns pose the next problem. You may be lucky and find one that conforms both to a style you would like and the tension requirements you must have, but more often than not, if you find one where the stitch tension is right, the row tension is wrong. Some commercial patterns fail to mention row tension at all, and the pitfalls will be many if you are unwise enough to use these. The best solution is to make a diagram, or a full-sized pattern of a jersey that will fit, and work from that.

MAKING A PATTERN FOR A JERSEY
WITH RAGLAN SLEEVES

Anyone who has done any dressmaking or knitting will know that garments are not made to fit the body tightly. (A certain amount of ease is allowed to make them more comfortable to wear.) For your first patterns measure yourself and also a garment that fits. By comparing both sets of measurements you will soon learn where to allow for ease and how much should be allowed.

Raglan Jersey Pattern — Taking Measurements

Body measurements / **Garment measurements**

1. Bust.

   Add 5-7 cm (2-3 in) ease. Divide the total by two, for the width of back and front.

2. Around head above the eyes

   and

3. around neck loosely.

   Neck measurement of jersey is approximately halfway between these two measurements.

4. Across back, from shoulder-to-shoulder.

   This measurement is divided into thirds for the two shoulders and the back neck.

5. Shoulder measurement

   and

6. shoulder to wrist.

   Together, these equal the total sleeve length from neck to wrist (fold line of sleeve).

7. Underarm to wrist.

   Subtract 4 cm (1½ in) for sleeve seam length.

8. Armhole depth.

   Subtract sleeve seam length from the total sleeve length to find upper sleeve length (underarm to neck).

9. Around upper arm.

   Add 5-7 cm (2-3 in) for ease.

10. Wrist measurement.

    One fifth all round garment measurement or, more usually, about two thirds of the full sleeve width.

11. Centre back from neck to where the jersey should come for length.

    For side seam length subtract the armhole depth from total back length of the jersey, or measure a garment which fits.

Next draw two diagrams for both the jersey body and the sleeves.

The first one should be marked in centimetres (or inches).

Mark the second one (using your tension sampler), and convert: measurement of length — to rows; measurements of width — to stitches (fig 62a).

Further Hints

Note. Garment-body measurement is the total bust measurement plus the allowance for ease.

Sleeve measurements

1. Armhole depth is approximately one quarter of garment-body measurement.
2. Sleeve width is approximately one third of garment-body measurement.
3. Wrist measurement is two thirds sleeve width, or one fifth of the garment-body measurement if a firmer band is desired.
4. Sleeve seam equals underarm measurement less 3.5 cm (1½ in) (adult).
5. Full sleeve width is reached at least 2.5-4 cm (1-1½ in) before the armhole shaping.
6. Ribbing depth — as desired, but 5-6 cm (2-2½ in) makes a firm band.
7. Top of sleeve usually measures 2.5-4 cm (1-1½ in) across.
8. Cast-off at underarm is approximately 1 cm (½ in) for children, 2.5cm (1 in) for women, 3 cm (1¼ in) for men.

Neck measurements

1. Back neck: use one third of the back (shoulder to shoulder) measurement. If the number of stitches will not divide evenly, put the surplus stitches in the neck section. (Check with shoulder measurement.)

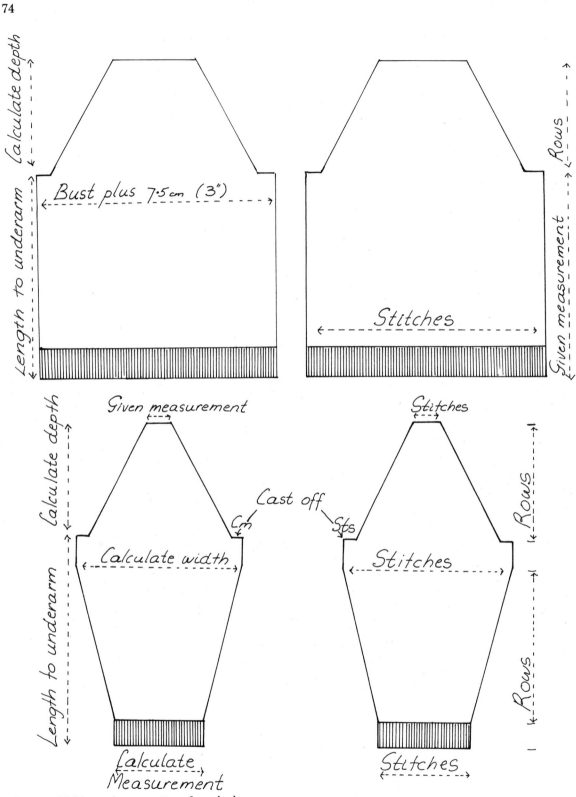

Fig 62a. Making a jersey pattern from body-measurements and a few calculations.

2. Front neck: use the same measurements and number of stitches as for the back neck.

To shape, cast off half these stitches in the centre front. The remaining half are cast off each side of the neck by knitting two together every alternate row. Then knit straight.

3. Round necks usually begin two thirds of the way up the armhole shaping.

4. V-necks usually begin level with the armhole shaping.

5. Neckband: add together the number of stitches in the neck — at the centre front, up both side fronts (one stitch for every row), across the sleeve tops and across the back neck.

Check carefully that the neckband will not be too tight — it must fit snugly but should not cause discomfort when pulled over the head. Printed patterns give measurements ranging from the actual neck measurement to 2.5 cm (1 in) less than the head measurement. Both these are rather extreme — halfway between them is better; about half the bust measurement is a good guide. Two-fifths of the garment-body measurement will give a slightly firmer band and is also a better method of calculating for extra large garments.

Making the Necessary Calculations

Sleeve increases

1. Calculate the available length for making the increases: the length of the sleeve seam, minus the depth of the cuff ribbing, minus 2.5-4 cm (1-1½ in) at the top of the sleeve below the armhole shaping.

Convert the result to the number of rows.

2. Calculate the number of stitches to be increased: the sleeve width minus the wrist width.

3. As half these stitches are increased on each side — halve the number of stitches and divide the result into the number of rows available for the spacing.

For example, let us suppose 24 stitches are to be increased in 72 rows. Each increase row has 2 stitches increased. Therefore the number of stitches to be increased is halved to find the

Fig 62b. For those who prefer to knit or calculate from the top down, directions are given for a sleeve pattern. Remember, the garment body-measurement is bust plus 7.5cm (3in) and the raglan slopes must match in both the sleeves and the body of the garment

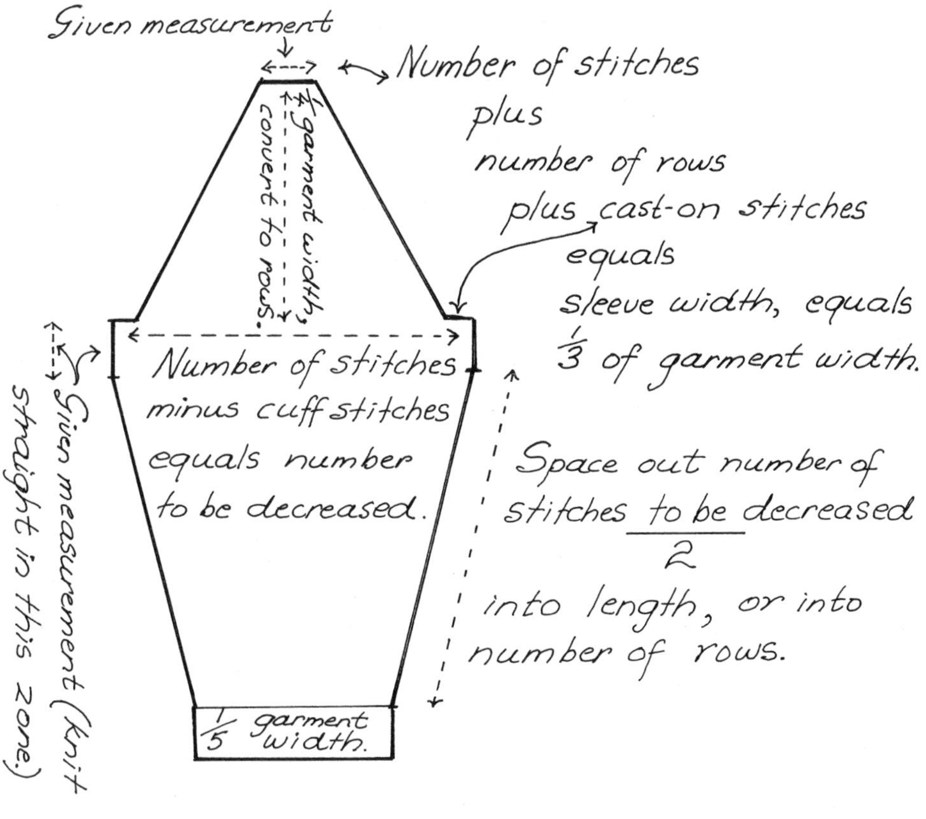

Given measurement

convert to rows

¼ garment width

Number of stitches
plus
number of rows
plus cast-on stitches
equals
sleeve width, equals
⅓ of garment width.

Number of stitches
minus cuff stitches
equals number
to be decreased.

Space out number of
stitches to be decreased
─────────────────
2
into length, or into
number of rows.

straight in this zone.

Given measurement (knit

⅕ garment width.

actual number of increase rows: $24 \div 2 = 12$. This result is then divided into the available rows to give the spacing: $72 \div 12 = 6$ — a stitch will be increased at the beginning and end of every 6th row.

Note. Sleeve increases are usually worked on the even rows 4, 6, 8 etcetera. Should the division for spacing not work out evenly, (e.g. $100 \div 12 = 8 + 4$ over) put the surplus rows into the rows which are knitted straight before the armhole. In this case you would increase every 8th row and knit 4 extra rows straight.

Sleeve decreases

1. Calculate the number of rows available for decreasing in the sleeve top (depth of sleeve top multiplied by the row tension).

   Calculate the number of stitches to be decreased: sleeve width minus the top of sleeve measurement.
2. Subtract the number of rows from the number of stitches to be decreased, and cast off half the remaining stitches on each side at the beginning of the armhole shaping.

The decreases for the front or back are worked out in the same manner. It does not matter which are done first, but the decreases on the sleeve must exactly match the decreases on the front and back, so that the seams can be joined neatly.

Just occasionally, when you are trying to get these decreases to match, the subtractions and divisions will simply not work out as they should. If this happens, make your first calculations in the usual way, from the bottom up and then work backwards, from the neck down, for the others. You may have to add instead of subtract and multiply instead of divide, but you will soon find where the adjustments to your pattern must be made (fig 62b).

Note. Work out the complete pattern before you start knitting.

KNITTING A JERSEY WITH A FAIR ISLE YOKE ON CIRCULAR NEEDLES

Seamless jerseys knitted on a circular needle are very popular with many handspinners, and a Fair Isle yoke provides an opportunity for using up all those small skeins of coloured wools.

Tension samples and calculations for measurements are done in the same way as outlined for the raglan jersey.

Circular needles must always be shorter than the all-round measurement of the garment they are being used for. Thus a 40 cm (16 in) length needle will be required for the neck and part of the yoke when sufficient decreases have taken place, but a longer needle may be more comfortable for the main part of the body. Sleeves will have to be knitted flat or on sock needles.

Sleeves

Begin with the sleeves. (This is a good idea for any jersey — there is less to unpull if you are not satisfied.)

Follow the instructions for the raglan sleeve as far as the armhole. If sock needles are being used, make the increases on either side but two stitches in from an imaginary seam-line. (A purl stitch can be used to mark the seam-line if desired.) The underarm cast-off must be double, to allow for the usual cast-off from either side of the sleeve.

Garment body

The body of the garment is knitted as a straight tube up to the armpits. Be careful not to twist the cast-on stitches; or, to avoid doing this, rib the band flat and sew it up invisibly afterwards. Again a purl seam stitch can be made on either side of the garment if desired. It provides a useful guide when casting off for the underarm, but can be more nuisance than it is worth if you read or watch television while knitting.

At the underarms, remember to cast off for both the front *and* the back, on either side of the garment. (If the castoff is normally 2.5 cm (1 in) then 5cm (2 in) must be cast-off on each side.)

Yoke

At this point the remaining stitches could all be put on to the circular needle and the remainder of the garment knitted in a cone shape up to the neck. However, a jersey made this way does not fit very well as the front neck is too high and the back neck is inclined to be low and draughty.

Normally the neckline begins two thirds of the way up the armhole shaping. For a plain jersey the neckline could still be made this way, but on a jersey with a Fair Isle yoke the pattern would be spoilt and another method of shaping must be used.

The back of a jersey is usually about 7 cm (3 in) higher than the front. Some of this depth can be acquired by building up across the back just before the ribbing for the collar begins and a further adjustment can be made on the front. For a few rows the centre front is not knitted while the rest of the jersey continues to be built up and shaped.

This shaping can be done on the circular needle, but for the first attempt it will be easier if the four pieces of the garment (the back, front and the two sleeves), are kept separate for the 5 cm (2 in) after the underarm cast-off — knit back and forth as in flat knitting.

Front adjustment

Knit about 12 mm (½ in) of the front in the normal manner of flat knitting, and make the decreases as usual at the armhole seam line. Continue these decreases throughout the following procedure:

Divide the front into thirds.

Knit across one third — turn and purl back.

Knit across the same third again but stop about 2.5 cm (1 in) short of the previous turn.

Turn again and purl back.

Repeat, making each plain row a little shorter than the previous one, until you have built up a shallow triangle at least 4 cm (1½ in) high at the armhole edge.

Make a triangle at the other side front in a similar way.

The sleeves and back should then be built up until the raglan seams match with those on the front (fig 63).

Fair Isle yoke

When Fair Isle knitting is done on circular needles, there is always a little jump in the pattern at the beginning of each new row. How obvious this will be will depend on the pattern, but it usually offends least when placed at the centre back. Adjust the stitches on the needle so the rows start there.

Break the wool. Starting at the centre back, pick up half the back stitches, then those of one sleeve, then right across the front; pick up the stitches of the second sleeve and finish with the second half of the back.

Decreases

Calculate the number of stitches that still have to be decreased for the neck.

To dispose of these, divide them by four or five and then make four or five decrease rows spaced evenly apart up the yoke; for example if you still have 20 cm (8 in) to knit to the neck, decrease one

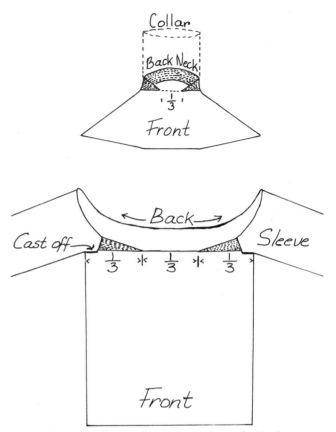

Fig 63. The shaded areas show where a jersey knitted on a circular needle should be built up to ensure that there will be sufficient difference in depth between the back and front necklines. The diagram has been drawn in two parts, showing the upper and lower sections separately

quarter of the unwanted stitches every 5 cm (2 in). Spread the decrease stitches evenly around the jersey. Try to place them on rows with no pattern, or between patterns where they will not show.

Some Fair Isle yokes have a large pattern at the base, and it may be impossible to decrease while knitting this. Just decrease as soon as you can and space the decrease rows from then on. Sometimes, particularly for a broad-shouldered person, the jersey is more comfortable when made this way. However once the shoulders are reached (about 13 cm [5 in] from the armpit), the decreases must be done at regular intervals.

Decrease one third of the stitches straight away, decrease another third halfway to the neck, and the last third at the neck.

Never make two big decrease rows close together. Always space them, otherwise the garment will pucker.

Fair Isle patterns

Design your patterns on graph paper. If you have never attempted to design before, start with smallish patterns that repeat every four or six stitches. Large patterns usually look better at the base of the yoke, and it is certainly easier to fit in smaller patterns nearer the neck where there are fewer stitches.

Avoid patterns that have skips of more than five stitches. If the pattern stitches do not divide into the number of stitches on your needle, make the necessary decreases, spaced evenly around the jersey, until they do. Sometimes it is easier to increase one or two stitches.

Building up the back neck

This is done when the yoke is finished but before the ribbing is begun. Divide the stitches on the needle by three. Mark off one third and centre it at the front.

Knit from the centre back, right across the shoulder to the beginning of the front. Turn.

Purl back to the other side of the front.

Knit backwards and forwards across these stitches always stopping 2-3 cm (1 in) short of where the previous turn was made, until the back has been built up 2.5-4 cm (1-1½ in).

Collar

Put the neck stitches on to a finer needle and rib up for the collar as usual (fig 64).

Fig 64. A handspun, handknitted jersey, designed by the knitter. A multicoloured fleece was used; the wool was flick carded, then spun from the assorted colours chosen at random. Some of the darker grey part of the fleece was spun separately for the yoke pattern. Apart from the flower motifs the Fair Isle yoke pattern consists of simple zigzags. However, the proportions of light and dark areas in the yoke were carefully planned. The weight of the garment is 310 g (11 oz) ★

Do not feel rigidly bound by these instructions; they should be used as a guide.

For example, if you know that an armhole depth of one quarter of your bust measurement is too large or too small, alter it. Home sewers are much more venturesome about altering patterns. They happily cut off parts they do not want and add extra where they need it.

Do learn to make your own patterns. Remember people had been knitting for hundreds, if not thousands, of years before commercial knitting patterns became available.

Weavers rarely buy patterns for kaftans, primitive jackets, tabards or ponchos. After taking measurements they cut a paper or calico pattern of the garment they wish to make, try it on for size and away they go. Knitters can work in exactly the same way and they have far more freedom than any sewer or weaver because of the elasticity of knitted fabric.

If you are interested in making fashion garments, keep an eye on the fashion industry to see what is being worn. Then take courage and experiment with your own ideas. This can be far more fun and much more rewarding than sitting hour after hour following someone else's pattern row by row.

Your own original ideas will be a fitting complement to your handspun yarn.

8 Spinning
Part II: More Advanced Spinning

INDIVIDUAL SPINNING STYLES differ considerably and this is very natural. However, it would be a mistake to assume that style alone is responsible for the variety of actions that can be observed when watching spinners at work. Different fleeces or projects demand different methods of working, and this includes preparation, drafting and spinning. So far only one method of drafting has been described but other methods will now be discussed and their uses explained. The spinner should then have a fuller understanding of the complexities of thread construction.

A SUMMARY OF DRAFTING METHODS

1. The Short Forward Draft
The rear hand holds the wool and remains stationary about 15 cm (6 in) from the orifice. The front hand pulls forward and slides back, between the fibre mass and the orifice, controlling the draft, and smoothing the fibres that have been twisted.

This is a traditional draft for a worsted spin; it is a very tightly controlled method and is relatively slow. The drafting and the twisting areas are sharply defined and never overlap.

2. The Short Backward Draft
The reverse of the first method — the front hand remains stationary. The rear hand (which holds the fibre mass), draws back to draft and then moves forward to allow the fibres to run through the fingers of the front hand, before they twist and wind on to the bobbin. The front fingers provide a smoothing action on the twisting thread and also control the separation of the twisting zone from the drafting zone.

This draft can also be used for a worsted spin. It too is relatively slow, and the drafting and twisting zones are again sharply defined. However, it is not so tightly controlled as the previous method as the drafting zone is more flexible.

A further advantage is that it leads naturally to other drafting methods which are used for making a variety of yarns. It is therefore an excellent method for beginners to learn.

3. The Medium Draft
The rear hand holds the fleece and drafts right back as far as is comfortable, keeping the drafting area just ahead of the gathering twist. The front hand can either work near the orifice or move back with the rear hand, but at a constant distance.

With this method not only the length of the draft, but also the rate, control the diameter of the yarn produced and the amount of twist it receives. Winding-on is usually rapid but can be controlled to insert extra twist in the yarn when necessary.

This is the most flexible draft of all. It is a very comfortable method of drafting, which involves both hands working for a quickly-spun, soft, airy yarn. The length of the draft from about the hip to the orifice makes it easy to see the yarn being spun before it is wound on to the bobbin. The twist is allowed to enter the drafting zone as in woollen spinning. However, whether the resulting spin will be more worsted or more woollen in character will depend upon the type of fleece used (long or short stapled), and the way it was prepared.

All preparation methods are suitable for this way of drafting. In brief — it allows complete freedom of fleece choice and preparation, for the speedy production of a light, airy general-purpose yarn, which is often called woolly-worsted.

4. The Long Draw
Both hands wait near the orifice for the twist to accumulate. One hand remains in this position, holding back then releasing the twist. The other hand draws the yarn sideways to full arm's length, keeping the draw just ahead of the twist. The thread is returned to the orifice at a fairly rapid but controlled rate, and both hands wait for the twist to gather and be released again.

This is the traditional draft for a woollen spin. The time spent on the hand-carding of short fibres, to get them arranged at right angles to the spin, is more than offset by the extremely rapid spinning that results from this method of drafting. It requires practice, but is well worth mastering.

WORSTED AND WOOLLEN SPUN YARNS

Worsted spinning

The spinning of a true worsted thread has not been popular for some time and this could be for several reasons. Until recently, information has been lacking about the combs and the procedures for preparing the wool. The finishing process for worsted cloth is beyond the capabilities of the average home-weaver, therefore the weavers have not been particularly interested in worsted yarns. The knitters, many of whom do spin a worsted-type yarn, find the beautiful, clean, free fleeces they use require only the minimum amount of preparation before they can be spun into a good thread. Naturally they hesitate to subject these fleeces to the heavy combing process which is necessary for the production of a true worsted yarn.

Anyone interested in worsted spinning can do no better than read Peter Teal's excellent book *Hand Woolcombing and Spinning*, which fully describes the whole process and the equipment required. A summary of worsted spinning is given below to enable the handspinner to understand the differences between a worsted and a woollen spin. (See fig 65a)

The longer-stapled fleeces are required for worsted spinning and during their preparation the fibres are kept as much as possible in parallel formation. A comb specially constructed for the purpose is clamped to a bench and the fleece is anchored in the tines. A second comb, which has been warmed, is then swung at the fleece to open up the staples and remove all the short fibre. This operation is repeated several times, then the combed fibres are elongated into a long sliver and are twisted into a roving, before they are spun.

During spinning a short draft is used, that is, the drafting takes place *before* the fibres are twisted. Worsted spun yarns are nearly always plied. The plying removes some of the twist and returns the fibres to as near parallel formation as is possible. Lying this way they reflect the light and so display the sheen that is always associated with a worsted spun yarn.

Fig 65a. *Upper*: woollen yarn consists of short fibres, first prepared by carding, and then spun by the woollen method. It is typically light, airy, elastic and rather fuzzy.

Lower: worsted yarn consists of longer fibres which are combed into parallel formation, and then spun by the worsted method. It is typically smooth, lustrous, and somewhat heavier than woollen spun yarn

Woollen spinning

This is another important method of spinning because the yarns so produced are used for the true woollen cloth. Woollen-spun singles are used for both warp and weft, and when the cloth is washed (or 'fulled') after weaving, the fibres cohere in a way that does not happen when the cloth is woven with plied yarns.

Wherever there has been a traditional production of tweeds, flannels, blankets and rugs, there has also been a tradition of woollen spinning. The spin can produce a firm but lightweight thread for woollens, or it can be plied to give a light air-filled thread for knitted garments that are warm and soft, but not heavy.

The shorter-stapled fleeces are required for this spin. They are hand-carded and rolled into firm rolags so that the fibres lie at right angles to the yarn being spun; the arrangement is like a long coiled spring entrapping a column of air. The whole spinning process is carried out in a way which will retain as much as possible of this air in the spun yarn. Drafting and twisting take place simultaneously.

SPINNING A WORSTED THREAD USING
THE SHORT DRAFT

The Crossbred wools are ideally suited to this type of spinning. Although few home spinners will own the more complicated preparation equipment necessary for producing a true worsted thread, it is still quite possible to achieve a worsted-type yarn by preparing the wool with an ordinary comb. The staples can be opened up with a heavy or light combing, then spun from the butt end; or drum-carded wool can be used with the batts torn lengthwise.

The aim of worsted spinning is to produce a smooth thread. This is achieved by removing all short fibres and by endeavouring to keep the long ones in parallel formation during both preparation and spinning. However, when the shorter fibres are not removed in the combing process, cohesion is better and spinning is easier.

A short draft is used when spinning. The twisting area is always separated from the drafting area, and usually it is better if the hand controlling the fibres and the drafting moves back and away from the hand controlling the twist. The fingers which control the twist also work at smoothing the yarn. The thumb rolls across the fingers, helping to tuck in any stray fibres. The basics of this method have already been described in the section on 'Learning to Spin'.

The short forward draft also produces a soft worsted spin. Its weakness lies not in the results that are achieved by using the method correctly, but rather in the restrictions it imposes upon the spinner — it does not lead naturally to other styles of spinning. It can be useful, however, for spinning very slippery fibres such as mohair and samoyed dog hair.

SPINNING A WOOLLY — WORSTED YARN
USING THE MEDIUM DRAFT

In the days when the cloth trade was dependent on the output of handspinners, this might not have been recognised as an acceptable method of making a yarn. Today, free from the restrictions imposed by the demands of commerce, we can use traditional practices when they meet our requirements, or we can adapt them and develop them as spinners through the ages must surely have done.

The medium draft follows naturally from the short worsted draft, and many spinners have discovered it for themselves when trying to spin more quickly. It provides an opportunity to become familiar with hand-carding and spinning the shorter stapled fleeces, and it also gives experience in controlling the fibres when the twist is allowed to run into the drafting area. In this way it leads naturally to the long draw required for a traditional woollen spin.

Preparation should be suitable for the type of fleece — both of which will affect the character of the final yarn.

A much longer draw is used than for the short backward draft, but its direction does not change. Attach the wool to the leader and start treadling; but instead of pinching and allowing the thread to wind on, keep drafting back in one smooth movement until the rear hand is above a point in line with your hip. Keep the thread horizontal.

The twist should be running into the fibres right at the apex of the drafting triangle and there will be both spun thread and drafted fibres between the two hands. There is no pinching off until the full length of the draft has been achieved (fig 65b).

The front hand can support the thread either by moving backwards or remaining near the orifice: its position depends somewhat on the way the wool has been prepared.

Note. Occasionally when this method of drafting is being taught, students are made to practise with one hand only. This is an excellent way to master the long smooth draw, but learners sometimes fail to grasp that for the final production of a good spinning thread two hands are needed.

The spinner must control the rate of winding on, so that the thread gathers sufficient twist for its diameter — it is all too easy to produce an undertwisted thread. Practise by counting the number of treadlings you use to draft back, and the number you use to go forward again. You must be consistent. Practise too until you can make the thread thick or thin.

Because this method of spinning produces a

light airy yarn it follows that the thread will also be plump. You will need to spin your singles a little finer than is necessary when using the short draw, to get a yarn of comparable diameter.

The tension on the wheel should be very light and treadling fairly rapid. The desirability of slow treadling is so impressed upon beginners that they often fail to realise they have outgrown the need for it. Nor is it always desirable. With these woollen-type spins more competent drafting can take place with a reasonably fast treadling speed.

Note. This spin is not achieved by using a picking movement with the front hand while the rear hand merely clutches the fleece and rests permanently on the hip or the lap. On the contrary, the drafting hand is constantly on the move, first drafting back while releasing the fibres *and then moving forward again*, so that the yarn can be wound onto the bobbin.

Fig 65b. Spinning a woolly-worsted yarn with the medium draw. Unlike worsted spinning there are both spun yarn and drafted fibres between the two hands. There is also a longer length of spun yarn visible with each draw, and this makes it easier to keep the size of the thread constant

SPINNING A WOOLLEN THREAD USING THE LONG DRAW

There are several things worth noting before this spin is attempted.
1. With a horizontal wheel it is usually more comfortable for the right hand to do the drafting. It draws from near the orifice — sideways across the body to full arm's length. The draw may be done with the left hand, but this can sometimes be more awkward — as a certain amount of extra room space is required!
2. The left hand, which is responsible for holding back and releasing the twist, usually works in an overhand position. It stays near the orifice throughout. The movement used for releasing the twist is a rapid opening and closing of the thumb and fingers.
3. Treadling must be much faster than for worsted spinning.
4. The draw takes place at a rate that keeps it just ahead of the ever-creeping twist; in other words, the twist is already running into the fibres as the rolag is drawn out.
5. The portion of the rolag which is to be drawn out is released before the draw starts. No

further fibres are released during the draw.

Note. The woollen spin can be done on either a Scotch tension wheel or a double band wheel, but it is more easily accomplished on the latter. The yarn is drawn out fairly quickly, but when fully extended is not sufficiently twisted. The extra twist is inserted on the return journey with a double band wheel. When a Scotch tension wheel is used, the spinner must wait with the arm fully extended and the yarn held taut, while it gathers the necessary twist, for it will receive none (or very little) on its return journey with this type of wheel.

Attach the wool to the leader in the usual way. Leave about 20 cm (8 in) of thread between the wheel and the front hand so the twist has somewhere to accumulate. The front hand (in an overhand position) will be pinching the thread about 2 cm (1 in) away from the end near the rolag.

The drafting hand holding the rolag waits beside the other hand with about 5 cm (2 in) of the rolag protruding (fig 66).

Treadle 1, 2, 3, 4, 5 — wait while the twist gathers.

Continue treadling — release the twist through the finger and thumb and —

At the same time extend the drafting arm sideways, drawing out the portion of rolag as the twist runs into it (figs 67 and 68).

When the thread is fully extended return it quickly, allowing the yarn to wind on. Do not smooth it with the front fingers.

Remember to hold back sufficient yarn for gathering the next lot of twist.

Expose the next 5 cm (2 in) of rolag — and repeat.

This is the most difficult draft to describe in words, as so much depends on 'feel'.

When the rolag is being drawn out a considerable amount of resistance is felt *between the two hands* (almost as if you were playing with a piece of heavy elastic). In other forms of drafting, the front hand supports the spin, whereas in the long draw the tension between the two hands alternates. Sometimes the hands actually work against each other — sometimes the tension between them is relaxed.

The twist-releasing movement is also one of touch. At first a rapid opening and shutting of the forefinger and thumb will be necessary, but with practice this becomes a more relaxed, rolling movement.

At the end of the draw the yarn will be very light and airy. Take care that it gathers sufficient twist on its return journey to the orifice. The thread must have definition.

If there are slubs in the extended yarn, gather it up on the return journey, while still in its light and airy state, and again use the tension between the two hands to draw out the slubs and even the thread. Poorly prepared rolags can be the cause of slubs because they make it difficult to achieve a steady draw. The rolags must have the fibres evenly distributed. However, a regularly occurring slub at the beginning of each draw is usually caused by slight hesitation at the moment of 'take off'.

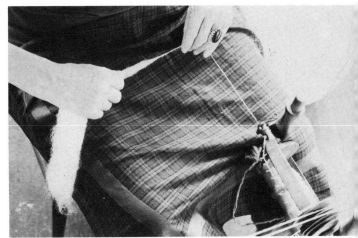

Fig 66. Spinning a woollen yarn with the long draw. Ready to begin — waiting in position while treadling. *Note*: 1. the length of the thread, between the hand and the orifice, in which the twist is gathering; and 2. between the two hands there is a short length of spun thread *and* the short exposed portion of the rolag

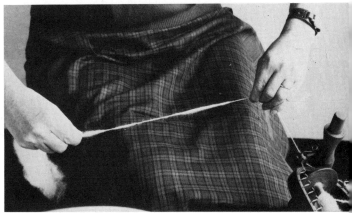

Fig 67. The twist has been released and the right hand is moving away from the left hand, which remains in the same position as before. At this stage there is considerable tension between the two hands and a good deal of pressure is being exerted by both of them. The thread is half formed

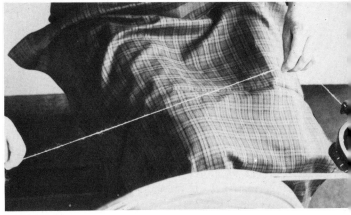

Fig 68. The right hand has moved away sufficiently far for the wool to have been drawn out into an even thread. The tension between the two hands can now be relaxed while the right hand moves back toward the orifice, allowing the thread to wind onto the bobbin

If the thread falls apart, not enough twist was collected before it was released. The front fingers must always be ready to pinch the thread should it be necessary to gather more twist.

A fine thread, however, can break through becoming overtwisted. If this keeps happening the draw must be quicker, particularly at its start, as the most vulnerable place is where the rolag joins the spun thread. Make sure you pinch a little away from this spot. There is of course a very fine dividing line between firm twist and overtwist, and more so in a fine thread.

If the woollen spun threads are to be used for woollen cloth the warp threads must be 'firmly' spun. A simple test is that they should snap, rather than fluff out and fray when you break them. Some woollen cloths are woven with both warp and weft yarns twisted in the same direction. However, in some localities it is traditional for warp and weft to be spun with the twist in opposite directions. (See Construction and Design of Yarns — singles — later in this chapter.)

SPINNING TO SUIT THE FLEECE

For every fleece there is one particular size of spun yarn which will best display the unique character of that fleece. The maxim that fine wool is required for a fine thread, and that stronger wool is more suitable for thicker yarns, still leaves much room for error when deciding *exactly* how fine or thick a thread should be.

Let the fleece itself be your guide. Study the crimp patterns in the staples and gauge the distance between them. Then pull out two or three staples and experiment. Draft them on your lap and twist them fairly firmly into a thread with your fingers. Fold the twisted thread in half so it plies back on itself naturally.

Make several little samples of varying thicknesses, then compare the results with the original fleece. The sample with the distance between the twists in the ply most closely related to the size of the crimp pattern is the one most appropriate for that particular fleece. Not only will it look and feel best, but it will also be the quickest to spin.

Note. — It takes a little practice to twist your yarn by hand to suit the diameter of the thread you are making. Don't be misled by overtwisting or undertwisting.

SPINNING FOR MAXIMUM EFFICIENCY, OR PRODUCTION SPINNING

After several years' apprenticeship on an ordinary spinning wheel, you may feel it has become too slow for you. Professional weavers often resort to electric spinners, believing them to be the only alternative. However, a treadle wheel may still be used although it may not be the one you already possess.

You will require a sturdy well-made wheel (preferably double band) with a treadle action that will allow you to treadle *comfortably* at 100-120 times per minute. It should have a high drive ratio — somewhere between 15:1 or 20:1. The wool must be washed and well prepared and it should be spun using a long draw as for a woollen spin. Spinning to suit the fleece helps further.

Drive ratio is relative not only to the amount of twist required by various yarns, but also to the speed at which the spinner works. High ratio can produce high twist, but coupled with quicker drafting, can produce low twist and more yardage.

CONSTRUCTION AND DESIGN OF YARNS

A whole new world of thread construction and design will open up for any spinner who has both a sympathetic understanding of the fleeces she is using and sufficient control of her spinning wheel to make the best use of their special characteristics.

Even a child can tell that, apart from differences in colour, woollen threads can be thick, thin, shiny, dull, hard, soft, smooth or textured. However, a spinner can go a step further and recognise that these differences stem from:

Fleece breeds.

Differences in fibre diameter within the breed.

Methods of preparation.

Methods of drafting.

Techniques used in spinning.

Techniques used in plying.

In other words, the differences are caused partly by the actual construction of the thread and partly by the choice of a suitable fleece to make the desired construction possible. Once this is understood it is not difficult to design and construct any woollen thread of your own choosing.

Thin or fine yarn

For fine soft thread use fine fleeces e.g. Merino, Halfbreds, Down, fine Romney etc.

For fine hard thread use stronger fleeces.

Preparation. This should be suitable for the fleece type.

Spinning. A very loose tension and quicker treadling are needed. The thread can be plied or used as singles. Take care that a very fine thread has sufficient twist to give it strength. This is particularly important if it is to be plied or used as a singles warp.

Thick yarn

Thick and bulky yarn requires a fleece with plenty of loft or puff — Cheviot, Perendale, Southdown, fine Romney. Weightier thick thread requires heavier fleeces — stronger Romney, Leicester, Coopworth etc.

Careful and thorough preparation of fibres is essential.

Spinning. Adjust the size of the fibre mass to the bulkiness of the yarn and make sure the fibres are free to be drawn into the draft and not clutched in the hand. Tighten the tension and treadle slowly to allow time for drafting the larger number of fibres without overtwisting them.

Competent spinners will be able to handle this spin using the medium draw — even for very bulky

yarns. Beginners will find it easier to use a quick short draft, very quick and very short.

Make sure the thread will go through the orifice if it is to be plied. A larger spindle pulley may help.

Shiny yarn

Fleece. Choose long-stapled lustrous breeds — Leicester, Romney, Coopworth.

Preparation. Comb, to keep the parallel fibre arrangement.

Spinning. Use a worsted spin. Plying will further enhance the sheen.

Dull yarn

Fleece. Choose from breeds that lack lustre — Cheviot and Down breeds.

Preparation should be suitable for fleece type.

Spinning. Use a woolly-worsted or a woollen spin.

Hard yarn

Fleece. Choose a coarse or strong fleece breed — Lincoln, Leicester, strong Romney or Coopworth.

Preparation. Comb or flick-card.

Spinning. Over spin and/or over ply, for thicker threads. A fine thread spun with only moderate twist will also be hard if a strong fleece is used.

Soft yarn

A very careful choice of fleece is needed to suit the diameter of the yarn being spun. A fine yarn will need a fine-fleece Merino, Halfbred, Corriedale etc.

A medium yarn will need fine to medium-fine fleeces — Corriedale, Romney, Perendale. For a thicker yarn use Romney — medium etc.

Careful preparation and spinning are needed to suit the twist to the diameter of the yarn. It may be plied or singles yarn.

A woollen-type spin will give a soft airy thread, but woollen or worsted spins at their best are both suitable.

Smooth yarn

Fleece. Long-stapled fleeces — Romney, Leicester, Coopworth.

Preparation. A heavy combing should be given to the wool.

Spinning. The smooth look is associated with worsted-spun yarn.

Singles yarns

The choice of fleece, preparation and spinning, will depend upon the use to which the yarn will be put; most of the yarns already discussed can be used as singles. Weft threads are often spun more softly than warp threads — but not always; for instance many tweeds use the same yarn for warp and weft. Weft threads are sometimes spun in the opposite direction from warp threads ($\overleftarrow{s}$ + $\overrightarrow{z}$ twists), but again this is not always the case (fig 69).

Twist in all singles yarns should be appropriate for the article for which the thread will be used. For example, upholstery yarns require more twist than yarns intended for stoles and shawls.

Slub singles

Yarns with regular slubs, to create texture in weaving or knitting, are spun by pinching *the drafted fibres* instead of the end of the twisted thread. This is exactly the opposite procedure from that used when spinning an even thread. (See fig 56.)

The size of the slub and the diameter of the yarn between the slubs are controlled by drafting and by the length of the staple. Slightly quicker treadling helps. All singles yarns must have their twist set by washing (fig 70).

Plied yarns

Plain plied yarns for knitting have already been adequately covered, but for other projects extra twist may be required. The more twist put into the ply the more will be taken out of the original singles.

If necessary, either adjust the amount of twist in the singles; or, alter the direction of the twist, in either the ply or the singles.

Crepe plied

1. Spin four or six spools of singles: $\overrightarrow{z}$ twist
2. Ply these together in pairs: $\overleftarrow{s}$ twist
3. Ply the plied yarns together: $\overrightarrow{z}$ twist

Plied coloured yarns and plied yarns with mixed fibres

There is a great scope for adding colour and creating texture with plied yarns. Yarns of different colours can be plied together. Yarns of different fibres can also be plied together, for example, wool and silk. Handspun and millspun yarns can be plied together, although this requires a little planning.

If an ordinary smooth plied yarn is wanted — the direction of the twist in the commercial yarn must be studied before the handspun yarn is spun. Break off a length of the millspun wool. Twist the end furthest away from you to the right (exactly as the spinning wheel would do). If the thread twists more tightly, it was spun in that direction

Fig 69. $\overleftarrow{s}$ and $\overrightarrow{z}$ twist

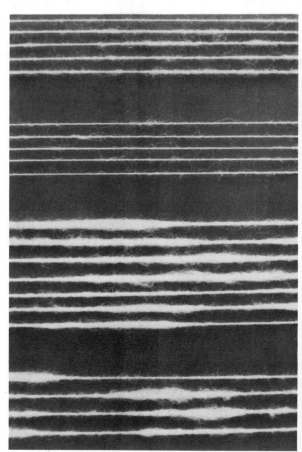

Fig 70. A close-up view of singles yarns. From the top down: Woollen spun, worsted spun, long slubs from long staples and short slubs from shorter staples. (Note how quickly regularly-spaced slubs begin to form a pattern even in this small area. If you wish slubs to appear less regularly in your weaving, spin them that way in the yarn.)

originally and it would be a Z⃗ twisted thread. If the twist comes undone, the original twist was obviously in the opposite direction and it would be an S⃖ twisted thread. Spin your handspun yarn in the same direction.

Textured plied yarns

Many of these textured plied threads will require the two yarns to be fed into the orifice at different rates. Hold the yarns in separate hands; a lazy-Kate on either side of the spinner is a great help.

Beads

Spin a bulky yarn Z⃗ twist.
Spin a yarn as fine as sewing cotton S⃖ twist. Ply together S⃖ twist but try —
1. letting them ply together evenly.
2. retarding the fine yarn and letting the bulky yarn feed in more rapidly.

In both examples the fine yarn will become more twisted and will therefore bite into the puffier yarn (fig 71).

Knots

Spin two singles Z⃗ with high twist (or they will break) and then ply S⃖.

Hold the threads in separate hands.

Make the knots as the hands move *forward* towards the orifice, by winding one yarn around the other until a little heap is formed. Use a little figure-of-eight movement with the winding yarn and hold it almost at right angles to the core thread.

Draw the hands *back* while the ply between the knots is forming so there is room to move forward for knot-making again. Yarns of two colours may be used.

If knots are made with alternate yarns and hands, equal amounts will be used from each spool.

Tufts

Tufts can be made from small bits of unspun fleece, small pieces of spun thread, or small pieces of a different fibre altogether. One hand is needed for dropping-in the tufts, so the other hand must be responsible for the plying. The yarns must be held as far apart as possible, so make use of several fingers. Drop the tufts in the space just as the twist is about to run in. Work while the twist is running back towards you.

Loops

1. Spin a single thread Z⃗ twisted — fairly fine, for the loop thread. Strong silky fleece and a worsted spin are essential for this thread.

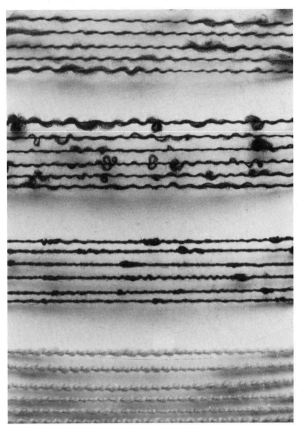

Fig 71. Some fancy plied yarns. From the top down: softly spun slubs plied with a very fine thread, loops, knots, and bead yarn

2. The support thread should be Z⃗ twisted, fairly fine, and softly twisted. A medium fleece is required: 50's/52's. (The support thread must be inconspicuous so do not use a bulky thread.)
3. Ply with Z⃗ twist also. Hold the support thread under tension and push the other thread into loops as you ply — they will look rather a mess at this stage.
4. Ply again, S⃖ twist, with a third thread (woollen spun Down thread is ideal), Z⃗ twisted. Retard the third thread slightly and arrange the loops as you go. The second plying holds them in place.

To Summarise

You need three singles threads from three different fleece types with three different spins — but all spun in the same direction Z⃗ twist.
The first plying is also Z⃗ twisted.
The second plying is S⃖ twisted.

Note. **All fancy yarns need washing to set the twist.**
They are better weighted while drying.

SPINNERS' GOSSIP

Recently an old wartime recipe for restoring shrunken woollens came to light:

Dissolve 90 g (3 oz) of epsom salts in boiling water.

Add sufficient cold water to cool and to make the solution up to about 9 litres (2 gal).

Soak the garment for two hours then pull it into shape.

Squeeze gently and dry.

It has been tested on a pure wool mountaineering shirt and a hand-knitted jersey and has proved most successful. However, it was not so successful on another jersey that had become matted through rubbing against machinery, and it had no effect at all on a cloth of a wool and cotton mixture.

Some spinners who spin washed fleece add one to two 5 ml spoons of olive oil to the final rinsing water and find this is sufficient to re-oil the fleece. However, the wool needs to be spun and re-washed fairly promptly. Sometimes a little oil on the fingers during spinning is all that is necessary.

The test used for judging the twist in spun yarn can also be used to observe the amount of twist that will be required in the ply. When a yarn is folded and allowed to ply back on itself it finds the natural balance between the twist in the spinning and the twist required in the plying.

An old knitting book came to light recently, but its age could be gauged only from the patterns, which showed little girls' long white gaiters finished with large satin bows above the knees, and long woolly combinations with a buttoned flap at the back.

From the handspinners' and knitters' point of view, the most interesting comment was in the foreword: the editors bemoaned the fact that knitting wool was in future to be sold by weight instead of length. It seems that previously the wool, regardless of whether it was 2, 3, 4 or 6-ply, was sold in hanks of a standard length of sixty turns.

It was also interesting to find that all the knitting instructions included drawings of the pattern pieces on graph paper.

Here are two ways to wind balls so that the yarn will pull out from the middle.

1. Leave a good length free at the beginning, then wind a butterfly, or figure-of-eight, around your outspread thumb and little finger. After half a dozen or so turns, fold the eight over on itself to make a nought. Continue to wind a ball in the usual way around this core, making sure the free starting end does not get caught in.

2. Slip a good starting length down the core of a small cardboard tube. Wind the rest of the wool into a ball around the tube and slip it off when completed.

This is an excellent way to treat leftover singles on your bobbins: in an emergency you can ply the wool from both ends of the ball as, contrary to popular belief, the twist in the spun yarn slopes in the same direction from both ends. This may be more easily understood if a length of plied yarn is studied — the slope of the twist is easier to see.

For those who have trouble remembering which way to spin an s spin and which way to spin a z spin: sit in front of your wheel and move your hand in one direction, across the top of your drive wheel. Your hand moves in the same direction to both turn the wheel and to write the first stroke of the appropriate letter. For example: the hand moves to the right — to turn the wheel in this direction and to write the first stroke of the letter z. The hand moves to the left, — to turn the wheel that way and also to write the first part of the letter s.

Fine, Medium or Bulky? Spinners are often confused about what yarn is acceptable when they are asked to spin a fine, medium, or bulky yarn.

The chart for millspun wools would suggest:

Fine:	100-200 m, per 25 g	(130-250 yd per oz)	equivalent of 2 + 3-ply.
Medium:	50-100 m, per 25 g	(60-125 yd per oz)	equivalent of 4-ply + DK
Bulky:	40 m or less, per 25 g	(50 yd or less per oz)	equivalent of TK + chunky

9 Dyeing Wool

PEOPLE involved in the textile crafts are usually interested in colour − they enjoy the challenge and the stimulation of working with a wider range of colours than those found in the somewhat neutral tones of natural fleece. Dyeing wool is an absorbing occupation and adds yet another dimension to the whole craft.

There are several ways of approaching the subject. If large quantities of wool are to be dyed it is often simpler and quicker to use synthetic dyes. A packet or tin of dye can be bought from the nearest store and the instructions that accompany that particular brand can be followed. Spinners and weavers however would be better advised to use the dyes manufactured specifically for the wool industry. These dyes are extremely fast to light and washing and are not difficult to use if the instructions are followed carefully.

However, when time is of no particular consequence and the dyer enjoys the benefits of outdoor life and involvement with nature, she may be more interested in that fascinating hobby of plant dyes.

DYEING EQUIPMENT

The following equipment is needed:
A set of accurate measuring spoons.
Scales for weighing the wool.
Two sticks for stirring (wooden spoons are ideal).
A bucket.
A colander − preferably with handles so it will sit astride the top of the bucket for draining purposes.
Dyepots. These may range from large enamel mugs or small pots (for mixing and sampling) to a much larger stockpot for dyeing. An old-fashioned washer boiler is ideal if you become really enthusiastic.
What you use will depend on what you can afford and what is available. For general use and cheapness, an enamel container is the most useful, but it must be unchipped. A lid is needed, but if necessary you can improvise this. Stainless steel is expensive but lasts well and is easy to keep clean. Aluminium brightens some colours when dyeing with plants, but the saucepan will be ruined if copper sulphate is used in it. Iron and copper pots dull, or 'sadden', your colours but can be useful if wanted for this purpose.

The pot of your choice should fit the ring or element on your cooking stove. Remember, a tall narrow pot is always better than a wide shallow one as it will be suitable for small as well as larger dyelots.

It is advisable to have on hand:
Some form of protective clothing.
Plenty of newspaper to cover kitchen benches.
An old cloth for mopping up spills.
Rubber or plastic gloves to protect your hands from dyes and poisonous chemicals.
For safety − use a dyepot that all the family recognise as such; and have a box or basin in which everything can be put away where it will be absolutely safe from small children.

Wool
Wool must be thoroughly washed, and wetted for at least 30 minutes, in warm water. It may be already spun and skeined (in which case it must have ties around it to prevent tangling), or it may be unspun and still in the fleece.

Spun and skeined wool
Many knitters prefer to dye skeined wool. Softly-spun wools take dye colour easily although care is needed for even dyeing. This is not a difficulty with two or three smallish skeins but can be a problem with a large amount of wool, unless a very large dye vessel is available. A 'dyeing disaster' may ruin enough yarn to prevent the completion of a project.

Fleece
Most weavers prefer to dye unspun wool. Fleece absorbs dye well, although some types of fleece do so more readily than others. Large quantities of wool can be dyed this way − either in one lot, if the dye vessel is large enough, or in separate lots in

smaller dyepots. Any unwanted unevenness in colour can be remedied later during the carding process.

Dyed fleece wool can be used for designing yarns incorporating several colours, or several shades of one colour, from different dyelots. A small amount of dyed wool will be lost in the teasing, carding and spinning processes.

SYNTHETIC DYES

Synthetic dyes are easy to work with, have a high degree of fastness to both light and washing, and can be used to reproduce a required colour more accurately than plant dyes. However, it is worth remembering that perfecting synthetic dyes is a science to which many people have devoted their whole working lives. The instructions in this book have been reduced to their simplest terms and when followed with care should give good results. But slapdash methods may bring failures and disappointments — don't blame the dyes!

The Names Of Dye Colours
Sample cards or catalogues for synthetic dyes usually list the colours in the following manner: the basic name of the colour, followed by several letters or numbers: Brilliant Red BL, Brilliant Scarlet RL, Yellow 3 GL.

The letters mean the following:

R = reddish tinge; 2R more red; 6R very red.

B = bluish.

G = yellow (from German *gelb*).

L means fast to light; LL very fast.

Therefore red GL — is a yellow-red and is fast to light.

Red 3BLL — is a very blue red and is very fast to light.

The L is not included in the identification system used for Panhue brand dyes. This does not mean they are not fast to light — merely that fastness in their dyes is an understood quality. CIBA dyes do include the information.

Note. Dyes especially for wool are manufactured by a number of firms, and brands available for the handweaver are advertised in weavers' magazines.

Recipe
The standard recipe is:

1-3% dye

1-2% acetic acid

10-20% glauber salts crystals

1-2% albegal A

In the dye industry dyeings are always de-scribed in percentages. In other words for a 1% dye, 1 kg of dye is used to dye 100 kg of yarn. This information does not seem of much value for our kitchen dyepot methods, but a little arithmetic breaks it down to a more useful calculation:

Dyeing at 1% strength, use one 5 ml spoon of dye for 500 g wool (1 tsp for 1 lb).

Dyeing at 2% strength, use two 5 ml spoons of dye for 500 g wool (2 tsp for 1 lb).

Dyeing at 3% strength, use three 5 ml spoons of dye for 500 g wool (3 tsp for 1 lb).

Most dye colours are at full strength at 3-4%. For medium and lighter shades use the smaller amounts.

The following chemicals are used in the dyebath:

Acetic acid — dyes perform better in slightly acidic conditions.

Glauber salts — a retardant which stops some parts of the wool grabbing the dye more quickly than other parts, thus giving a patchy result.

Albegal A — a levelling agent which stops uneven dispersal of the dye. It also helps to keep the fibres open. If it is not available, substitute a good neutral detergent.

Water
The proportion of water to wool is not a critical relationship. You need enough water to distribute the dye evenly, but not so much that it will boil over when it comes to full heat. A litre to every 25 g of wool (1 quart to 1 oz) is a very comfortable amount to work with, but you may be able to use a little less with large dyelots.

Your kitchen dye recipe now reads:

For 500 g (1 lb) wool (weighed dry, then scoured, rinsed, and wetted out):

Water: 18 litres (4 gallons) in the pot and brought to 50°C (warm).

Add: Acetic acid — 2, 5 ml spoons (2 tsp).

Glauber salts	– 10, 5 ml spoons (10 tsp).
Albegal A	– 2, 5 ml spoons (2 tsp), dissolved in boiling water.
Dye:	Measure 1 to 4, 5 ml spoons (1 to 4 tsp) depending on the desired depth of colour.

Method

1. Mix the dye to a smooth paste with cold water.
2. Add enough boiling water to dissolve the paste – 0.25 litre (½ pint).
3. Pour the dye solution into the pot and stir so that the dye spreads evenly.
4. Put the wool in the pot. Make sure it is completely immersed.
5. Bring *slowly* to just under boiling point over a period of 30 minutes and simmer for 30 to 60 minutes depending on the desired depth of colour. At the end of this time the water should be clear of dyestuff, which means that the wool has absorbed all the dye. (If it is not clear add a little more acid.)
6. When the wool is dyed, strain it into a colander and leave it to cool before rinsing.
   Spin-dry in a bag and dry as quickly as possible away from strong heat.

Points Worth Noting

In factories the wool is put into the water before the dye is added – but special apparatus is used for adding the dye. At home it is much safer to put the dye in first. Factories also have special cooling apparatus, all carefully controlled. At home, **never** use running water on the hot wool, and **never** take the yarn straight from the hot dyebath and plunge it into cold rinsing water.

The most important time to turn the wool during dyeing is just before the dye comes to full heat. This is when the wool is grabbing the most dye. Hold the temperature at this level (about 85°C) for another ten minutes if the dyeing looks very uneven. Then raise the temperature to full heat and continue to turn the wool regularly for another five to ten minutes. After this it need not be turned so often, although it will still require a little movement from time to time.

Some kitchen pots seem to overheat on the base (where they are in contact with the stove) in comparison with the heat being distributed through the water. As it is important to have an even temperature throughout the liquid, try using a rack to keep the wool away from the bottom of the pot, and improvise something to keep it under water at the top.

The contents of the dyepot froth rather vigorously, so do not overfill the pot. Wipe up any spills promptly so that you do not find yourself needing a new stove and a new linoleum after your first few experiments.

Some red dye colours are better dissolved in hot (rather than boiling) water – the boiling water can cause them to gel.

WARNING: **Always put the water in the dyepot first and then** ADD THE ACID TO THE WATER. **If done the other way the acid could sputter with sufficient force to cause eye damage.**

MIXING COLOURS

Spinners sometimes hesitate to use synthetic dyes as they believe the colours will be harsh and crude. However, these are the dyes the textile industry uses and from them can be mixed any of the countless colours seen in the fashion trade. There is no need for the result to be garish. With a little skill in mixing you can learn to duplicate even the most subtle vegetable dyes. The following basic rules for choosing dye pigments and mixing colours should meet all your immediate requirements. The list of colours can be altered to suit particular needs as you gain experience.

Buying Dyes

Because dyes are expensive many people prefer to buy a minimum number of colours:

yellow
red   the primary colours
blue
and black

Theoretically any colour you desire can be mixed from these primary colours; but with dyes, if too many pigments are mixed together, the results tend to become rather muddy. You will get more satisfactory results if you slightly extend your colour range. The best choice of colours is much the same as you would find in a basic paintbox.

3 yellows	green yellow
	yellow
	orange yellow
2 reds	yellow red
	blue red
2 blues	red blue
	green blue
	black
	brown is also useful

Basic Rules For Colour Mixing

Mixing the primary colours produces secondary colours

yellow and red	=	orange
red and blue	=	purple
blue and yellow	=	green

Changing the proportions of the primary colours also changes the resulting secondary colours. For example, equal proportions of yellow and red produce a tomato shade of orange; but a lot more yellow and less red give a true orange.

Equal proportions of red and blue produce blue purple. More red and less blue give true purple.

Again, equal proportions of yellow and blue give blue green. More yellow and a smaller portion of blue produce mid-green.

It follows that:
1. It takes a large amount of a light colour to alter a dark colour.
2. Conversely it takes a small amount of a dark colour to alter a light colour.
3. The greater the difference between the light and dark colours, the more important it is to remember this. (The greatest care is needed when the darkest colours — black, purple and blue — are added to the pale colours.)

The colour wheel

Most people are already familiar with a colour wheel. The colours used in the standard wheel are the primary colours and their secondaries, and the arrangement follows the sequence of the colours in the rainbow (spectrum) (fig 72).

More important from the dyer's point of view is the fact that particular colours always lie opposite certain other colours:

Yellow is opposite purple.
Red is opposite green.
Blue is opposite orange.

The colours opposite each other on the circle give a grey when mixed together. Many a weaver has discovered this accidentally — when hoping to produce a bright fabric — a green warp has been intertwined with a bright red weft — but the result has been a grey not a gay cloth.

This knowledge, used in the proper way, can be useful when mixing pigments, as frequently soft or grey tones are what are required.

For example, used in the right proportions, pure yellow and pure red produce a hard orange colour

If a paler orange is wanted — use less dye pigment.

If a *darker* orange is wanted — use more dye pigment and/or black.

When a *softer* orange is required however, add blue (which is opposite orange on the colour circle) to grey the original orange.

Similarly, red and blue when mixed together produce a hard purple; but — red and blue and a touch of yellow produce a softer, greyer purple.

Yellow and blue mixed together produce green, but yellow and blue with a touch of red produce a softer, greyer green.

Note. Only *very* small amounts of the opposite colour should be added otherwise, like the poor weaver, you will get a full grey.

This is when the extended range of dye pigments comes into its own, for instead of mixing three colours you need mix only two. Apart from being simpler it gives better results. Yellow and red (with a touch of blue) produce a soft orange Or — yellow and blue-red can be mixed to produce the same soft orange.

By applying the above principles to all your colour mixings you will be able to obtain all the dark or light, hard or soft colours, that you require. You will be able to match any colour that any plant will give, and with careful measuring and accurate recording you will be able to dye any quantity of wool to any colour you wish, at any time of the year (fig 73).

When mixing two or three dye colours it is better to dissolve each colour separately first. These solutions can then be mixed in suitable proportions before they are poured into the dyepot. Give the dye liquor a thorough stir before you enter the wool.

To assess the colour mixed, dab drops of it on to blotting paper or clean white newsprint. (The appearance of the liquid in the dyepot does not give an accurate indication of the colour.)

Do not be concerned, when two or more colours have been used in the dye liquor, if halfway through dyeing only one colour has attached itself to the wool. Different colours exhaust at different rates. Have patience and judge the results only when the dyeing is completed. If you do have to make any alterations, cool off the dyebath first.

If the wool comes out of the dyepot patchy (some parts blue, some yellow and some green), the patchiness was probably caused by one (or all) of the following:

The wool was not wetted out evenly before dyeing began.

The dyes were not thoroughly dissolved and stirred.

The levelling agents were in short quantity or were left out altogether.

The dye liquor was brought to simmering point too quickly.

If you have dyed fleece wool, the fault can be corrected when it is carded. However if you are dyeing skeins of spun yarn, obviously all care must be taken in the first place.

A *recipe for brown.*
3 parts yellow, 3 parts red, and 1 part blue.
For small lots use   1.35 ml sp (¼ tsp).
For medium lots use   2.5 ml sp (½ tsp).
For larger lots use   5 ml sp   (1 tsp).

The exact colour this recipe produces depends upon the particular yellow, red and blue that are used. Remember brown is a deep colour and you will need plenty of dye and a long simmering time.

Black
This is the only dye pigment that is likely to cause you any trouble. It is usually sold at 200% strength, which means it is twice as strong as other dyes. This is necessary for a good black dye, but it can cause complications when it is added to other colours, particularly the light colours. In small dyelots it is almost impossible to measure accurately a small enough amount of the black powder.

A reliable way to deal with this problem is to measure (in the usual way) 1.25 ml (¼ tsp) of black

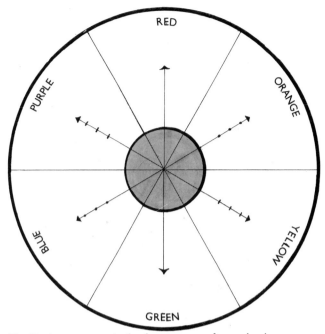

Fig 72. Arrangement of colours on a colour wheel

and mix it to a paste with cold water, then dissolve in .25 litre (½ pint) of boiling water. Add this black *solution* by the spoonful — 15 ml (or 1 tbsp) — to the dissolved main colour. Better still, pour the black dye solution into a disused baby bottle and use the graded markings as your measuring guide. Any leftover solution can then be corked and kept for a short while until it is needed.

A lovely range of greens can be made from yellow and black using the above method.

Olive Green
For 100 g (4 oz) of wool:
7.5 ml (1½ tsp) of yellow dye — yellow FGL mixed with cold water and dissolved in boiling water.
1.25 ml (¼ tsp) black — mixed with cold water and dissolved in boiling water.
For chartreuse colours, add about one third of the black solution to the yellow; for moss greens to mid-olive greens, add about two thirds; for dark olives, add about four fifths of the black solution to the yellow. Remember the particular yellow you use will vary the green colour slightly.

PLANT DYES

While synthetic dyes cater for our colour requirements, plant dyes provide the missing touch of magic. It is doubtful if there are many spinners who have not at some stage fallen under their spell. Most stay bewitched. Even the general public finds a fascination in the association of the modern spinner and her wheel and that era when all colours came from the countryside.

Few of us these days are lucky enough to dwell in the heart of the country, but enthusiastic plant dyers seldom let their environment inhibit them for long; they quickly discover where the plants they are seeking are most likely to be found. Many dyers take pleasure in keeping a special corner of the garden for their favourite dye plants, but for those who are denied this joy there are still plenty of weeds and wildflowers, orchard and tree prunings, vegetable discards, and debris from storm and tide.

Have no hesitation about interrupting the journey of any plant on its way to the bonfire or compost heap. Don't hanker after plants you cannot get hold of easily — it's always fun to try something new; but most experienced dyers, whether they live in the bush, by the sea, on farms, or in cities, have their favourite recipes and these are repeated year after year. The enchanting thing is that the results are never quite the same. There is always an element of excitement that comes with each new season with its differing amounts of sun, and rainfall, and variations in plant health or soil content.

The Mordants And Mordanting

Theoretically plant dyeing is putting the plant, the wool and the water into a pot and simmering them gently together for about an hour. This is a suitable way to use some plants but, on the whole, more successful dyeing takes place when a little more assistance is given to both the wool and the plant.

Through centuries of experimenting dyers have found that unless the wool is treated with certain chemicals, the dye from many plants remains in the water instead of attaching itself to the wool; or, if the wool does take up any colour, it tends to fade rapidly.

The chemicals which are used are known as 'mordants'; they can all be bought or ordered from the local chemist. The few plants that do not need chemical assistance probably provide their own natural mordant.

Before wool is mordanted it must be:
Scoured and *thoroughly* rinsed.
Weighed dry.
Thoroughly re-wetted in warm water for at least 30 minutes.
As plant dyeing is often a spur-of-the-moment occupation, it is a good idea to have a bag of clean washed wool always ready.

The mordants most often used are:
  alum (potassium aluminium sulphate)
  chrome (potassium di-chromate)
  copper sulphate
Later you may like to try:
  Tin crystals (stannous chloride)
  iron (ferrous sulphate or copperas).

Additives

Other useful chemicals which you will probably already have in the home are:
Acids: cream of tartar (potassium bi-tartrate); acetic acid or vinegar (4% the strength of acetic acid).
Alkalis: baking soda; ammonia.
And salt.

Except for cream of tartar (which also assists in mordanting) additives are most often used in small amounts during the actual dyeing process. With some plants they either assist a colour to flow more freely or deepen the strength of a colour already produced. Occasionally they bring about a dramatic change of colour. Use them in small amounts — a pinch of baking soda or cream of tartar to 25 g (1 oz) of wool and no more than a 5 ml spoon to about 250 g (1 tsp to ½ lb).

Acetic acid and ammonia can be used in about the same proportion — a few drops to a 5 ml spoon. You may be a little more free with salt if you are using it to bring out a red or blue colour.

Mordants can be used in three ways:
  1. Before dyeing.
  2. During dyeing.
  3. After dyeing.

Mordanting before dyeing

Pre-mordanting is the most usual method of mordanting. It is particularly useful when test-dyeing as several batches of wool, all mordanted separately with different chemicals, can be put together in the one dyepot to give an indication of the varieties of colour that can be coaxed from the one plant.

Mordanting during dyeing

Mordanting during dyeing means that the water, wool, mordant chemical, and the plant are all simmered together. It is more successful with some mordants used with particular plants, than it is with others.

Mordanting after dyeing

Mordanting after dyeing is not practised very often. When it is, it is more in the nature of a short afterbath of about ten minutes duration. It can be used for both mordanted and unmordanted wool, but the original colour is definitely changed.

Alum

This is the most commonly-used mordant. It is nearly always used in conjunction with cream of tartar in the proportions of three parts alum to one of cream of tartar.

Method

Dissolve the alum and cream of tartar in hot water.
Tip them into the pot with enough extra water to cover the wool.
Place the wet wool in the alum bath.
Simmer for ¾-1 hour.
Cool.
Strain.
Store the mordanted wool in the dark for three days for peak performance. It may be used before the third day, or it may also be dried and stored for future use (in which case it will need re-wetting).
Alum is best used before dyeing but it may also be used with the plant and wool during dyeing. Sometimes this makes no difference, but often the colours are less strong.
Too much alum makes wool harsh.

Chrome   A POISON

Chrome is the most useful mordant. The orange crystals should be stored in a dark bottle as they are sensitive to light.

Method

Dissolve the crystals in hot water.
Tip the solution into the pot and add sufficient water to cover the wool.
Place the wet wool in the chrome bath.

Simmer for ¾-1 hour. Keep the lid on the pot to stop evaporation, splatterings on the stove, and light penetration.
Cool.
Strain.
Rinse in fresh water and use straight away. (The wool may also be dried and stored for future use.)
Chrome brings out the richer, deeper colours and these are often faster. It also keeps the wool soft and silky.
Chrome is poisonous — by mouth or skin contact — so take all possible precautions.

Copper Sulphate   A POISON

Copper sulphate may be used before dyeing but works just as well during dyeing — it is excellent for bright fast greens. Drying the wool in the open air or sun often brightens the colours further. If the wool is simmered for a long time the bright greens will turn bronze. Copper sulphate can also produce some unexpected fawns and browns.
Follow the pre-mordanting procedure for chrome.

Tin   A POISON

Tin is sometimes used before dyeing — but it is often added near the end of dyeing, even though another mordant has already been used. It should be used in conjunction with cream of tartar to counteract the harsh brittle qualities tin gives to wool — 1 part tin to 4 parts cream of tartar. Dissolve and simmer for one hour when pre-mordanting, or dissolve and add to the dyebath 20 minutes before the end of dyeing.
Tin nearly always brightens yellows, and is often useful with reds and blues.

Note. POISONOUS SUBSTANCES SHOULD BE CLEARLY LABELLED AS SUCH AND STORED SAFELY.

Iron

Iron is used before and during dyeing to dull and darken colours, but it has a tendency to make wool hard and tender. Rinse the wool very thoroughly after using iron. Regrettably, it can also ruin your dyepot as it can be difficult to remove all traces of it. On many occasions, an old iron pot, if you have one, is just as useful as the chemical.

MORDANTING CHART
FOR 100 G OR 4 OZ OF WOOL

Chemical	Percentage of wool weight	Gramme weight	Approximate amount of one 5 ml spoon (1 teaspoon)
ALUM	20%	20 g	4 spoons
with cream of tartar	5%	5 g	1 spoon
CHROME	1½-3%	2 g	¼ spoon
COPPER SULPHATE	3-5%	5 g	1 spoon
TIN	3%	3 g	¼ spoon
with cream of tartar	12%	12 g	3 spoons
IRON	3%	3 g	½ spoon

For those without suitable scales for weighing such small amounts, the following may be of interest or use. One 5 ml spoon of:

Alum weighs	5 g
Chrome	8 g
Copper sulphate	6 g
Tin	8 g
Iron	4 g
Cream of tartar	4 g
Baking soda	5 g

Multiplication should not be too difficult for dyers who wish to mordant in larger amounts. 100 g (4 oz) seems the most suitable basic weight both for those people using metric equipment and for the many home dyers who are still using their old Imperial scales.

PLANTS AND THEIR PREPARATION

All parts of a plant are worth trying for dye colour — the flowers, fruit, berries, pods, seeds, leaves, stalks, twigs, bark, and roots or tubers.

With some plants such as small flowering plants the same colour is usually obtained from the whole plant; with others, only one special part of the plant will give any colour. Trees and shrubs on the other hand often give a variety of colours, one from each different part of the plant. A few plants give very little or no colour at all. More frustrating from the dyer's point of view perhaps are those plants which give beautiful colours that prove to be fugitive (not fast).

There are as well other variable factors which affect the colours given by even the most worthwhile dye plants — the climate, and whether it is warm or cold, wet or dry; the seasons; the time of day when the plant is picked; the growing place and whether it is sunny or shady; the soil content, the general health of the plant; and last but by no means least — the cook!

Proportion Of Plant Material
The proportion of plant material to wool is variable, but the **volume** is a *much more constant factor* than the **weight.**

A 9 litre (2 gal) plastic bucket holds the old fashioned measure of one peck, a word which is frequently mentioned in old dye books. **Five hundred grammes (or 1 lb) of wool to a bucket or a bucket and a half of plant material** should give reliable results.

Fig 1a. Upright spinning wheel (J. Beauchamp)   Fig 1b. 'Little Peggy' (J. Rappard)

Note: Some figures in this colour section are also
included in the text. (See black and white photos
marked with stars.)

Fig 2. 'Pipy' horizontal double band
spinning wheel (Pipy Craft)

Fig 3. Ashford kitset spinning wheel
(Ashford Handicrafts)

Fig 6a. Nagy wheel (I. Nagy)

Fig 6b. Carlisle wheel (E. A. Wildy)
(Both wheels in 6a and 6b carry five bobbins.)

Fig 7. Princess Indian Spinner (Sleeping
Beauty Craft Products)

Fig 8. Polywheel (Pipy Craft)

Fig 22. Faults in fleece *Top, left to right*:
a. Log stain from burnt land.
b. Seeds in neck wool.
c. Moit i.e. twigs and sticks.
d. Canary stain visible in washed staples.
   Both b and c are acquired during grazing.
Lower, left to right:
f, g and h are tender wool.
f. The most miserable staple from the most miserable sheep. It is short, it is tender throughout its length, and has a localised weak spot or 'break' as well.
g. The crimp pattern is uneven throughout the staple length.The staple formation is not well defined and the wool has an obvious break.

h. A very severe break. The upper parts of the staples are coming adrift of their own accord.
i. 'Tippy' wool.
j. A portion of a badly cotted canary-stained fleece. It was quite impossible to separate a smaller portion for the photograph.
Middle left:
e. A not-so-obvious break in an otherwise beautiful fleece. Testing proved its presence, however. An experienced spinner used this fleece — it was hand-carded and woollen spun.

None of the fleece on the bottom line would be worth spending time on.

Fig 26. Fine wools
Top, left to right:
a and b. Merino (a is finer than b).
c. Polwarth.

Lower, left to right:
d. Corriedale.
e, f and g. Halfbred wools (e has been washed)

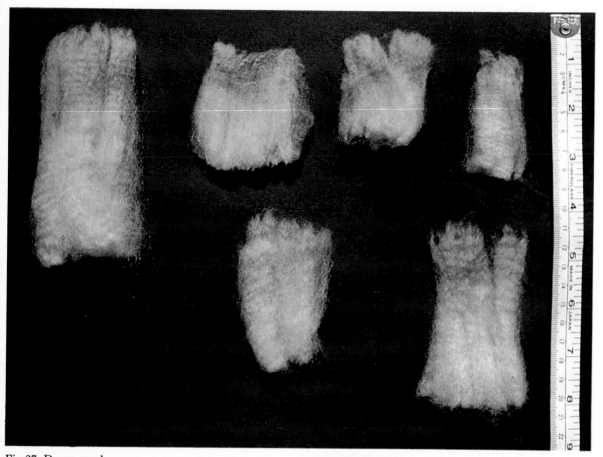

Fig 27. Down wools
Top, left to right:
a. Suffolk.
b. Southdown.
c. South Hampshire.

d. Dorset Horn.
Lower, left to right:
e. Polled Dorset.
f. Cheviot (a Down type).

Fig 28. Crossbred wools

Top, left to right:
a and b. Perendale.
c and d. fine Romney.
e. medium Romney.
f and g. strong Romney.

Lower, left to right:
h and i. Coopworth.
j. Border Leicester.
k. English Leicester — an unusually short staple but enough to show the very pronounced crimp and flatter staple formation than in the Border Leicester.
1. Drysdale (six months' growth) used in the carpet industry.

Fig 61. A basket of knitting wools and wooden knitting needles

Fig 64. A handspun, hand-knitted jersey, designed by the knitter. A multicoloured fleece was used; the wool was flick carded, then spun from the assorted colours chosen at random. Some of the darker grey part of the fleece was spun separately for the yoke pattern. Apart from the flower motifs, the Fair Isle yoke pattern consists of simple zigzags. However, the proportions of light and dark areas in the yoke were carefully planned. The weight of the garment is 310g (11 oz)

Fig 73. Weaving yarns with synthetic dyes

Fig 74. Handspun yarns dyed with garden flowers. The henna colours are from dahlias, the dark red from coreopsis

Fig 75. Handspun yarns dyed with weeds, tree prunings, vegetable parings, etc. The yellows and golden tans at front right are from beach lupins

Fig 76. Handspun yarns dyed with New Zealand native plants. The colours at the front are all from lichens. The very dark brown skeins and the colours in between are from native flax; other tan colours at the top are from tanekaha. Plants used for the other colours were: puriri, pepper tree, kowhai, coprosma, five-finger, native privet, and manuka

Fig 111. Two cushions woven with natural black, white and grey wool

Fig 113. Primitive jacket; this can be woven on a simple loom 30cm (12 in) wide

Fig 114. Hudson Bay jacket, designed to be woven on small looms

Fig 120. The ruana, of South and Central American origin, is an all purpose unisex cover-up. Like an old Highland plaid, it can also be used as a blanket at night

Fig 123. Textured fabric for chair seats

Fig 128. A sturdy shoulder bag woven of carpet wool in weft-faced plain weave

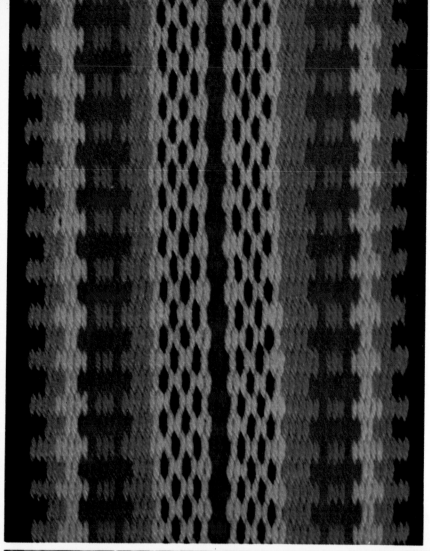

Fig 130. Warp-faced plain weave braids can be woven on the inkle loom or the conventional loom. (*Weaver: Sarah Ward*)

Fig 133. Upholstery fabrics with stripes in the warp are quick to weave with a one-colour weft

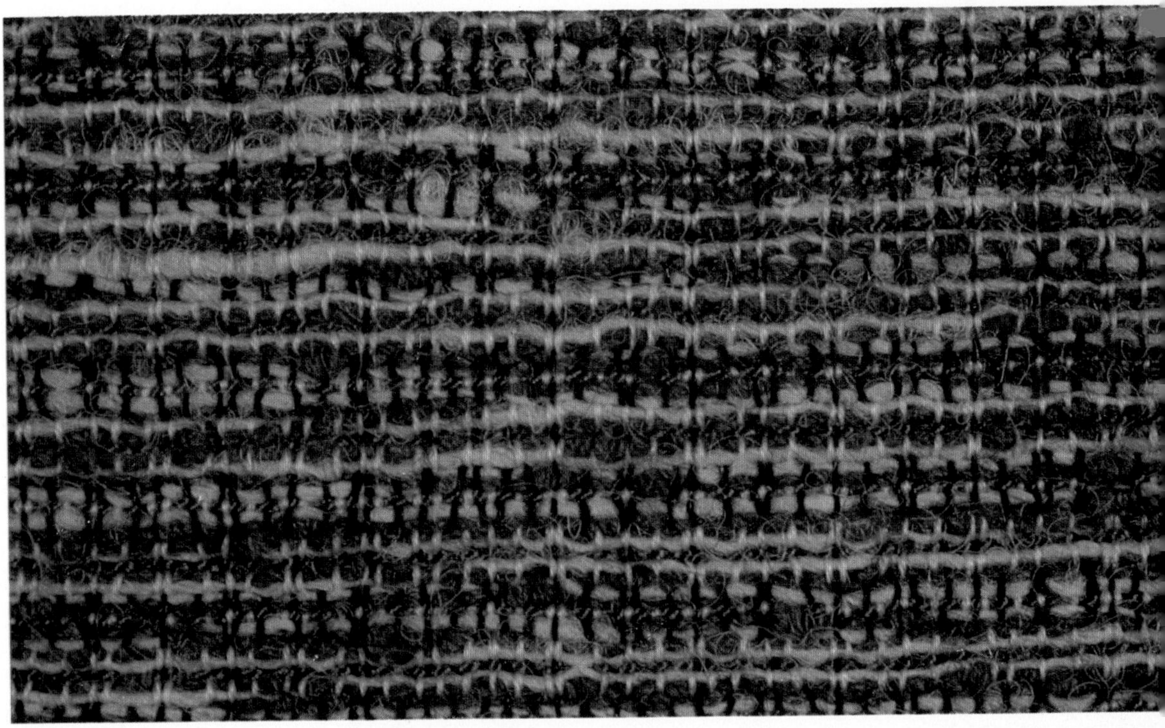

Fig 135. Black, white and brown yarns, both plain and
textured, make an understated upholstery fabric

Fig 141. A textured yarn has been used as a supplemen
tary warp forming 'floats' in the warpwise directio
This idea is capable of many interesting interpretation

However, although we often mordant wool in these quantities, dyeing, particularly of the experimental type, is more often carried out in smaller lots. The corresponding ratio for these smaller amounts is: *25 grammes (or 1 oz) of wool to one standard size preserving jar of plant material (1 litre or 1½ pints).*

Note. It is very important to be generous with plant material. Skimping is one of the main causes of fading.

Preparation Of Plant Material

After the plants are gathered they often require a little preparation before they are used for dyeing. This helps them to release their colours more quickly but it also helps to reduce their bulk and makes them more manageable in the dyepot. Most flowers can be used whole, but berries are usually better mashed, seeds chopped, leaves cut up, and bark pounded. Treat the plant in whatever way seems the most appropriate.

Put the plant material in containers, take careful note of the volume, then cover with cold water and soak. Soft plant material, such as fennel or flowers, usually benefits from 2 hours to 3 days soaking. Harder things such as nuts or bark need from 3 days to a week or even longer.

If it is your first experiment, start with a 3-day soak for everything, and shorten or lengthen the time as you become more experienced. Some plants take a long time to release their dye. The pounding and soaking will help to shorten the actual dyeing time and will keep fuel bills down.

If the plant material is likely to become entangled in the wool, pop it into muslin bags for distribution throughout the wool.

Dyeing Methods

There are two generally accepted methods of dyeing wool:

Method 1

Put the wet mordanted wool in with the cold soaking plant material and bring *slowly* to the boil.

Simmer them together until the full colour is released.

Then either leave the wool in the pan to cool overnight, or strain the hot wool in a colander and leave it to cool before rinsing.

Rinse in cool to lukewarm water.

Put the wool in a bag or pillowslip and spin-dry in the washing machine.

Spread the wool out to dry as quickly as possible without subjecting it to strong heat or sun.

Method 2

Simmer the plant alone for as long as you think is necessary for full colour — the time varies from 20 minutes to 2-3 hours or even longer; the hardness or softness of the plant may give you some indication.

Cool the dye liquor.

Either put the wet mordanted wool into the dyepot as before, or strain out the dyestuff and put the wet mordanted wool into the remaining dye liquid, topping up with more water if necessary. Then proceed as before.

Each method has its advantages and disadvantages. The size of your dyepot will be one controlling factor; another will be the amount of wool you want to dye. When trying a new plant, the first method gives some indication of how long it takes for the full colour to be released. If you find it is going to take hours you would do better to first simmer the plant alone in future dyeings.

Some other points worth noting are:

It is not good for the wool to sit on the bottom of the pot, and it is also desirable to have something on top of the wool to keep it under the water. As there is no doubt that dyes are stronger if there is at least some plant material left in with the wool, try to leave a pad of plant material on the bottom of the pot and use another one on top of the wool.

If you are dyeing cloth, a jersey, or other bulky goods where evenness of dyeing is of great importance, strain the dye liquor of all plant material and make bottom and top pads of something else, such as muslin or cheesecloth.

Water

Make sure you have plenty of water in the pot — at least a litre for every 25 g of wool (1 quart to 1 oz), and more if you need it. Remember, the depth of colour depends on the ratio of plant material to the wool. Increasing the water does not affect this ratio. The function of the water is to dissolve the dye and distribute it evenly throughout the dye vessel. Sufficient water reduces the need for stirring and the probable consequence, felted wool.

Never ever overstuff the pot with wool. You may have mordanted 250 g (½ lb) of wool but if you find, when you come to dye, you have room in the pot for only 100 g (4 oz), leave it at that. One hundred grammes of wool, well dyed and fast to light, is far more useful than 250 grammes which is likely to spot-fade where the dye was unable to penetrate.

Keeping Records

Try to keep records of what you do. There is not much point in having a room full of beautifully dyed wools if you cannot remember how any of the colours were produced. Some dyers keep beautiful record books with a pressed flower or drawing of the plant as well as notes of other relevant information, such as the plant's botanical and common name, where it was growing, the date it was picked, the mordants that were used, the exact recipe used for dyeing, and samples of the coloured wools.

Most of us get great pleasure from looking at other peoples' record books but somehow never get around to keeping one ourselves. However, some system is needed for recording results and here are a few suggestions.

Mark your skeins before they are put into the dyepot. Tags of clean unmordanted, white carpet wool are excellent for this purpose. Put one knot in the tag if the skein is mordanted with alum, two knots for chrome, three for copper sulphate etc. Stick to the same method of marking and leave the tags on the skeins when they are taken out of the dyepot.

If you finish with six skeins of wool all dyed with the same plant — tie all these together. Pierce a hole in an envelope and thread the tie through. Mark the envelope quickly with the name of the plant, the date or season, and anything special you did when dyeing, such as adding baking soda, using twice as much plant material as usual, or allowing some extra soaking time. If you want to use the wool, put samples of the colours attached to the tags inside the envelope.

If you dye with fleece, tag it in exactly the same way but bag up the separate colours when it is dry. Put all the small bags into one big bag and tie at the top with your label. Then, if the day comes when you want to make a beautiful sample book or maybe just check on something you did before, you can do so.

Tests For Fading

Testing for fading is of vital importance. Some plants give a fast colour with one mordant but fade with others. Some colours soften a little on exposure to light and sun but do not fade badly. A few colours change completely. In a decorative basket of coloured wools this does not matter very much, but in a knitted garment, woven material or a wall hanging, a change in even one colour can spoil the whole balance of a colour scheme.

Really fast colours are important and these are the ones you should strive for. The easiest way to test for fading is to put several lengths of wool hanging half in and half out of a tightly closed box, on a sunny windowsill.

Strangely enough, most of the bad fading occurs quickly but the gentle softening can take longer. A test of 6-12 months should be given to any dyed wool which will be used in an article for sale.

RECIPES

Note about the recipes: the recipes in this book have been chosen for the following reasons. Firstly, so that there would be a few basic recipes for everyone to follow, regardless of environment. Secondly, to give a variety of dye methods. Thirdly, in a New Zealand publication it was felt our own native plants were worthy of special mention.

Read all the recipes, even if you have no immediate hope of using the particular plant mentioned. The methods used are applicable to hundreds of plants, not only the ones mentioned in this book. Experiment for yourself and have fun — that's what plant dyeing is all about.

Trees

25 g (1 oz) Wool —   1 litre (1½ pints) plant material

Silver Dollar Gum (Eucalyptus cinerea)
No mordant — brick red
Summer and autumn
Use twigs and leaves.

Pound and chop up the leaves and twigs.
Cover with water and soak.
Simmer until the red dye is released in the water.
Cool.
Enter the wetted wool (try to leave most of the plant material in the pot). Add more water if necessary.
Simmer again until the wool is well dyed.
Either cool the wool in the dyepot; or strain it into a colander and leave to cool.
Rinse the wool and dry.

Further experiments

1. Try boiling a second batch of wool in the liquid you have already used. If any plant material was removed to make room for the wool in the first dyeing, exchange it now with what is in the pot.
2. Try a third boiling.
3. Start from the beginning again, using fresh plant material, this time using mordanted wool. Use wool mordanted with one chemical — or, more exciting in a test dye, use several lots of wool, each mordanted with a different chemical — alum, chrome, copper sulphate.

   Compare these results very carefully with the unmordanted wool, both for colour and for colour fastness.
4. Start again, using your best recipe, but this time use dry leaves from the ground under the tree.

Poplar Aspen or Lombardy (*Populus tremula* or *nigra*)

Alum — yellow; Chrome — gold; Copper sulphate — green
Summer
Use leaves.
The mature leaves picked from midsummer onwards can be used fresh, or dried and stored, but fresher colours come from the fresh leaves.

Chop up the leaves.

Cover with water and soak.

Simmer using Method 1 (plant and wool together) or Method 2 (simmer plant alone first). Better still, try both methods.

Use the three mordants if possible as they are all worth trying.

If you have plenty of leaves repeat the first recipe using pale grey mordanted wool, instead of white wool. This will give you six colours that combine well, instead of only three, and is a useful exercise with the other recipes as well.

Poplars discard their leaves and twigs with abandon in high winds. If the leaves are immature, as they frequently are when we get our equinoctial gales in spring, mordant with chrome — the resulting yellow-gold is so bright that it is almost fluorescent.

Garden Flowers (fig 74)
25 gm (1 oz) Wool —   1 litre (1½ pints) of plant material

Dahlias
Alum — orange; Chrome — henna
Summer and autumn

Use flowerheads or seedheads.

Gather flowers from the garden or vases. Enjoy the blooms before you use them for dye, as faded flowerheads and seedheads do just as well as fresh flowers. It is the central part of the flower that contains the dye.

Cut up the flowers, cover them with water and soak.

Simmer, using whichever method you prefer, for about ¾ hour.

With alum you will get orange and with chrome a red orange.

Extract some of the wool to keep for samples — then put in a pinch of baking soda (it will froth). The orange will turn to pumpkin colour and the red orange to brilliant henna.

Simmer for a few minutes then cool the wool, rinse and dry.

Dahlias have a mixed reputation among dyers. One of the secrets of success is to use a very strong dye brew. By *weight* there should be at least five or six times the weight of dahlias to the weight of wool. Simmer for a good ¾ to 1 hour — the colour will not spoil.

You should get a good strong fadeless dye at whatever time of day you pick the flowerheads, but do try at least one experiment using flowers that have been picked in full sun.

Coreopsis
Chrome — orange-red to dark red
Summer
Use flowers.

Gather the flowers.

Cover with water and soak for three days.

Simmer with the wool if possible.

Just before the end of dyeing add one of the alkaline additives (either ammonia or baking soda), or remove the wool from the dyebath and rinse in a bath of fresh water and ammonia.

Rinse and dry in the usual way.

Coreopsis is an excellent dye plant. The colour is even deeper and redder than that produced by dahlias. A spoonful of salt may further deepen the red.

In general, dyeing in either an enamel or an aluminium pot will not affect the colour of the wool. However, if baking soda is added with Coreopsis, the colours from the aluminium pot are several shades deeper, they really have to be seen to be believed. Alum-mordanted wool becomes tomato orange and chrome mordanted wool changes to a very deep ox-blood red. The colours with chrome are fast but with alum slightly doubtful.

Other garden flowers worth trying

Golden Rod — Flowers or flowers and stalks, (yellow to tan).

Marigolds (all kinds) — golds.

Cinerarias — greens and pinks.

Iris — enjoy the flowers, the leaves give good dye — dark olive green.

Geraniums — browns

Vegetables

25 g (1 oz) wool —   1 litre (1½ pints) of plant material

Onions

Alum — gold; Chrome — brown gold

Not seasonal

Use the skins, golden or purple. (The deeper the colour of the skins the better the dye.)

Cover the dried onion skins with water and soak.

Simmer with at least some skins in with the wool for ¾ hour to 1 hour.

Cool rinse and dry.

Try for a second cooking but test carefully for colour fastness, as second boilings sometimes fade.

Strong coloured onion skins, a strong dye solution, and a good long simmer should prevent any fading problems.

If you grow your own onions, try using the leaves also.

Carrots

Alum Chrome Copper — all give brilliant yellow greens

Not seasonal

Use the tops.

It is not good gardening practice to leave carrot tops lying on the carrot patch, but before they are composted put them into the dyepot. Simmer them for about an hour, then let the mixture stand for about a fortnight. The brew will turn slightly mouldy but it will be thick and strong. Simmer the wool in the usual way.

Wildflowers and Weeds

25 g (1 oz) Wool —   1 litre (1½ pints) of plant material

Fennel *(Foeniculum vulgare)*

Alum and Chrome — yellows; Copper Sulphate — greens

Spring

Use plant-tops.

Pick the fennel while it is still young — (no more than about 20 cm [8 in] high). Older fennel gives sadder colours, but as long as the plant has not flowered the colours are not necessarily weaker.

Fennel which has been sprayed with weedkiller is useless.

You may do a test dye with alum, chrome, and copper sulphate mordanted wools but, for variety, also try adding copper sulphate straight to the dyebath, using unmordanted wool.

Cut up the fennel and soak. Make sure you have plenty of plant material.

Dissolve 5 ml (1 tsp) of copper sulphate for every 100 g (4 oz) of wool.

Pour this into the pot with the fennel and water. Stir.

Add wet unmordanted wool.

Bring very slowly to simmering point.

After a few minutes begin removing portions of wool. Repeat every few minutes until you have shades of green ranging from pale blue green to full apple green to bronze green. Cool and rinse.

Dry outside in the open air and sun.

Test all colours for fastness.

Other plants which are good for green colours are:

Iris leaves — very dark olive green.

Parsley — a glorious bright green — but like fennel, a lot of plant is needed.

Purple prunus leaves in early spring — mid-olive green.

Any berries, flowers, leaves or stalks with a purple tinge are worth a try.

Spring is the best season to try for green dye colours.

Buttercups

Alum — soft yellow; Chrome — ginger-tan

Spring

Use the flowers.

Pick the flowers — a few stalks won't matter — but do try to pick the flowers from a sunny spot.

Soak for three days.

Simmer the wool, with the plant if possible, for ½-¾ hour.

Cool.

Rinse and dry.

A pinch of baking soda added to the dyepot at the end of dyeing will change the soft yellow to gold and the ginger tan to henna. The ginger-tans are fast but the yellow softens (evenly) after a short period of time. The leaves and tips of the plant give paler muted shades of the flower colours.

Fig 73. Weaving yarns dyed with synthetic dyes ★

Fig 74. Handspun yarns dyed with garden flowers. The henna colours are from dahlias, the dark reds from coreopsis ★

Fig 75. Handspun yarns dyed with weeds, tree prunings, vegetable parings, etc. The yellows and golden tans at front right are from beach lupins. ★

Fig 76. Handspun yarns dyed with New Zealand native plants. The colours at the front are all from lichens. The very dark brown skeins and the colours in between are from native flax; other tan colours at the top are from tanekaha. Plants used for the other colours were: puriri, pepper tree, kowhai, coprosma, five-finger, native privet, and manuka ★

Yellow Beach Lupins *(Lupinus arboreus)*
Alum — yellows; Chrome — gold to ginger-tan
Early summer
Use the flowers.

Gather the flowerheads and soak very briefly — a few hours is plenty. The colours dull with a longer soak.

Simmer the mordanted wool and plant together.

The colours produced seem slightly variable. Sometimes alum gives clear baby yellows and chrome — old gold but, at other times, flowers picked from the same area give very bright yellows with alum and a ginger-tan with chrome. These differences may be related to the maturity of the plant, but a more likely reason perhaps is the amount of rainfall in the days before picking.

Whatever the cause, all the colours are clear and lovely. The yellows are particularly useful as so often yellows from other plants are fugitive.

The black seedheads also give an old-gold colour with chrome, but the colour from the flowers is better.

Other wildflowers and weeds to try:
Bindweed tubers.
Dandelion flowers.
Plantain leaves — use fresh or try the carrot-top recipe.
Docks — the roots are the strongest dye part so if you use the leaves, which give brilliant colours, double the plant ratio.
Foxgloves — all parts of the plant can be used.
Nasturtiums.
Blackberry leaves.
Yellow oxalis flowers.

Some of these give their best, or only, dye in early spring. Others do better when the plants are more mature. Experiment at different seasons (fig 75).

New Zealand Native Plants (fig 76)

Flax *(Phormium tenax)*
Flax is an excellent dye plant, all parts of it. If you live where there is an abundant supply of the plant, try the flower buds, flower stalks, flowers, green seedheads, the base of the leaves, and the roots if any bushes are being dug up. If you live where the plant is less plentiful, leave the flowers until the tuis have finished with them and then use the seedheads for dyeing.

Flax will dye well without any mordants but they can be used to extend the colour range. The seedpods, without a mordant, give an earthy brown with vague purplish overtones; with chrome, a very dark brown; with copper sulphate a very rich purplish dark brown. (This colour will produce gasps of admiration from your friends, but it is a colour that is often difficult to use in colour schemes with other plant dyes.)

Flax is a strong dye. Six seedheads can dye up to 3 kilos (6 lbs) of wool but the pods need a thorough soaking — from a week to ten days. It makes no difference to the colour if the empty pod cases are used without the seeds, but some dyers feel the inclusion of the seeds in the dyepot makes the wool softer.

The dye froths rather vigorously, so do not overfill the pot.

Do start cooking before the mixture ferments. Plant dyers develop a certain immunity to the wicked smells that issue from their brewing pots. However the smell of fermenting flax stewing on the stove is so foul that not even a compulsive dyer could find it acceptable.

Kowhai *(Sophora spp.)*
Blossoms and seed gathered from beneath the trees produce yellows and tans.

Peppertree *(Macropiper excelsum)*
This tree has young purple shoots which produce different greens with chrome and copper sulphate.

Coprosmas
These trees and shrubs are members of the madder family and several are worth using for dye. *Coprosma australis, C. aerolata, C. robusta* (karamu), *C. lucida* (shining karamu), *C. rhamnoides,* and *C. rotundifolia.* The bark and roots give the best colour. The brightly coloured berries give stains which rapidly fade.

C. australis is the member of the family from which red is produced and is a dye plant that was known to the Maoris. Although this tree seeds itself on the edge of the bush and in garden patches in bush areas, it is unfortunately extremely susceptible to drought, and without a canopy of protective forest it is almost impossible to keep even quite big trees alive during hot summer months. It has perhaps become one of those plants that dyers should know about but refrain from using.

Tanekaha *(Phyllocladus trichomanoides)*
The bark of this tree is another old dye plant. You are unlikely to want to attack a tree, but sawmills in some areas can be very cooperative. It is a tree

that, like the kauri, sheds small dead branchlets and, if you live near the bush, these can be gathered easily and give a reasonable dye.

Simmer the plant material alone first to extract the gum, then pour off this water as the gum makes the wool hard. Add fresh water and proceed in the usual way. The dye becomes stronger with keeping.

Mordants are not necessary but their use extends the colour range.

Five-Finger Tree (Pseudopanax arboreum)
This tree is rather a teaser. For some lucky people the very ripe berries produce exciting colours. The birds do not seem to like the berries very much — neither will your family; make sure the windows are wide open to get rid of the choking fumes.

If you cannot get the purple and wine colours you are seeking, add some copper sulphate to the dyepot. You will be compensated with a good green which is fast.

Ferns
Ferns can give good colours, as any housewife who has had to dry her sheets where they slap against new ponga fronds will know. (In this case, of course, one moves the sheets not the ponga frond!) However, the smaller ferns, particularly those of the *Blechnum* family, are good dyeplants too. The older fronds give a dark olive green when used with copper sulphate.

Puriri (Vitex lucens)
Fuchsia (Fuchsia excorticata)
Totara (Podocarpus totara)
The bark from these trees is worth trying with alum and chrome — as are bracken and the shoots of **manuka (Leptospermum scoparium)**, which are much easier to gather.

Native Privet (Geniostoma ligustrifolium)
With the three common mordants the bright green shoots of this small tree give dark muted colours which are rather beautiful and useful at times.

Many of the **pittosporum** trees have purple flowers or berries which give greens with copper sulphate, as do the berries of the **putaputaweta (Carpodetus serratus)** a member of the Escallonia family.

There are several New Zealand native plants belonging to the buckthorn family — **kumarahou (Pomaderris kumeraho)** is probably best known in the north.

It does not always follow that dye can be obtained from a native plant, just because it belongs to a plant family which is well known as a dye producer elsewhere, but it is an indication of a possibility and is always worth a try.

Lichens
Lichens have long been favourite dyeplants but, alas, they are now so scarce in many places that it is considered wrong to use them. There are still plenty of lichens in New Zealand, but treat them with respect and gather them only from places such as orchards where they are not welcome. As well as being precious, lichens are fairly strong dyeplants, so you can use less plant material and keep your dyelots small.

Usnea — Old Man's Beard
Winter, spring and summer
This lichen is the hairy-looking green-grey lichen which hangs like a beard from trees and fenceposts. Often it shows tints of the beautiful henna colours it will give in the dyepot.

The best lichen for dyeing usually comes from areas with warm wet climates or from places near the sea. After a long summer drought, resist the temptation to collect the lichen after the first rains; the best colour will have been washed away.

Gather the lichen and cut it up into small pieces so that it will 'bleed' easily in the water, otherwise it may take hours to release its colour.

The simmered lichen becomes soft and slimy like seaweed, so either boil the plant until the dye is released, then strain it and add the wool; or, if you want to cook the wool and lichen together, put the plant material into muslin bags first. No mordant is needed.

The strongest colour comes from the plant and wool together, but it is then often difficult to get an even colour distribution. This is not a disturbing problem with unspun fleece but it could be with yarn.

A little acetic acid helps to release the colour if you have problems. In poor seasons an afterbath of chrome deepens the colour considerably and brings out the pinkier tints.

Parmelia family
Spring, tan colours
There are several lichens belonging to this family that give colour to wool. They grow in flat frilly circles on rocks and trees, and range in individual colour from blacks through greys to greens.

Smaller twigs are often entirely encircled by the lichen and it is these twigs which snap off old trees and fall on to roads and footpaths during storms. It is quite easy to prise the lichen off while it is still wet. Indeed sometimes the wind itself loosens big pieces of lichen from trunks of trees in wet weather.

Competition is keen for this plant as it gives the wool a heavenly scent. If the supply of spinners in your area exceeds the available lichen supply, you may not be able to get enough for the dyepot all at once; store your little bits carefully (making sure they do not become mouldy) and your collection will soon mount. However, limit storage time to about two months, for the colour does weaken eventually.

If the lichen pieces are dry, cover them with water and soak overnight, otherwise put them straight into the pot. This is a contact dye and gives the best colour when mixed with the wool — a layer of lichen and a layer of wool throughout the pot. Most of the lichen shakes out (with some fairly vigorous shaking) when the wool is dry, and the rest comes out during teasing and carding. No mordant is needed.

Sticta hirta (formerly known as S. coronata)

Sticta hirta must surely be the most fascinating of all dyeplants. It is a lichen of the forests — particularly the beech forests of the South Island's west coast.

Most dyeing with lichen is done in small lots through necessity, but happily this is just what *S. hirta* seems to prefer, if it is to give that beautiful sequence of colours starting with pinks or purples, and progressing through browns, golds and greens.

Either cook the wool direct with the lichen, or put the lichen in a bowl and pour over it 1 litre (1 quart) of boiling water. Leave it soaking for about 10-15 minutes by which time the water will have turned the colour of red wine. Pour the liquid off and use it for dyeing your wool.

Try to keep the lichen whole; broken lichen usually, although not always, releases the yellows.

While the first lot of wool is dyeing and cooling, several more kettles of boiling water can be poured over the lichen and put aside in jars. Each jar of red liquid will dye small lots of wool — each result beautiful, but becoming a progressively paler mauve. Do not throw away the used dye liquid — keep it for topping up the pot later on.

When the red liquid becomes too pale to be useful, put the lichen in the pot with the wool and simmer them together in the usual way. However, instead of throwing away the plant and liquid each time a dyelot is completed, pop in fresh wool to replace the old.

When the colour becomes really insipid, rest the dyepot overnight or even for a couple of days — while you catch up on your housework. *S. hirta* dyeing is a lengthy business! When started again the dyepot will have renewed vigour after its rest and will reward you with a completely new colour range.

Continue in this way, dyeing then resting, until you have gone through the full sequence of colours — purples, browns, golds and greens.

If pinks are wanted instead of purples, add half to one 5 ml spoon of ammonia the first time boiling water is poured over the lichen. Once seems sufficient. Again you will get the full sequence of colours, but the order in which they appear will be different.

You can further extend the colour range by using mordanted wools; frequently the colours are then brighter and more permanent.

S. hirta, when fresh, is rather like a flabby cabbage leaf in colour and texture but is bright yellow on the underside. It has a cousin rather similar in appearance but which lacks the ability to produce the same range of dye colours. If you are in any doubt over identification, a small drop of acetone placed on the back of the thallus will turn pink immediately if the plant is *Sticta hirta*.

DYERS' GOSSIP

There seems to be a strong seasonal trend in the colours produced by plants. Spring brings with it fresh chartreuse greens and yellows which become warmer colours as summer approaches. From summer to autumn come the golds, the hot oranges and the orange reds. From autumn through to winter the tans and browns are more common. There are many exceptions of course, but if you are hunting for a particular colour, this observation may be useful.

The full colour a plant will give seems more likely to be permanently fast than a pastel version of the same colour (usually produced by either too weak a dyebath or too short a simmering time).

There are few true yellows (not golds or khaki) on the list of fast colours. This is a surprise considering how many plants produce a yellow dye.

Chrome has a much higher success-rate for producing fast colours than does alum.

Ammonia fumes from dyepots are POISONOUS and can also damage the kitchen paintwork. Ammonia is no kinder to the wool than it is to the dyer. If you use it, make sure there is plenty of ventilation, that you work quickly, and that you rinse the wool thoroughly straight away.

Tin and iron are two other chemicals that should be used with discretion. If you are colour hunting for a competition, or just for fun, they are necessary, but there seems no sense in using them with soft handspun wool.

When using and storing chemicals do not leave them standing around in open jars. Many are very unstable and a steamy dye kitchen will make them deteriorate even more quickly.

Buy chemicals in small amounts and replace them frequently.

Alum is usually sold in bags containing 500 g.

Chrome and copper sulphate: 50-100 g is an adequate supply.

Tin cannot usually be bought in amounts smaller than 100 g.

Iron, 25-50 g should be adequate.

It seems the fashion at present to leave the wool to cool in the dyebath when dyeing is over. The wool treated this way may deepen a little in colour, but this practice can also change a beautiful even dyeing into a patchwork mess. This is most likely to happen if plant material is present in the dyepot. While the dye is simmering there is sufficient water movement to prevent this happening.

Straining the wool into a colander and leaving it there to get cold before rinsing it, leaves a good many globules of liquid throughout the wool, from which it can still draw colour while cooling, with-

Fig 77. Ready for the wool sale at Wiri Wool Brokers

out risk of streaking. This also frees the dyepot for another cooking.

Flax. If you are hacking at flax roots, wear glasses. Juice squirting into your eye can cause an agonising pain.

Do not leave wet mordanted wool lying around for longer than three days — it can become mouldy. Dry it thoroughly and put it into labelled bags, then re-wet it when needed.

Always use the correct measuring spoons for all dyeing. That is, use a 1.25 ml spoon (¼ tsp), a 2.5 ml spoon (½ tsp) and a 5 ml (1 tsp). It is quite impossible to measure accurately without them. This is particularly important when using synthetic dyes.

10 Weaving

Weaving is an ancient art which has developed in so many different ways in various parts of the world that even a brief survey of all the many types would fill hundreds of pages. In order to limit the subject to a reasonable length it has been necessary to concentrate on one aspect of weaving only: learning to weave on a conventional loom, utilising the basic structures of woven cloth.

Wool has been chosen as the primary fibre and, as so many spinners want to use their handspun wool in weaving, many of the projects given for practice-work specify handspun wool for the weft. For those who do not spin, some of the yarns manufactured in imitation of handspun wool may be substituted. The final section looks at the use of handspun wool in both warp and weft.

Read through the whole of the text first in order to get a general knowledge of the weaving process, then return to the instructions for learning to weave. Consult the glossary (Appendix D) for any unfamiliar terms.

Looms and other items of weaving equipment are made in either metric or imperial measurements according to the country of origin. Weavers with imperial equipment will find it convenient to work in yards and inches, but those with metric equipment should work in metres and centimetres. Those with a combination of both kinds will be involved in some extra arithmetic.

In the text one metre is sometimes equated with one yard, and one centimetre with half an inch. These measurements are, of course, not exactly equivalent, and it must be left to the good sense of the reader to choose whichever is appropriate in the particular case.

Almost every part of a loom, and almost every process in weaving, has more than one name. In many cases the names are regional variations on the same theme. We have tried to use the terms which will be most readily understood by the complete novice who wants to learn to weave from the pages of a book.

EQUIPMENT FOR WEAVING

Reduced to its essentials, weaving is an interlacement of two sets of threads at right angles to each other. There are many rich and complex variations, it is true, but most weavers find that the fascination of weaving as a craft lies in the satisfaction to be found in the exploration of simple structure, colour and texture.

Relatively rigid materials, such as vines and the stalks of plants, can be manipulated by the hands alone and worked into a woven form; but very flexible materials, such as spun yarn, are difficult to manage unless a loom of some kind is used.

A loom is essentially a sturdy framework upon which the lengthwise threads (warp) can be held in tension while the crosswise threads (weft) are interlaced through them (fig 78). Some weavings, such as tapestries, wall hangings and similar art pieces, are still woven by a hand process on relatively simple frames, but the techniques for these are too lengthy and specialised to be included here. The following chapters concentrate on the

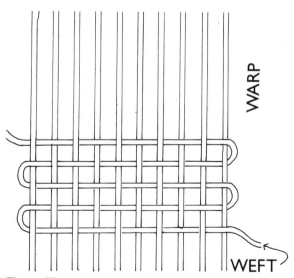

Fig 78. Warp and weft interlacing at right angles

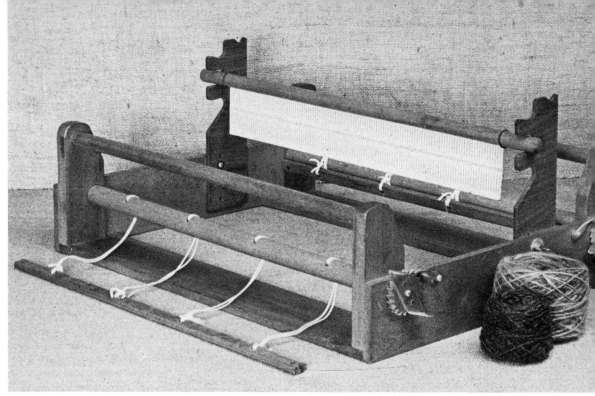

Fig 79. Rigid-heddle loom (Pipy Craft)

type of loom which attracts most beginners to weaving — the loom equipped with some form of laboursaving device to speed up the work.

The simplest of the laboursaving looms is the rigid-heddle loom, followed by the four-shaft table loom and then the treadle loom. Prices vary considerably, depending on type, size, sophistication, and the amount of work involved in the making.

You may be tempted to build a loom at home as a means of reducing the cost. This is not without its hazards but, if you use a good plan and follow it exactly (you will need to be able to read technical drawings), and have the tools and the necessary skill, you may be able to make a worthwhile loom. The greatest danger is in making alterations to the measurements given on the plan. A loom is a deceptively simple-looking piece of folk technology; its measurements and tolerances have been refined over hundreds of years, and ill-considered 'improvements' can affect its performance adversely.

It would be wrong to give the impression, however, that good work can be done only on an expensive loom. We need only look at some of the looms used in undeveloped countries to know that true craftsmanship can triumph over unsophisticated equipment. The folk loom is often made to large measurements, particularly in the length from front to back, and these generous dimensions can overcome the disadvantages of crude joinery, rough-hewn timber, and so forth. The more compact the loom, the more likelihood there is that

such crudities of construction will affect its functioning; and, as compactness is often valued in a loom for household use, we should give preference to one that is well made.

If a loom has been made with superb craftsmanship, has a beautiful finish, and comes with lots of gadgets, it will naturally cost more than a plain workmanlike job — but it may not weave any better. It is the weaver who sits at the loom who is largely responsible for the quality of the weaving, not the loom itself, and many a good weaver uses a loom which others would dismiss as quite inadequate.

If the loom has an identifiable fault which impedes the work it should be altered or repaired, but otherwise you should get on with the business of weaving, making the best and most suitable use of the equipment at hand.

Types Of Loom

Rigid-heddle loom (fig 79)
This loom is relatively cheap, light to carry and easy to understand, but it has some limitations. The working part of the loom consists of a metal or wooden heddle-reed perforated with holes and slots.

The function of the holes and slots is to raise or lower alternate warp threads so that a shuttle wound with weft may be passed through the

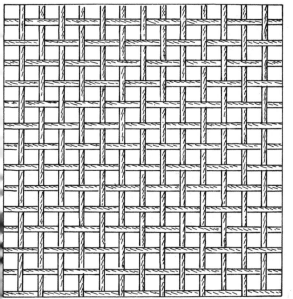

Fig 80a. Plain weave, showing the interlacement of the weft over and under alternate warp threads

Fig 80b. Weaver's conventional diagram of plain weave, the white squares representing warp threads, the black squares weft

opening thus created — the 'shed'. The heddle-reed is also used as a beater to beat the weft rows into place, and as a spacer to keep the work an even width from beginning to end.

The size of the holes and slots (through which the warp threads must be passed) restricts the type of yarn which may be used, and because the holes and slots occur at fixed intervals it will weave fabrics of only one rather coarse nature. Because of its design it is capable of plain weave only (fig 80), but with the use of finger-manipulated techniques a number of decorative effects can be achieved. In the hands of an inventive craftsman it can produce most attractive work, and is a useful learning tool.

Four-shaft table loom (fig 81)

This has several hundred individual heddles (fig 82) arranged on four racks placed one behind the other in the loom. It has a separate steel reed (a comb-like device) to beat the weft and to keep the work an even width. Each warp thread is passed through the central eye of a heddle and then through a dent (space) in the reed, according to a predetermined plan. The heddle-frames are lifted, one, two or three at a time according to the pattern or texture to be woven.

The four-shaft table loom can weave twill (fig 83) and any pattern or texture which can be woven on a four-shaft treadle loom, but it will not be capable of heavy work. A table loom more than 80 cm (32 in) in width will be heavy to carry, and when placed on a suitable table will occupy al-

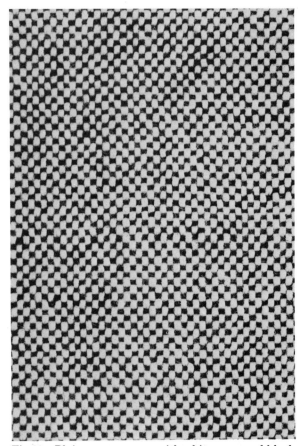

Fig 80c. Plain weave woven with white warp and black weft.

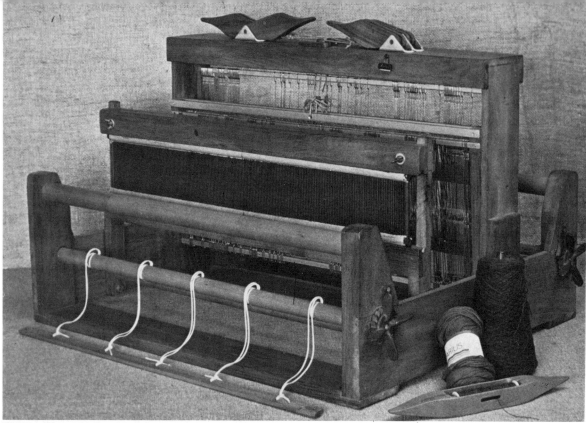

Fig 81a. Four-shaft table loom, one shaft shown lifted (Pipy Craft)

Fig 81b. Diagram (not to scale) of a table loom. 1, warp roller; 2, back beam; 3, cross-sticks; 4, four heddle-shafts inside central castle or heddle box; 5, four levers for lifting the shafts; 6, beater and reed; 7, the shed through which the shuttle is passed; 8, breast beam; 9, cloth roller

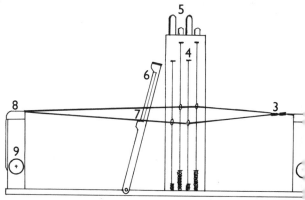

Fig 82. *Top*, reed. *Centre*, heddle-reed. *Lower centre*, steel heddle and string heddle. *Left*, threading hook, reed hook, hook for heddle-reed. *Right*, carpenter's level

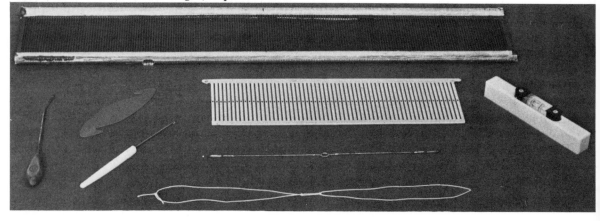

nost as much space as a modest treadle loom. A
oom up to 60 cm (24 in) wide is suitable for
earning and hobby purposes, and will remain
useful for samples and experiments, even if you
eventually buy a treadle loom.

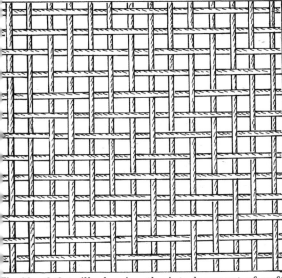

Fig 83a. 2/2 twill, showing the interlacement of weft
over two and under two warp threads. Note that the
interlacement moves sideways by the distance of one
warp end in each pick, and that this movement creates
a diagonal line in the weave

Fig 83b. Weaver's conventional diagram of 2/2 twill,
white squares representing warp, black squares representing weft

Fig 83c. 2/2 twill woven with white warp, black weft

Two-shaft table loom

This type of loom weaves plain weave only but,
because the heddles can be moved closer together
or farther apart, it is more versatile than the
rigid-heddle loom.

Treadle loom

The treadle loom is the ultimate choice of serious
weavers. The action is more rhythmical and the
weaving goes at a faster pace because the feet are
used to operate the shafts (heddle frames) leaving
the hands free for handling the shuttles and
beater. A lightly constructed treadle loom is suitable for fabrics and light work, but it is not suitable for heavy work or floor rugs. A large, heavy,
well-made loom should be able to weave anything
from delicate fabrics to firm rugs.

Whether you decide on a rigid-heddle loom, a
four-shaft loom, or a treadle loom, depends on
how much weaving you plan to do, the size and
type of article you wish to make, how much room
is available for a loom, and how much you can
afford to spend. If it is possible to borrow or hire
one at first you will be able to make a more intel-
ligent choice when it comes to buying, as an
understanding of looms and their capabilities can
be gained only by practical experience in weaving.

Other looms

Several other types are commonly used: the
tapestry loom, the back-strap loom, the inkle
loom (for narrow warp-faced bands), and the
upright two-shaft rug loom. Bands can be woven
just as well on an ordinary loom, and rugs can be
made better and faster on the conventional horizontal type. Tapestry may also be woven on a
conventional loom, but as this slow work occupies
the loom for a long time, and as the weaver wishes
to see the design as a whole, the tapestry frame is
usually preferred. Lack of space is often a consideration in choosing one of these looms.

The so-called 'off-loom' weaving is, in fact,
frequently done on a frame of some kind, and may
involve twining, knotting, netting, wrapping and
other fibre techniques. There is no reason why a
weaver attracted to this form of fibre art cannot
begin straight away on off-loom weaving, but it is
usually found that weavers who have first learned
to weave on orthodox looms have a better understanding of warp tension, the relationship
between warp and weft, and the manipulation of
fibres. To the casual observer, off-loom weaving
looks easy; in fact, it is very time-consuming and
demands a high degree of skill if it is to be
successful.

Buying A Loom

Buying a table loom

A table loom has limitations but within those
limitations it should be capable of working well.
The maximum width which can be woven is controlled by the width of the reed; allowing for
shrinkage in finishing processes, a loom with a
reed 75 cm (30 in) wide will produce cloth not more
than 68 cm (27 in) wide. The maximum length of
warp which can be wound on a table loom is
usually about 7 metres (7 yds), but naturally this
varies with the thickness or fineness of the yarn
used. The woven cloth is more bulky than the
warp alone and it may build up very rapidly on the
cloth roller. Apart from the fact that a table loom
is not strong enough for the weaving of rugs, the
finished rug may be too bulky to be accommodated on the cloth roller.

Some table looms are capable of being converted for treadle operation; such a loom should still
be thought of as a type of table loom and not
forced into work for which it is not suited.

If a loom is to be taken to and from classes,
check that you can get it in and out of a car, and
that it is not too heavy or awkward to carry. (A
loom that is semi-folding is useful in this respect.)

If it is to be used at home only, check that it will go
through a household doorway, as you may not
always wish to use it in the same room. If it
measures less than 60 cm (24 in) from front to
back it is unlikely to work well, but a loom that is
75 cm (30 in) long will need its own sturdy table.
New weavers often plan to use the diningtable,
but having to move the loom at mealtimes is very
inconvenient.

Check the position of the levers or other devices
for operating the shafts. Levers placed on top of
the castle (centre structure containing the shafts)
are better than those placed on the side of the
castle. Some have a pair of levers placed either side
of the loom at table level — check that you can
reach and use one or more of these levers simultaneously without being spread-eagled across the
weaving. Few table looms can be used comfortably by a seated weaver, and this is one of the
reasons why many weavers say they find table
looms tiring.

Examine the quality of the timber, the accuracy
of the joinery and the smoothness of the finish.
Examine the ratchets — they should be strong,
firmly attached, and easy to use. Check that the
reed is removable so that it may be replaced by
one of another dentage. Check that the heddles
can be moved on and off the frames — some weaves
require more heddles on one shaft than another. A
shuttle race (a small ledge of timber level with the
base of the reed) is desirable if you envisage using
small boat shuttles.

How noisy is the loom when it is in use? Table
looms are often noisier than treadle looms, and an
especially noisy one can be very irritating to the
weaver's family, if not to the weaver.

Above all, *check the warp-line*. Most table
looms are jack looms: that is, the shaft which is
operated is lifted upward while the rest remain
stationary.* The heddle-eyes should be located at
a level *below* a horizontal line drawn from breast
beam to back beam. When the warp is at rest the
threads should lie at the base of the reed. When a
shed is made the threads in the upper layer must
be at the *same* angle from the horizontal line as
the lower threads. In fig 84 the solid line represents the correct warp-line. The dotted line
represents the imaginary horizontal line, and the
dashed line represents the upper layer of the shed.

If the heddle eyes are incorrectly placed on the
horizontal line, the upper threads are stretched
very tight when a shed is opened, and the lower

* Table looms are sometimes of the counterbalanced type, and
these follow the rule for counterbalanced looms, see fig 87.

threads become slack (fig 85). This slackness causes the warp threads from the lower layer to buckle up when the pick is beaten, and a ridged effect appears in the weaving. The slackness also makes it difficult to pass the shuttle through cleanly, and mistakes in the weaving ensue.

The commonest fault in jack looms (whether home-made or professionally made) is the failure of the maker to realise that the warp-line should be as described. Possibly the fact that most books illustrate the warp-line for counterbalanced looms has given rise to this misapprehension — and the loom maker has not read the text carefully.

Look at any jack loom, whether table or treadle model, from a side view to check the warp-line. A faulty loom may sometimes be corrected by adding an extra layer of timber to raise the height of the breast beam and back beam. If this is not possible, try lowering the shafts until the heddle-eyes are in the correct position: this will probably mean that the beater height will need to be altered also, and this in turn may affect the cloth roller and the knee-beam (if there is one).

Buying a treadle loom

Treadle looms, although varying considerably in general appearance, fall into three classes: jack looms, counterbalanced looms, and countermarch looms (fig 86 a to e).

A treadle loom may have a top-pivoted beater (overslung) or a bottom-pivoted beater (underslung). Both work well but, in either case, the pivot point should be as far away as practicable from the actual reed — close to the floor for the underslung type, and well above head level for the overslung type. The long, easy swing thus obtained is much more satisfactory than a short, close swing.

There are two methods of using an overslung beater. In the older method the beater is hung so that it is close to the fell (the last row or pick woven) of the work. The shed is opened, the beater is pushed away from the weaver, the shuttle is thrown, and then the beater is allowed to swing forward with its own momentum.

In the second method the beater is hung so that it is about 20 cm (8 in) from the fell, and it is pulled forward after the shuttle has been thrown. Try both methods and see which you prefer. The second method is better if any finger-manipulated work is to be done.

The treadles are attached by cords, wires or chains to the lamms (fig 86 f and g). The lamms, in turn, are tied to the shafts. The purpose of the

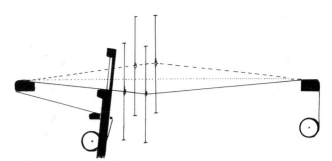

Fig 84. Warp-line for rising-shed jack loom. The solid line shows the correct position of the warp when it is at rest. The dotted line represents the incorrect warp line often seen on jack looms. The dashed line shows the upper layer of the warp when the shed is open. Note that the upper and lower layers of the shed form a similar angle from the horizontal

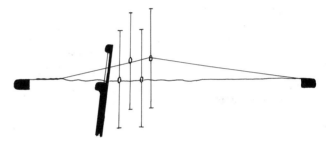

Fig 85. If the jack loom has been made with the warp-line in the (incorrect) horizontal position, the lower layer of the warp becomes slack when a shed is made

lamms is to enable a single treadle to operate more than one shaft at a time, and also to exert a more central pull on the shafts than could be obtained without them. Treadles may be hinged at the back of the loom (rear hung) or at the front of the loom (front hung). Front hung treadles are easier to find with the foot but they do not exert as much efficient leverage as rear hung treadles, unless they are hinged at a point under the weaver's bench (stool). If the loom actually treadles easily, forget the mechanical theory; but if treadling is difficult, consider it carefully.

The width of the loom controls the width of the cloth that can be woven but, if space is not a problem, one that is wider than you think may be needed is useful, because surplus heddles can be stored at the ends of the shafts. If a narrower loom is used, and if there are too many heddles for the piece being woven, you must either distribute empty heddles throughout the threading, or take them off the shafts altogether for the time being.

Treadle looms work best if they are not less

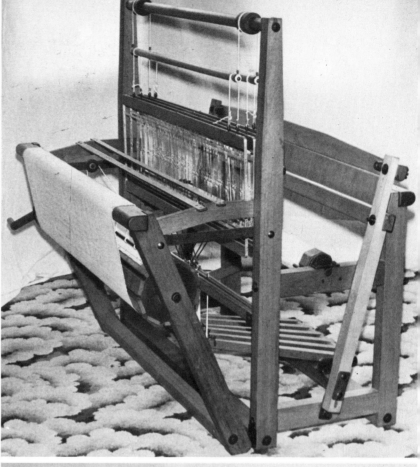

Fig 86a. A compact counter-balanced loom, viewed from the rear (Charles Fuller)

Fig 86b. A traditional counterbalanced loom with an overslung beater (David Thorp) (*Photo: Andris Apse*)

Fig 86c. A countermarch loom with two sectional warp rollers (Sunflower Looms) (*Photo: L. C. Scott*)

Fig 86d. A jack loom which can be folded up to occupy a small space. The shafts run in guides and are pushed up by levers attached to the upper surface of the lamms (Heritage Looms)

Fig 86e. A jack loom operated by levers situated within the centre castle. One treadle is shown depressed to indicate the action of the jacks

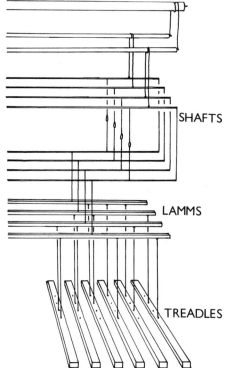

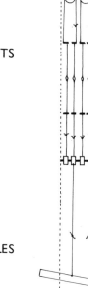

SHAFTS

LAMMS

TREADLES

Fig 86f. Diagram (not to scale) of a treadle loom, in this case counterbalanced, showing the treadles connected to the lamms and the lamms to the shafts

Fig 86g. The side view shows the places where adjustable cords should be used

than one metre (39 in) from front to back — they may measure almost two metres (6 feet). Some looms are semi-folding so that they occupy a relatively small space when not in use, but the ability to fold can result in a loss of rigidity in the loom and this point should be considered carefully if you intend doing other than light work.

The breast beam should be removable so that the weaver can sit on a chair or stool inside the loom while threading.

The heddles and reed should be easily removable for the same reasons as noted for table looms.

Depending on the design of the loom, a knee-beam may be needed to prevent the woven cloth from being rubbed by the weaver's knees. Provision of a knee beam is an integral part of the loom design, and it can seldom be added afterwards.

Some looms, even large ones, have a disappointingly small amount of space between the cloth-roller and the lamms — consequently long lengths cannot be accommodated on the cloth roller.

A loom which has some means of rolling the work forward and retensioning without the weaver having to stand up and turn ratchets is a great time-saver.

The dimensions of the timber used to build the loom should relate to its size and the heaviness of the work for which it will be used. (A linen rug warp is said to exert a tension of 1000 kg or 1 ton.)

Any loom should be well-made and true, and should have first-class ratchets and/or brakes for adjusting the tension.

The height of the weaver's bench is important, so a built-in bench should be adjustable. If the breast beam was renamed the waist beam perhaps more weavers might be encouraged to sit at a better height. The thighs should slope slightly down toward the treadles, and the arms (from elbow to wrist) should be able to rest comfortably on the breast beam. Sitting too low is tiring, prevents the shuttle from being thrown easily over a wide width, and means that the weaver must lift the knees to treadle. Poor posture at the loom can be a cause of back-ache. Being especially short or tall can be something of a disadvantage, so do sit at the loom and try it for size before buying. Ideally the loom maker should have a warp on the loom so that prospective purchasers can weave on it, otherwise it's like buying a car without a test drive.

Naturally, the question of where you are going to use the loom will have to be considered. A spare

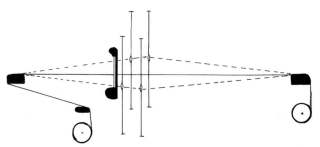

Fig 87. The warp line for counterbalanced and countermarch looms. The solid line represents the correct position of the warp at rest; the dashed lines represent the upper and lower layers of the opened shed

room, or perhaps a studio, sounds wonderful, but if the weaver is a woman she will find that much more weaving can be accomplished if the loom is in or near the kitchen.

Once you have satisfied yourself that the loom is well built you must consider whether it is the best type for the work you have in mind.

Treadle-operated *jack looms* are of two general styles.* In one style the shafts are lifted by means of levers located at the top of the castle and connected to the lamms and treadles by cords. In the other style the shafts are pushed up by levers located under the heddle-frames. The latter type has no need of any superstructure, so it is less massive in appearance but, because of the greater precision needed in design and manufacture, it is more expensive than the simpler type. The importance of the correct warp-line for the jack loom has already been discussed in the section on table looms. A very tight warp tension (such as that used for a linen rug warp) may have the effect of lifting the heddle-eyes up from their proper position, and for this reason jack looms, no matter how large, are not ideally suited to rug weaving.

The warp-line for counterbalanced and countermarch looms is different from that required for jack looms — it follows a straight line from breast beam to back beam and passes through the reed halfway up its height (fig 87). When a shed is opened *all* the shafts move, some up, some down (according to the pick being woven), and the lower layer of the warp then lies at the base of the reed. This action is usually described as a sinking shed, but it could also be thought of as a rising-and-sinking shed.

Of the two sinking-shed looms the *counter-*

* A few jack looms have the shafts suspended on springs, and the shafts are pulled down by the action of the treadles. For this type the warp at rest should be near the top of the reed, and the heddle-eyes should be above the imaginary horizontal line.

balanced loom is easier to use and understand. As the name suggests, the sinking shafts pull the rising shafts up by means of the rollers or pulleys on which they are suspended in pairs, in much the same way that a cablecar travelling downhill pulls another car uphill. The loom therefore works best when two shafts sink, their weight pulling the remaining two shafts up.

The balance is disturbed if one shaft is operated against three. The shed is then either too shallow for a shuttle to be thrown through accurately, or it is so high in the reed that the shuttle gets no support from the shuttle race and can fall through the warp to the floor. Think back to those cablecars: one car coming downhill cannot be expected to pull three up. You may feel there are hundreds of patterns and textures which can be woven using only the two-by-two sheds and that difficulty in using the three-by-one sheds is therefore of no consequence. You may change your mind when you realise that the double weaves employ the unbalanced sheds. Some weavers claim they are able to achieve all the sheds without any difficulty, but others have not been so fortunate.

Apart from this probable restriction on obtaining unbalanced sheds, the counterbalanced loom is delightful to use and is the simplest and cheapest type for the handyman to make.

The *countermarch* loom has two sets of lamms (marches). One set pulls down those shafts which are to sink, and the other set, working in conjunction with overhead jacks, pulls up those shafts which are to rise. Both sets are tied to the treadles, so twice as much tying-up is involved. The countermarch loom combines the rising-and-sinking action of the counterbalanced loom with the ability of the jack loom to open any shed, whether balanced or unbalanced. It is somewhat more troublesome to tie up and understand than the other two types, and it frequently occupies more space. This loom, more than any other, needs to be of roomy dimensions, both in length and height, to give plenty of clearance for efficient action. It is the favourite loom of many highly skilled weavers.

Looms are available with more than four shafts (although four could keep you occupied for a lifetime) and the additional shafts extend the range of pattern and texture possible. The counterbalanced loom is not normally used with more than four shafts, but *The Technique of Weaving* by John Tovey illustrates methods of modifying the loom provided it has a suitable superstructure. Certain design problems arise with all multi-shaft looms, however, and a loom designed with four shafts cannot necessarily be fitted with any more.

A second warp roller is useful when weaving with yarns of different rates of elasticity or in weaving for certain special effects.

Some looms are equipped with a sectional warp roller. This is a roller of 1 metre (1 yd) circumference which is divided by pegs across its width into 5 cm (2 in) sections. Each section is warped directly from yarn spools arranged on a rack — there must be as many spools as the number of warp ends required for each section. A roller of large circumference is a great advantage on any loom, but whether the sectional system is convenient depends on the weaver's needs and circumstances. If yarn can be obtained only on very large cops, the weaver is then faced with the task of winding it off on to the number of spools required for the warping. The time spent doing this may equal the time spent making a conventional warp, but there are other advantages (see Chapter 16). A warping board is not needed for the sectional method and is replaced by a spool rack, a spool winder, a tensioner, and a device for counting the number of metres or yards wound.

If you plan to weave many handspun warps you will probably find that counterbalanced and countermarch looms suit this yarn better than the jack loom. Handspun warps behave better with the positive pulling-apart of the two layers of the shed obtained with the rising-and-sinking action. If a jack loom is used and the shed is difficult to open (because the handspun threads stick together) try lifting one shaft at a time until the number for that pick has been raised.

Reeds

A major cause of friction with wool yarns is the dents of the reed. Denting with two or more ends per dent in a coarse reed is unquestionably better than one thread per dent in a fine reed. A denting plan using a regular sequence of ones, twos and threes per dent extends the capabilities of a small collection of reeds. Bouclé yarns are often given a dent to themselves, partly because they are rough or bulky and partly because they often puff up a great deal during fulling. Reeds made in imperial measurements are described by the number of dents per inch; metric reeds are described by the number of dents per 10 cm. The most useful dentages for handspun wool are 24 to 40 dents per 10 cm, or the imperial equivalent of 6 to 10 dents per inch.

Heddles

The length of the heddles varies with the type of loom. Suggested lengths are as follows:

Table looms and jack looms: 24 cm or 9½ in (steel)
Counterbalanced looms: 27 cm or 10½ in (steel) or
   30 cm or 12 in (string)
Countermarch looms: 33 cm or 13 in (string)

The choice between steel or string heddles is not entirely one of preference, as is so often erroneously stated. In practice it will be found that jack looms work best with steel heddles. The weight of the steel heddles is needed to keep the warp down in the proper position at the base of the reed, and this is particularly true of handspun warps. String heddles are much lighter, and you may need to add springs or weights to the shafts to help them to fall back to the proper position. It is often difficult (or impossible) to add weights or springs to the push-up jack loom.

Countermarch looms work best with string heddles: the weight of steel heddles causes problems in balancing the rising action against the sinking action when tying up the loom. In addition, countermarch looms generally require longer heddles than can usually be obtained in steel.

Counterbalanced looms can be used with either steel or string heddles. The wooden slats forming the top and bottom rails of the shafts usually used with string heddles take up more room than steel runners, and this accounts in part for the difference in the lengths suggested.

Well-made steel heddles are no harder on the yarn than string and may even cause less friction damage, but beware of steel heddles with twisted wire eyes as these can catch the yarn. The eyes should be perfectly smooth and oval.

String heddles are best threaded by the fingers alone — a hook can be more hindrance than help. They are rather fiddly to slide along the shafts but are otherwise no harder to thread than the steel kind. If old heddles are limp and floppy, starch them, and thread the eyes on a rod to dry. Treat all the heddles from the loom at the same time in case the starching causes shrinkage.

If you make every tenth heddle from a different coloured thread counting is easier, but if you are dyeing thread for the purpose do so before making the heddles, again in case of shrinkage. Every tenth steel heddle can be marked with a tiny dab of paint or coloured nail varnish.

The total number of heddles required depends entirely on the fineness of the work to be done. It is essential for the warp to have a good clear space

Fig 88a. Home-made warping board, well used but still serviceable

Fig 88b. This board is capable of measuring a 7-metre (yard) warp

to work in on the shafts, so on no account allow surplus heddles to rub against the edges of the weaving — take them off the loom.

Other Equipment (figs 88 and 89)

Warping board

This is used for measuring out the warp. It may be bought ready-made or made at home. A typical modest-sized warping board consists of round wooden pegs about 15 x 2 cm (6 x ¾ in) set firmly in a thick plank. The pegs may be removable (which makes the board easier to store), but because there must be no possibility of the pegs leaning over or falling out during warp-making, the handyman may find it best to glue them in permanently. The pegs in the board illustrated (fig 88) are placed at 25 cm (9 in) centres on the top and bottom rows, and at 8 cm (3 in) centres at the sides.

This board is suitable for the hobby weaver — it will measure warps up to 7 m (7 yds) long, and can be hung on a wall for storage. A larger board, or a warping mill (a vertical or horizontal reel serving the same purpose) is needed for longer warps. However, unless you plan to do a great deal of weaving on long warps you may not feel justified in giving a mill the amount of houseroom it requires.

Warping pegs

Individual wooden pegs clamped to a table are an alternative to a warping board, but are neither so

Fig 89. Accessories used in weaving. *On shelf:* single warping peg and clamp, bobbin winder. *Below shelf, from the top:* raddle and raddle cap, ski shuttle, rug shuttle, boat shuttle, two stick shuttles

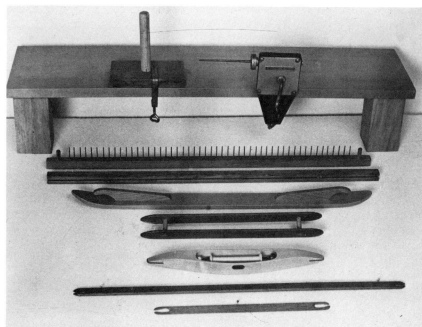

cheap nor so satisfactory in the long run and may mark the table.

Warping equipment must be very strongly made as the cumulative tension is much greater than might be imagined. Flimsy equipment will fall apart very rapidly, usually at the least convenient moment.

Raddle

A raddle is a kind of coarse-toothed comb, used to space out the warp to its proper width as it is wound on the loom. It should be wide enough to span the loom. It may be bought ready-made or you can make one yourself by hammering flooring nails into a piece of dressed pine. (Pine is suggested because harder timbers are inclined to split and the holes for the nails would need to be drilled.) The most useful spacing between the nails is 1.25 cm (½ in). A spacing of 2.5 cm (1 in) is too coarse and a 1 cm division is not especially convenient unless your reeds are metric and all your calculations are made in metrics.

Some small accessories are needed: a threading hook, a reed hook, one or more fret clamps, scissors, tape-measure, ruler, pins, needles and so on.

The threading hooks supplied with rigid-heddle looms are very flimsy. Go to a shop selling domestic knitting machines and buy a latch hook used for repairing runs in knitting. Pull the latch off with pliers. This hook is very satisfactory and long-lasting.

For counterbalanced and countermarch looms you will find a small spirit-level (as used in carpentry) of great value when preparing the loom for use.

A magnet attached to the loom is useful for holding a few pins and needles ready to hand.

A new loom comes equipped with cross-sticks and warp sticks. Shuttles are usually extra, and as the choice of a shuttle is very closely bound up with the weaving process, discussion of the various kinds is postponed until Chapter 13.

The weaver's bench (apart from being the right height) should be comfortable to sit on and large enough to hold notebook and pencil, spare shuttles and bobbins, scissors, and possibly a coffee cup.

Good lighting is essential — an anglepoise lamp attached to the loom is well worthwhile.

11 Yarns and Sett

YARN

ALMOST ANY YARN can be used in handweaving, and much imaginative work has been done with very unlikely materials. Beginners will find, however, that the natural fibres are the easiest to use and give the most pleasing results.

For the first projects in this book the yarns are suggested, but later on the weaver is expected to make his or her own judgments, basing the decision on the materials available and the effect preferred. There is no great skill involved in copying blindly from a book, but it can be very helpful for the beginner to have a recipe for the first attempts, just as it is usual to have a recipe book in the kitchen. The real creative joy comes later, when you feel confident enough to dispense with books and design the whole project from start to finish.

Wool
Wool is the true miracle fibre, easy to use, endlessly versatile, and, in knitting qualities at least, abundantly available. For those who spin, handspun wool may be used as weft by the novice and as both warp and weft by the more experienced. Millspun (factory-spun) yarns especially manufactured for weaving are not always so easy to come by, as they are seldom sold in shops.

The best plan is to join the nearest weavers' guild or other similar society — many of these have cooperative buying schemes operating. Weavers' magazines frequently carry advertisements for mail-order yarn outlets. Weaving yarns are usually cheaper than knitting yarns and give much better results. Use them whenever you can.

Cotton
Cotton has less elasticity than wool but is still easy to use. It is available as a knitting or crochet yarn, and other types of cotton for a variety of craft uses, including weaving, may sometimes be found in hobby shops.

Linen
Linen is beautiful, but it is inelastic and therefore difficult for the new weaver to handle as a warp; it may be used as weft, however. Heavy linen for rug warps is sold in craft supply shops, ships' chandlers, and so on, but fine linen for handweaving is usually available only through guilds or specialist suppliers. Reels of linen thread sold for stitching leather are not suitable — the thread is too smoothly and tightly twisted, it may be waxed, and it is often hard and slippery.

Other fibres
Mohair and other animal fibres, and the various plant fibres, whether millspun or handspun, are all used in handweaving. Silk is beautiful, expensive, and hard to obtain, but if the opportunity arises, use it. Synthetics such as orlon may be used, but these have the disadvantage in fabric weaving that they do not 'full' as wool does.

Combinations of fibres, whether natural or synthetic, when used in one piece of weaving, can lead to tension and unequal shrinkage problems, so be sure to make careful samples first.

For the most part this book deals with wool, and a word of caution is needed. A great deal of the wool yarn sold in craft shops is carpet wool, although it is often falsely described as 'economy knitting wool'. While it would not be true to say that this yarn should never be used except in the making of carpets, it is certainly true that many beginners are tempted to use it far too often because it is cheap, easy to obtain and easy to handle.

Carpet wool is not only thicker than normal yarns, but the fibres themselves are coarser and hairier. These are desirable qualities on the floor, but if cloth is woven from this yarn it will very likely be far too heavy and cumbersome, and will give a completely false idea of what constitutes an acceptable handwoven fabric. Use it with caution and discrimination.

The weaver who lives in an isolated area often feels at a disadvantage when buying yarn, although in fact towndwellers are often not much better off. Watch the advertisements in weavers' magazines and the For Sale columns in local newspapers. Examine every yarn about the house and district with an open mind — baler twine, synthetic strings used around the farm, fishing twine, garden supplies, fibres such as raffia and native grasses, cellophane and paper strips, bamboo, narrow braids, ribbons — everything can be pressed into service in the learning process. The finished product may or may not be handsome, may or may not be useful, but the knowledge gained of the way in which warp and weft intersect will be of great value. The time spent actually weaving, with whatever materials, is much more worthwhile than time spent sitting back waiting for a miraculous supply of fabulous yarns.

When the opportunity arises to buy real yarn, buy it. Do not hesitate too long, or it may be gone by the time you have made up your mind. Buy more than you think you will need, as yarn can seldom be matched. Remnants of yarn arrayed on a shelf can inspire colour and texture combinations which might otherwise never have been thought of.

YARN COUNTS

The biggest problem facing a new weaver is deciding which yarn to use. Books which refer to 'medium' or 'fine' without further explanation are not very helpful, and a yarn which is bought easily by brand name in one country is completely unknown in another.

Yarn used for knitting is often sold as 2-ply, 3-ply or 4-ply. The ply number tells us nothing about the *diameter* of the yarn — all it tells us is that x number of singles yarns were twisted together to form the finished yarn. A sewing thread may be 2-ply, but so may rope. When a spinner/weaver uses the term it is often intended in the sense of 'a yarn of a diameter similar to the traditional 2-ply knitting wool'. Many manufacturers now make all their yarns from two singles plied together, and from a technical point of view this is 2-ply; but, depending on the size of the singles used, the final diameter may vary from fine baby yarn to chunky sport yarn. Some more precise description is needed.

Until recently, spinning mills used a means of identifying the size of yarns by the number of yards per pound, and as this system is still used in older books it is necessary to be familiar with it in order to identify the yarns mentioned. Details of this system are given in Appendix A.

Latterly an international system known as Tex has been introduced. In this system all yarns (except continuous filaments) are described by the weight in grammes of 1000 metres. A size 10 yarn (R 10 Tex) is spun so that 1000 m weighs 10 g. A size 200 yarn (R 200 Tex) is spun so that 1000 m weighs 200 g. The number given refers to the final size of the yarn regardless of how many singles were twisted together to achieve that result — the ply number, if stated, is given only for information. R 100 Tex/2 therefore means that two singles

yarns were plied together and that the resulting yarn weighs 100 g per 1000 m. The direction of twist ($\overleftarrow{s}$ or $\overrightarrow{z}$) may also be noted on the label.

Under the old system a low number indicated a thick yarn and a high number a fine yarn. Under the Tex system a low number indicates a fine yarn, and a high number a thick yarn.

In practice, handweavers are seldom able to buy yarn of a known count (size). The cardboard cones on which yarns are wound are used over and over again, and the label inside may refer to some totally different yarn. It is wise therefore to use your own judgment when examining yarn and not to rely too heavily on the label.

The yarns known to knitters as 2-ply, 3-ply and 4-ply may also vary in length-weight from country to country, and for this reason a chart of commonly used yarns is given in the knitting section.

Given the necessity of using both metric and imperial measurements, it has been difficult to know what to do for the best in endeavouring to specify the yarns to be used for the weaving projects. The most sensible compromise seems to be to state the number of metres per 500 g (0.5 kg) and the number of yards per pound. A metre is a little longer than a yard, but 0.5 kg is a little heavier than a pound, and the measurement works out very nearly the same.

If you do not know the length-weight of the yarn you have bought, wind off a small ball (20 g or 1 oz), weighing it as accurately as possible, and measure the number of metres or yards with the aid of warping pegs or a niddy-noddy. Simple multiplication will give you the number of metres/yards per 0.5 kg or per pound.

If the yarn you have available is not the same size as that suggested for the project, you will have to use a different sett.

SETT

Sett is the word used to describe the number of warp ends and weft picks in any given area of cloth. In imperial measurements the inch is the unit of measurement, and the number of ends per inch and picks per inch (abbreviated epi and ppi) is stated. In metric calculations the unit is ends per centimetre (epc) although Scandinavian weavers work on the basis of a 10-centimetre unit. In this book, to avoid arithmetical confusion, the unit used is the nearest metric/imperial equivalent, 2.5 cm or 1 inch. To find the number of ends in 10 cm (if that unit is preferred) simply multiply by four.

The sett of a piece of weaving is very important and makes the difference between a successful and an unsuccessful result. It is an aspect of weaving all too often ignored by novices, and lack of attention to it is the cause of a great deal of disappointment. If the warp ends are too close together the warp will dominate the weft (warp-predominant); if the warp ends are too far apart the weft will dominate the warp (weft-predominant). Colours and textures planned for either warp or weft may either be overwhelmed or become unexpectedly conspicuous. In extreme instances the warp may cover the weft entirely (warp-faced), or the weft may cover the warp entirely (weft-faced). Warp-faced and weft-faced weaves are very firm, possibly stiff, and are reserved for braids, rugs and wall hangings. Fabrics which are warp- or weft-predominant are useful when a firm but not inflexible cloth is required, such as upholstery fabric. A cloth in which there are as many warp ends as there are weft picks in any given square area (2.5 x 2.5 cm, or 1 x 1 in) is called a balanced or square cloth.

Strictly speaking, the classic balanced cloth is one in which the warp yarn and weft yarn are of the same (or nearly the same) size. A cloth made with one fine yarn followed by one thick yarn in the warp, and balanced by one fine and one thick in the weft, or similar variations, also qualifies as a square cloth. A cloth with a fine warp supporting a thick weft is not balanced. Handweavers, especially those using a handspun weft, often allow themselves a little latitude here, depending on the nature of the project in hand, but if you weave an unbalanced cloth, make sure you do so from choice rather than from miscalculation.

A fabric which is designed to be cut and sewn into a conventional garment should be balanced, otherwise it will fray in the cutting, give way at the seams, will not drape easily, will not hang properly on the bias, and will not sit well on the body. The popular 'primitive' garments, which involve very little cutting and sewing, do not demand a balanced weave, but nevertheless a balanced cloth probably gives the best results. Cushion covers, table runners, and so on, may also be unbalanced, depending on the effect the weaver wishes to achieve. Curtains hang best if they are either balanced or warp-predominant.

To a limited extent the balanced cloth may be achieved by adjusting the strength of the beat to suit, but this may result in a cloth which is either softer or firmer than was intended. The solution lies in choosing an appropriate sett for the yarns to be used.

Estimating Sett

Estimating the sett required to produce a balanced cloth (whether plain weave, twill, pattern or texture) is an important part of designing. In the long run the only infallible method is to make a sample, washed and finished. If the sample, when counted, shows 16 warp ends per unit, and only 12 weft picks, add the two figures together (28) and divide by 2 (14). The correct sett for those yarns, in that weave, is therefore 14.

For an important project samples should always be made, and in the first instance a simple and fairly reliable estimate of sett can be obtained by winding the yarns to be used around a ruler, as follows.

Plain weave

Take a length of the warp yarn and a length of the weft yarn and wind the two simultaneously around 2.5 cm (1 in) of a ruler. Each yarn should lie flat and snug beside its neighbour with no overlapping or twisting. None of the ruler should show through the yarn, but avoid pushing the rounds artificially close together with the fingers. Now count the number of times the *warp* yarn only passed around the ruler, ignoring the weft. The answer gives an appropriate sett for plain weave.

Twill (2/2 and 3/1)

Take *two* lengths of warp yarn and *one* of weft and wind as before. Count the warp turns only, noting that each turn of the two warp yarns counts as two, not one.

Note that twill requires a closer sett than plain weave, owing to the different way in which the yarns intersect.

You will probably find that yarn of a diameter similar to that of 4-ply knitting wool needs a sett of 12 for plain weave and 14 to 16 for twill. Yarn similar in size to 3-ply needs 14 for plain weave, 16 to 18 for twill; and yarn similar to double-knitting wool needs 8 for plain weave and 9 or 10 for twill.

Hopsack
Hopsack is usually given a sett the same as for twill or slightly closer. If a particularly soft or firm cloth is wanted, adjust the figures up or down to suit.

Weft-faced plain weave
Wind *one* of the warp yarn and *two* of the weft around the ruler — count the warp yarn only.

Warp-faced plain weave
Wind the warp yarn only around the ruler, and multiply the result by two.

Estimating Quantities
Once an appropriate sett has been established it is an easy matter to work out the total number of ends needed for the warp. Simply multiply the number of ends in 2.5 cm (1 in) by the number of sections needed to make up the width of the planned piece of weaving. From the total number of ends the quantity of yarn needed can be worked out — the number of ends multiplied by the length of the warp. Thus, if a warp has 300 ends, each 5 m (5 yds) long, the total length required for the warp is 1500 m (1500 yds).

The amount of weft required can also be calculated, although not quite so accurately. A very rough guide, for a warp 5 m (5 yds) or longer, is to allow the same weight for weft as for warp, provided the weave is balanced and the yarns reasonably similar.

A more accurate method, especially for shorter warps, is to work out the length of yarn needed for one pick, and to multiply the number of picks needed for the length to be woven. The result will be a large number of centimetres or inches, which will need converting to metres or yards to be manageable.

If you are still doubtful after weaving has commenced, weigh out 25 g (1 oz) of weft yarn as accurately as possible, and take note of the length which can be woven with this known weight of yarn. (A byproduct of an interest in weaving is an improvement in elementary arithmetic!)

A word of caution is needed here: if the threading draft to be used requires (perhaps) 18 ends to a repeat, it will be necessary to wind a number of warp ends divisible by 18, and this may mean adjusting the precise width to be woven.

Emphasis has been laid on correctness. Does this mean that correctness is all-important in weaving? Of course it does not; a perfectly correct piece may also be perfectly boring. Imagination counts most in weaving, but creative work succeeds best when combined with sound technique.

12 Getting Ready to Weave

THERE ARE PROBABLY as many opinions about weaving as there are weavers, and there is no subject which reveals more divergence of opinion than the best method of making up a warp and getting it on to the loom.

The method given below is not the only one commonly used, but it is reliable, can be done by the weaver working entirely alone, and suits all fibres, including handspun wool. Only one method is described in order to avoid the confusion often felt by novices when offered several choices.

There are several steps in producing a piece of weaving. In order they are:
1. Planning the warp and measuring it out on the warping board.
2. Spreading the warp out to the desired width and winding it on to the warp roller.
3. Threading the warp through the heddles and reed and tying it to the cloth roller.
4. The actual weaving.
5. Washing and 'finishing' the cloth.
It will be seen from the above that the weaving itself, interesting though it is, is only one part of the whole. All the processes are of equal importance, and failure to give each one the care that is due to it will result in disappointment. Good weaving cannot possibly result from a badly planned or badly wound warp. The warp constitutes half of the finished cloth, so do not begrudge the time spent on it.

Planning The Warp

The first process in weaving is to measure out the warp with the aid of the warping board so that all the threads are of the same length and tension. Warp-making seems a tedious chore at first but, with a little practice, making it and winding it on the loom become quite easy.

The length of each warp thread (properly called an end) depends on the length of the article to be woven, plus certain allowances. Several centimetres (inches) of every warp are wasted in tying it to the cloth roller at the front of the loom, and there is also certain unavoidable waste at the end of each warp. An allowance of about 10 cm per metre (3 in per yard) must also be made for the contraction of the weaving after it is cut from the loom and for shrinkage in finishing. The extra length for wastage on table looms is about 45 cm (18 in), and 90 cm (36 in) for treadle looms. The wastage allowance and the length allowed for contraction and shrinkage when added together are called loom allowance.

The wastage (but not the contraction) is the same for a short warp as for a long one, but, in spite of long warps being therefore more economical of yarn, the learner is advised to make short warps at first until thoroughly familiar with the mechanics of 'dressing' the loom.

The width of the warp is the width of the piece of weaving required plus an extra allowance of perhaps 1 cm in 30 cm (½ in per foot) for take-up and shrinkage. The width allowance is difficult to estimate, as a good deal depends on the yarn, the weave, and the weaver's technique.

The exact number of threads which must be measured out to make up the desired width of cloth is a matter of sett, as explained in the previous chapter. The heddles of the four-shaft loom can be crowded together or moved apart, so a variation in sett is possible to suit the size of the yarn. The rigid-heddle loom, on the other hand, has a restricted sett because the holes and slots in the heddle-reed cannot be adjusted. With this type of loom the weaver must choose the yarn to suit the heddle-reed, and it is often very difficult to find a yarn of a suitable type and size. Knitting yarn is not entirely suitable for weaving but beginners are sometimes obliged to use it because they do not know where to buy anything else. Some compromise may have to be made — perhaps the use of a weft a little thicker than would otherwise be desirable, to compensate for the too-thin warp.

Whatever type of loom is used, the warp yarn must suit the size of the holes and slots in the heddle-reed, or the heddle-eyes and reed of the four-shaft loom, because yarn which is too thick, too fuzzy, or too bumpy to slip up and down readily in these confined spaces will prevent the loom from working properly and will cause endless frustration.

Making A Warp

A warp is not made by cutting individual pieces of yarn to the required length: it is made by winding yarn around pegs set the desired distance apart until as many threads as needed have been measured thus. The warp remains as a continuous skein

126

until the moment arrives when one end of the skein is cut for threading the ends through the heddle-reed or heddles. This is a very ancient procedure, tidy and efficient and, in some parts of the world, warps are still made outdoors around wooden stakes hammered into the ground.

The modern handweaver uses a compact ready-made warping board or a series of pegs clamped to a table. Various lengths of warp (up to the maximum possible on the board) can be made by using fewer of the pegs. It is a good idea to practise the circuit to be taken in making various lengths of warp with a ball of string.

If a warp is planned for two cushion covers (allowing one metre or 40 inches for each cover) the length of the warp is:

Metric	Imperial
200 cm for the two covers	80 in
45 cm for loom waste (table-loom)	18 in
20 cm for contraction	7 in
265 cm	105 in

Because of the fixed position of the pegs in the warping board it is not always possible to make the warp the precise length required, so take the yarn to the next nearest peg, or farther if you wish to have extra for making samples. The warp for the two cushion covers might therefore be 3 m (3 yds). If the width of the cloth is to be 45cm (18in) and if the sett is 12, 216 warp ends will be needed, plus an extra 4 for selvedge strengthening. If the sett is 10, 180 will be needed, plus 4 for selvedges.

Take a ball of the warp yarn, make a loop in the end and slip this loop over peg A. Place the ball of yarn in a bowl or carton on the floor near your feet.

Pass the yarn around the pegs in the sequence shown in fig 90: that is, from peg A, down between B and C, up between C and D, around E and across to F, and up between X and Y. This completes the outward journey and measures 3 m (3 yds).

Continue by leading the yarn around Z, up between Y and X, around F and across to E, down between C and B, and back to A. This completes one return journey, called a 'portee', and measures out *two* of the threads required for the warp.

Continue making these return journeys until 10 threads have been measured out (5 portees). Take a piece of strong contrasting string 1 m (1 yd) long and pass it around this first group of 10 as shown in fig 91. Leave the ends of the string lying on the board ready to tie the next group. (Tying in groups

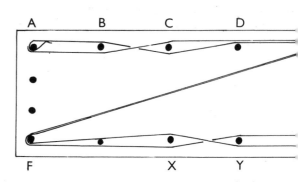
Fig 90a. Making a 3 metre (yard) warp on the board

Fig 90b. Push the accumulated threads to the base of the pegs at intervals

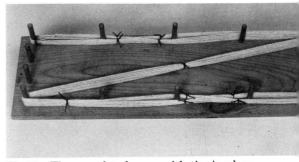
Fig 90c. The completed warp with ties in place

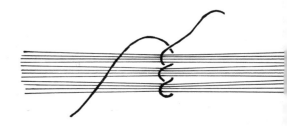
Fig 91. The counting tie

representing one dent of the raddle is an alternative to tying groups of 10; both are an aid to counting as it is tedious to count individual warp ends to ascertain how many have been measured out.) This 'counting' tie is best made at a place in the warp where it is not confused by the crossing-over of the threads, as otherwise the novice is inclined to count either twice as many, or only half the number, of threads required.

Continue to make the warp, pushing the accumulated threads to the base of the pegs at intervals.* When the first ball of yarn runs out, knot another to it, close to either peg A or peg Z — no knots should be allowed in the warp except at these two places. When the required number of ends have been measured, break off the yarn, leaving enough to make a loop to slip over peg A, as at the beginning.

The two 'crosses' in the warp, between B and C, and X and Y, are *essential* to the warp and *must be preserved at all costs*. The crosses could have been made between A and B, and Y and Z, but this leaves an inconveniently short length of yarn to thread with, so make them where suggested.

Without the crosses it is not possible to thread the warp ends in the correct order and, if the correct order is not maintained, the warp may become so tangled that it is unweavable.

The tension at which the yarn is passed around the pegs does not need to be great, but it should be even.

When the warp has been completed it is tied with temporary string ties (to secure the crosses) *before* it is lifted from the board. Use knots, not bows. Make ties in four places at each cross (fig 92), and one each at A and Z. Make very tight ties around the warp at 1 m (1 yd) intervals along the length of the warp.

If you feel confident of being able to crochet a chain which can be pulled undone later you may now crochet the whole warp into a thick chain, beginning from A, and using your hand as the hook. However, as so many beginners manage to make a chain which will not come undone when required, the tight ties at intervals (choke ties) will suffice. Lift the warp from the board, chaining or not as you choose, beginning from peg A.

Take two of the cross-sticks (distinguished from warp sticks by the hole bored in each end) and pass them carefully through the cross at X-Y. Tie the two sticks together with shoelaces, leaving a

* A wide warp may need to be made in two sections, and indeed this is the best procedure if the loom has cords from overhead jacks in the centre of the loom.

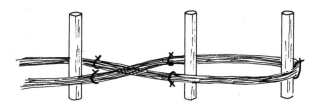

Fig 92. Securing the cross with ties

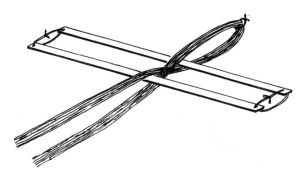

Fig 93. The cross-sticks inserted in the cross. The sticks have been tied together and the temporary cross ties have been discarded

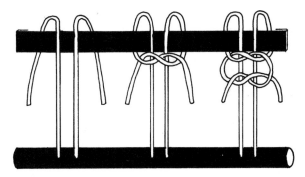

Fig 94. Three steps in making the knot attaching the apron stick to the warp roller

finger's space between them (fig 93). These sticks now take the place of, and serve the function of, the pegs at X-Y.

Raddling

Carry the warp to the loom. Remove the whole heddle-box (castle) if possible, or push the heddles aside so that there will be adequate space for the width of the warp. Remove the beater.

With the rigid-heddle loom, lift the heddle-reed out and set it aside. Untie the cords securing the warp stick to the warp roller, noting the type of knot used (fig 94), and slip this stick through the loop in the end of the warp.

Re-tie the stick to the warp roller, using the outer cords only, and make sure that the cords (or canvas apron) pass over the back beam. The remaining cords are left undone for the time being. Be sure that the stick is parallel to the roller or the weaving will not be straight.

Remove the four temporary ties around the cross, and remove the tie around the end loop at Z. Tie the cross-sticks to some convenient part of the loom so that they remain steady during raddling — nothing is more irritating than sticks that see-saw about. From this point on, the method differs a little according to whether a four-shaft or a rigid-heddle loom is used. Separate instructions for each are given.

Rigid-heddle loom

Tie the raddle to the brackets that normally support the heddle-reed. (It must be admitted that it is not usual to use a raddle with this loom, but you are recommended to do so because the method can be applied to any future loom you may own.) Place a piece of stiff folded paper over the teeth of the raddle to prevent snagging, then lift the warp over the covered raddle and let it hang down to the floor at the front of the loom.

The warp must be centrally placed in the loom, so take a piece of chalk and mark the raddle evenly either side of the centre — 22.5 cm (9 in) either side for this warp. Select threads from the cross, strictly in order (fig 95) beginning from the right, and place a number of threads equal to 1.25 cm (½ in) of warp in each dent of the raddle.

If the sett is 12 this will mean putting 6 threads in each raddle space; but if the sett is 10 put 6 in the first space and 4 in the next, and repeat this sequence, thus making a total of 10 in 2 spaces. (The reason for not putting 5 in each space, as might seem logical, is that the pairs of threads which make up each portee should not be separated.)

Continue to place groups of threads in the raddle (fig 96), moving the folded paper aside as necessary, until raddling is completed. Tie the raddle cap on, or twine string around the nail-heads of the home-made raddle (fig 97) to prevent the threads jumping out of the spaces. Spread the warp out neatly on the warp stick so that it is the same width as in the raddle, then tie the remaining cords from the warp roller to the stick.

Four-shaft loom

In preparation for winding the warp on to the loom, place the raddle across the loom frame in a position handy to the cross, and secure it with

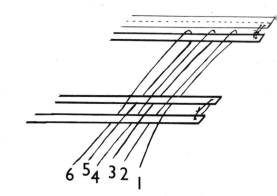

Fig 95. The cross, showing the first 6 threads separated from the bulk of the warp ready to be placed in a dent of the raddle

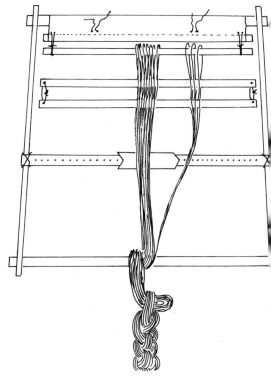

Fig 96. Bird's-eye view of raddling in progress. The heddle shafts and reed have been removed and the raddle is supported by angel sticks. The warp chain has been wrapped around the breast beam to provide the tension needed to make it easy to detect the correct order of threads in the cross

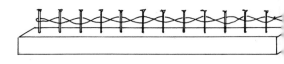

Fig 97. Twining the home-made raddle

string ties, or by any other convenient means, so that it cannot possibly fall down. The exact position cannot be stated with any certainty because looms vary a good deal in design detail.

Find the best place on *your* loom. This may be on the breast beam, on the back beam, on top of the castle, or in the beater in place of the reed. Two sticks (often called angel sticks), long enough to reach from front to back of the loom, may be a suitable means of supporting the raddle (fig 96). The warp may even be raddled on the table and carried to the loom afterwards, but if this is done the raddle cap must be a very good fit. In any event, make sure that the raddle is placed a little higher in the loom than the cross-sticks, as otherwise the threads are inclined to jump up out of the spaces. Place a piece of stiff folded paper over the teeth of the raddle, and then proceed as for the rigid-heddle loom, noting fig 95.

If it is difficult to detect the correct order of ends in the cross, exert some tension on the warp chain or hang a weight on it, and the order will become clear. You will notice that the ends are arranged on the cross-sticks so that they emerge alternately over and under the sticks. If the correct thread is chosen from the cross it is able to slide along the cross-sticks, and along the warp stick, without being obstructed by any other thread. Make every effort to work from the cross in the correct order of warp ends — one or two mistakes may not matter, but more may spoil the warp.

Winding the Warp on the Roller (Beaming)

Clamp the loom to the table and engage the warp roller ratchet. Stand at the front of the loom, grasp the warp at the first choke-tie and give it a good shake and a pull, or even slap it briskly, so that any disturbance to the even length and tension caused by raddling is corrected. The first choke-tie may then be cut and discarded.

Take a 5 cm (2 in) section from the right-hand side of the warp, give it a firm pull, and then place the section gently on the breast beam directly in front of the position it occupied in the raddle. The warp must at all times pass in a straight line from the roller through the raddle to the breast beam. It should never be allowed to taper toward the front.

Tension the rest of the warp in this way, working in small sections to the left-hand side. Move to the rear of the loom and wind one turn of the roller *without touching the warp in any way*. A dot of coloured chalk or paint on the roller will help to

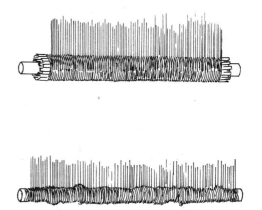

Fig 98. *Upper*, a well-beamed warp. *Lower*, a badly beamed warp

establish when one complete turn has been made.

Allow the ratchet and pawl to click while you wind as a precaution against turning in the wrong direction. Rollers usually wind clockwise, but this is not invariable, and the pawl will not hold if the roller has been wound the wrong way.

If the cross-sticks have moved toward the roller, push them back toward the centre of the loom. Return to the front, and tension the warp in sections as before, but begin from the left side this time. The warp should be unchained as necessary and any temporary ties should be removed. If there is a tugging sensation during beaming, stop and look for a thread which may have caught on the raddle or cross-sticks and be in danger of breaking. If a thread breaks, knot in a short replacement length of yarn and deal with the knots during the weaving, as described later.

From the very first turn it is essential to cover any cord knots or other bulges on the roller with a layer of warp sticks or corrugated card, because the warp must be an even smooth roll, without any suggestion of humps and hollows or tangles. Great care must also be taken to prevent the warp from spreading out at the edges or forming a thicker roll toward the centre, as this fault causes tension problems in the weaving. At the slightest hint of any such trouble, wind in more sticks or card so that a fresh smooth surface is presented for the next round of warp (fig 98). Aluminium venetian blind slats are sometimes used as packing, and so is paper, but both are virtually useless.

Winding the warp on the loom is of critical importance. Good weaving cannot be done on a badly beamed warp, and very little can be done about a bad warp once the work is in progress.

Treadle looms have fairly large rollers, so beaming can be done quickly and efficiently; but table looms usually have rollers of small diameter, and extra time and care should be taken.

It is sometimes said that warping a loom cannot be done by the solo weaver unless the sectional beaming method is used. This is not so. If you have an interested person to help, well and good; but if the only person available is not really interested in what you are doing, you are far better off working alone.

Continue to wind the warp in this way until about 45 cm (18 in) remains. Tie the cross-sticks to the loom so that they cannot fall out of the warp. Cut through the entire loop of yarn at the front of the warp and remove the ties securing the second cross.

At this point you might ask why the second cross was made if it was not used. The second cross has several functions which will become apparent later in your weaving career. At the learner level it is like the spare wheel of a car — useful in emergencies. It is needed if the first cross is accidentally spoiled or lost, and it is also needed if the warp yarn turns out to be 'sticky' and refuses to slide through the cross-sticks while beaming.

If the yarn is sticky, remove the cross-sticks and wind on through the raddle only, re-inserting them in the second cross when you come to it, as described in Chapter 17. (Many weavers always remove the sticks while beaming to reduce friction on the warp.) A cross is essential for threading, so *never* remove the sticks unless you are sure you have another cross in reserve.

Some warping boards have insufficient pegs to make two crosses, but if you intend working with wool have the board altered and get into the habit of making two crosses — the second one will save you many grey hairs.

Threading

Remove the raddle. Position the cross-sticks so that the sequence of the warp ends is clearly visible as you sit at the front of the loom. Put the heddle-box back into the four-shaft loom, and tie the heddle-reed to the supporting brackets in the rigid-heddle loom.

Rigid-heddle loom

Mark the position the warp will occupy in the heddle-reed. For a 45 cm (18 in) warp this will be 22.5 cm (9 in) either side of the centre.

Select the first two warp ends from the right-hand side of the cross-sticks, take the threading hook and pull them through the hole nearest the right-hand mark. Select the next two threads and pull them through the slot immediately to the left of the hole just filled. These two double threads are for selvedge strengthening. The remainder of the threads are used singly in the holes and slots until the left selvedge is reached, when two double threads are used again.

Be sure to select the warp threads in the correct order from the cross. Do not miss any of the holes or slots, and do not use any double threads apart from those forming the selvedge. Check frequently for errors, and tie each checked group in a loose slipknot as a precaution against threads being pulled out accidentally.

Four-shaft loom

Count the number of heddles on each shaft. Calculate how many are needed on each shaft for the piece of work to be threaded. For instance, if the warp has 216 ends, 54 heddles are needed on each for plain weave. Count out the number required and push any surplus heddles evenly to the sides of the shafts so that they remain balanced. The edges of the warp should not be crowded by spare heddles and it may be necessary to remove the surplus from the loom.

For a first project the loom should be threaded as in fig 99.

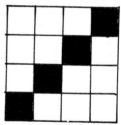

Fig 99. Simple threading draft, commonly known as 'the straight draw'

This diagram (weaving drafts are always read from right to left) means that the first thread of the warp is threaded through the eye of a heddle on shaft 4 (nearest the back of the loom), the next through the eye of a heddle on shaft 3, the third through shaft 2, and the fourth through shaft 1 (nearest the front). Each thread is taken through one heddle-eye only. This is the simplest and most basic threading sequence or draft.

Take each thread in strict order from the cross, hook it through the appropriate heddle-eye and draw it to the front of the loom (fig 100a). Check frequently for errors, tie each checked bunch in a loose knot for safety, and push each group of threaded heddles to the right where they will be out of the way.

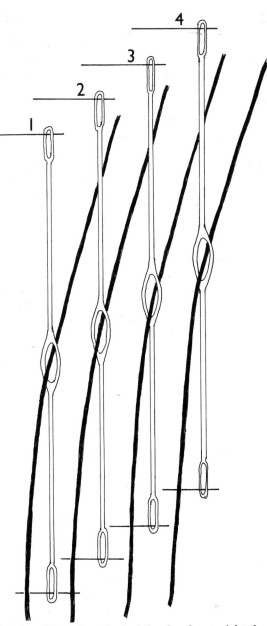

Fig 100a. Threading the heddles for the straight draw

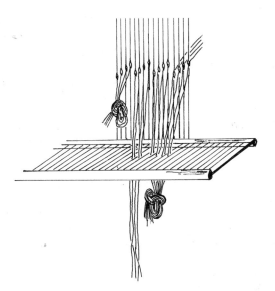

Fig 100b. Placing the reed in a horizontal position makes sleying easy

two horizontal spaces instead of four. The top row represents holes, and the lower row slots.

When all the warp ends have been threaded and checked, repeating the sequence given in the diagram, replace the beater in the loom, minus its cap. Tie the reed to it, in a horizontal position if possible, otherwise tie it upright. The angel sticks may come in handy again for supporting the reed (fig 100b).

Sleying

The process of threading the warp ends through the dents of the reed is called sleying. Check the sleying for errors at frequent intervals because if you miss a dent, or put too many threads in a dent, these irregularities will show as flaws in the work.

Taking each of the threads in turn, as they were threaded through the heddles, pull each through a dent in the reed with the flat reed hook. If the sett of the work is 12, and if the reed is 12 dent, place one thread in each dent except that the first four and last four threads are sleyed two per dent for stronger selvedges. If the reed is 8 dent, thread the main part of the work with two in every second dent so that there are 12 threads in every 8 dents. Four-shaft loom selvedges are strong because they are closer woven than the rest of the cloth; rigid-heddle selvedges gain their strength from the use of doubled threads.

As each group is checked for errors, tie it in a loose slipknot. When sleying is completed, lift the reed to its vertical position, put the cap on, and tighten any bolts.

You will find it helpful to count out four heddles, one from each shaft, and thread these four before going on to the next group. With practice you will learn to count out several from each shaft according to the number needed for the particular draft. This careful counting-out also acts as a check on the accuracy of the threading.

Threading drafts are not usually given for the rigid-heddle loom, but if a draft was required it would be written in a similar fashion but with only

Making the Front Tie

The warp, on either loom, is now ready to be tied to the cloth stick. This is attached to the front roller by cords or by a canvas apron. Unroll the cords or canvas and bring the stick in front of and over the breast beam.

Untie the slipknots in the warp groups. Take a group of threads representing no more than 2.5 cm (1 in) of the warp, and stroke the threads through the hands until they are all of equal tension. Pass the group over the cloth stick, divide it in two, bring the two halves up to the top of the stick, and tie the first part of a reefknot (fig 101). When all the groups have been dealt with, run your fingertips across the warp in front of the reed to ascertain if the whole warp is at an even tension. If some groups are slacker than others tighten them, then complete each tie with a half bow.

Believe it or not, you are now ready to weave!

The procedures described necessarily seem lengthy when written down in sufficient detail to avoid misunderstanding. In practice, however, the making, beaming and threading of a warp is quite straightforward and logical, and should not take more than two or three hours.

Quick Reference Guide for Dressing the Loom

1. Calculate the warp length and the number of ends required.
2. Wind the warp on the board, making a cross at both ends.
3. Tie the crosses, tie the end loops, and make choke-ties.
4. Insert the cross-sticks into the cross at X-Y.
5. Raddle the warp and wind it on to the warp roller.
6. Thread the heddles and reed (or heddle-reed).
7. Tie the warp to the cloth stick and check tension.
8. Weave a heading and check for errors.

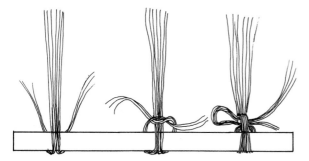

Fig 101. Tying groups of warp ends to the front apron stick

13 Learning to Use a Loom

PUSH THE CROSS-STICKS toward the back of the loom as far as they will go. (Once you are satisfied there are no threading errors you may take them out altogether with advantage, as table looms are so short from front to back that these sticks can prevent the warp from having enough length in which to make a shed with ease.)

Turn the ratchet on the cloth roller until the warp is at a moderate tension; a slack warp will not give a good shed — the space between the threads through which the shuttle is passed.

Weaving a Heading

The first few rows (picks) of weaving are done with any scraps of thick yarn you have on hand, and are for the purpose of spreading the warp to the correct width and closing up the gaps between warp groups. This heading, which is pulled out of the finished work, is also used for checking for errors in threading and sleying, and for detecting any irregularities in the tension.

Weaving a heading on the rigid-heddle loom

Lift the heddle-reed to the upper notch in the heddle-holder bracket. You will see that the threads in the holes are pulled up, while the threads in the slots remain in the lower position, thus opening a shed through which the shuttle can be passed. Pass the shuttle, wound with a few turns of thick yarn, from right to left through the shed (fig 102). Do not worry if the shed is not very clear yet — it seldom is for the first few picks.

For the second pick, place the heddle-reed in the lowest position in the bracket; this causes the threads in the holes to be carried down to the lowest level while those in the slots slide to the top, thus creating a second shed, the countershed. Pass the shuttle from left to right.

Repeat these two rows once more, then grasp the heddle-reed centrally and press it forward against the four picks of weft. Be careful to hold it parallel to the breast beam.

During the actual weaving the heddle-rèed is used to beat *every* pick, but for this initial heading, using it after every fourth pick helps to close up the gaps between the warp groups faster.

Weaving a heading on the four-shaft loom

Operate the levers (or other devices) attached by cords to the top of shafts one and three. These are

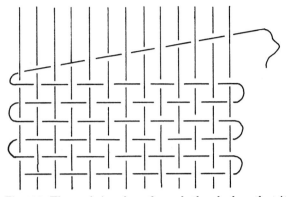

Fig 102. The weft is taken through the shed so that it lies at an angle of about 30°

commonly found on the right-hand top of the castle. The threads in the heddle-eyes on these shafts are raised to the upper position while those on shafts two and four remain stationary, thus creating a shed. Pass a shuttle wound with any thickish yarn through this shed (fig 102), right to left. (It is not always easy to work up a satisfactory rhythm on a table loom; depending on the placement of the levers or lifting devices it may be better to start the shuttle from left to right. Study your loom and try to find a method which allows you to change the shed and beat without putting the shuttle down.)

Lower shafts one and three, lift shafts two and four, and pass the shuttle through this new shed. Repeat these two picks once more.

Grasp the beater centrally with one hand, draw it forward and press it against the four picks of weaving. In the actual weaving the beater is used after *every* pick but using it after only every fourth pick for the heading will close up the gaps more effectively. Eight or twelve picks should be sufficient for a heading.

Placing the weft

The weft should pass through the shed and lie at an angle (fig 102). If the yarn is carried straight through there will not be enough slack in it to allow it to pass comfortably over and under the warp ends, and this will cause the work to 'waist' or become progressively narrower (fig 103).

Checking the tension of the warp

If a group of warp threads has been tied too tightly, the weft in that area will form a hollow; if

133

a group is too loose the weaving will form a hump. Loosen or tighten the groups accordingly, then weave a few more picks. Continue until you are satisfied that the picks of weft lie in a perfect horizontal line, parallel with the breast beam, and the same width as the warp in the reed.

Checking for Errors in Threading and Sleying

Is the weave in a perfect over-and-under sequence? Correcting errors in threading or sleying is tedious, but it must be done or your work will be blemished. Correction may involve partial re-threading or re-sleying, which proves how necessary it is to check carefully at the time.

It is sometimes possible to correct a threading error by tying in a string heddle in the appropriate place, thus avoiding the necessity of re-threading a good deal of the warp. An error in the reed means that the warp ends must be re-sleyed from the place where the mistake was made.

Throwing the Shuttle and Beating

When you are satisfied with the heading, wind a shuttle with the weft yarn chosen for the project, and begin the main weaving.

Pay attention to achieving a balanced weave. With each pick draw the shuttle through the shed until the weft trailing from it touches the outermost warp thread snugly. Do not finger the selvedges in an effort to make them neater. Neat selvedges come with experience and rhythm; fingering them will only delay the time when they come naturally, and will make the weaving process slow.

The sequence for weaving on a table loom is as follows:

Draw the beater forward and, while it is still pressed against the last pick, close the shed which has just been used and open the next shed. Push the beater back, pass the shuttle through the shed, beat, open the new shed, and so on. (This sequence is used for fabric weaving — other types of weaving may require a different technique.)

When you have woven from 5 to 8 cm (2 in to 3 in) release the ratchet on the warp roller, wind forward a little more warp, then re-tighten the tension. The weaving itself should take place in the middle third of the distance between the shafts and the breast beam.

Weaving too far before rolling forward can contribute to warp breakages and cause horizontal streaks in the cloth. Adjust the warp to the same tension each time (you'll soon get the feel of this), and use an even, steady beat. When the

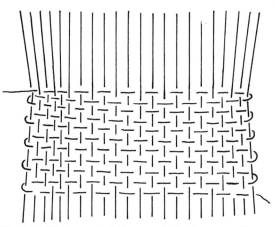

Fig 103. If the weft is taken straight across, the work becomes progressively narrower

woven cloth has sufficient length to begin rolling around the cloth roller, pad the roller with sticks or corrugated card, just as you did on the warp roller, so that knots at the beginning of the warp do not cause bumps in the cloth and consequent tension problems. It is seldom necessary to use any packing after the initial round or two.

Resist the temptation to unroll your work and look at it — it is difficult to re-wind evenly. Keep a record of the distance woven by tying small cardboard price-tags to the selvedge at intervals, each marked with the measurement to that point.

The measurements should be taken either with the warp slack, or with the warp at weaving tension, but be consistent. Do not measure on a slack tension one time and on a tight tension the next. Keep notes concerning the width of stripes or other design features so that you can match the pattern at the other end of the work if desired. Remember to allow about 10 per cent for contraction and shrinkage when calculating the length to be woven.

As a matter of policy, relax the tension on the warp at the end of a work session. It is generally advised that a wool warp should be woven off in a week but, in fact, wool warps which have been on a loom for months have survived without any detectable damage. If a warp is beamed at a very tight tension damage could perhaps occur, but an even tension, not a very tight one, seems to suit wool best.

Keep a notebook listing everything you weave, with samples of the yarn, details of sett, draft, length, width, amount of contraction and shrinkage, and any other relevant details. Include comments on the work, what you liked about it, what you did not like, what you would do differently another time, and any ideas for further projects which may have occurred to you during the weaving. These notes are invaluable and will teach you more than half a dozen textbooks.

Work in Progress

Beginning the weft
Leave a tail of yarn about 5 cm (2in) long hanging from the selvedge of the first pick, then catch it around the outer warp thread and carry it back into the shed as shown at A in fig 104.

Ending the weft
At the end of the work tuck the weft around the selvedge thread and back into the last shed as shown at C in fig 104.

Joining in new weft
When the first shuttle runs out, overlap yarn from the new shuttle for about 2 cm (¾ in) in the same shed, as shown at B in fig 104. Joins are best made near the selvedge rather than in the centre of the work. Ends which have been broken make a less conspicuous join than ends which have been cut, and very thick yarn should be tapered before making such a join.

To change to yarn of a different colour
Finish off the old colour by tucking the end back into the same shed, as at C in fig 104. Begin the new colour in the next shed, leaving a small tail of weft hanging from the selvedge. Tuck this end back into the work in the following pick. Very narrow weft stripes do not need to be cut and joined each time: simply leave each shuttle lying on the work until needed again. Broader stripes are cut and joined if the selvedge is to show in the finished work, otherwise they are treated in the same way as narrow stripes.

Broken warp threads
Withdraw the broken thread from its place in heddle and reed. Take a piece of matching yarn at least 1 metre (1 yd) long and thread it through the empty dent and heddle. Place a pin in the work at the place where the warp thread was last woven in, and wrap the end of the new thread around it, figure of eight fashion (fig 105).

At the back of the loom tie the other end of the replacement piece to the broken end with a bow knot. Match the tension of the rest of the warp when tying the bow, and keep the bow as far away from the heddles as possible. Weave about 10 picks.

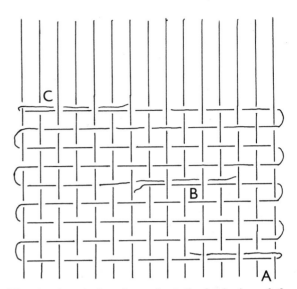

Fig 104. A, starting the weft at the beginning of the work. B, joining in new weft when the first shuttle runs out. C, ending the weft on completion of work

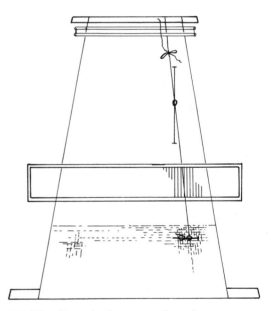

Fig 105. Mending a broken warp thread

Remove the pin from the work and darn in the new end beside the old one, matching the weave, for about 2.5 cm (1 in). Trim the ends closely.

Continue to weave, untying the bow and moving it toward the back of the loom at intervals until the original thread coming from the warp roller is long enough to reach the fell of the cloth. Pass this thread through the heddle and reed, darn it in as before, and discard the remainder of the replacement thread.

Knots in the warp should be cut out and treated as a broken thread.

Cutting off

If you plan to weave several articles on one long warp, and to cut each off as finished, allow at least 15 cm (6 in) extra length for each cutting and tying. Cut in front of the reed after slackening the tension on the warp so that the cut ends do not jump back through the reed and heddles.

Hemstitching or overcasting

This is easiest done while the work is still under tension on the loom. A knotted fringe is done after the work is taken off the loom — allow at least 10 cm (4 in) extra length for this. Be sure to push the overhand knots right up to the fell of the weaving — nothing looks worse than a higgeldy-piggeldy row of knots.

Some Problems

Poor shed

Are you working too close to the reed? Are the cross-sticks too close behind the shafts? Do you need more tension on the warp? Do the cords from shafts to levers need tightening? Is the yarn sticking in the reed because it is too thick or too fuzzy for the reed chosen?

Mistake in the weave

Is a thread in the wrong heddle? Or not in a heddle at all? (This kind of error can be corrected by tying a string heddle at the correct place.) Is a knot in the yarn sticking in the heddles or reed? Has a thread broken? Is a thread crossed around its neighbour between heddles and reed? (Look through the open shed from the side of the loom to detect this kind of error.) Have you missed a dent, or entered two threads in a dent where there should be only one? Is any thread much tighter or looser than its neighbours?

If a mistake is made in the weaving it is best to cut the weft in several places and draw the pieces out gently. It is possible to unweave the work but this is tedious, and involves moving the beater back and forth to clear the shed. The extra friction causes fluffing of the warp, and this may show in the finished piece.

Warp threads breaking

Fragile yarn will break if the warp is not wound forward frequently because the movement of the reed is damaging to the yarn. This is especially true of wool yarn single-sleyed in a fine reed in-stead of double-sleyed in a coarse one. Selvedge threads break if the work is allowed to waist; observe the action of the reed, and notice that each time it is drawn forward the outer threads are stretched and damaged.

Careless use of a stick shuttle can also be responsible for broken threads; and, of course, weak places in the yarn are very likely to break.

Tight or slack selvedge threads

More often than not troublesome selvedges are the result of poor beaming, and the only real solution is to re-wind, and to take more care next time.

If the outer threads of a warp were permitted to spread out on the roller beyond the planned width of the warp, or if the warp sticks were not really long enough to support the warp effectively, the selvedge threads will be tighter than the main body of the warp. The warp roll should always be as neat, tidy and as near perfect as you can make it.

Small humps just at the selvedges in the woven cloth, spoiling the perfect horizontal line of the weft, may mean that the selvedge groups need to be tied a little tighter. These humps also occur if the selvedge is sleyed a little too closely — the closeness of the threads prevents the weft from bedding in quite as well as it does in the rest of the cloth.

Selvedges

Selvedges seem to cause more discussion among new weavers than any other subject. If the selvedge is not visible in the finished article, its neatness or otherwise is not very important, yet most of us feel dissatisfied with poor selvedges, and if the untidiness is the result of poor technique we are right to be concerned.

A selvedge is generally thought to be for the purpose of making a strong edge where the cloth is most likely to get hard wear, but from the weaver's point of view it also provides a firm edge for easier weaving.

In most cases the selvedge is threaded 1, 2, 3, 4 (read from right to left) even if the body of the work is threaded to a pattern draft. (There are exceptions to this rule of course.) A selvedge allowance of four threads per side is usually sufficient, sleyed one and a half times or twice as close as the rest of the warp. If a selvedge of eight is used it may be threaded 11, 22, 33, 44, using a total of eight heddles.

Single threads sleyed closely in the reed give a neat flat selvedge, whereas double threads are inclined to give a coarse selvedge. However, some weavers use one doubled thread per side, because they feel it gives an especially firm edge which enables them to weave faster. Some use one end of a fine sewing thread at the extreme edge each side, and pull this out of the finished work if it is obtrusive.

There is no need to make the selvedge of cotton twine, as is so often suggested. Wool selvedges are not difficult provided a weaving technique suited to wool is used. If a singles wool warp is used, the selvedge may be made of a matching 2-ply wool, but this is not really necessary.

Good selvedges come with experience in operating the loom and using the shuttle. Beating while the weft is still under tension can spoil the selvedges — allow the hand holding the shuttle to move back toward the work, thus relaxing tension, before beating. Failure to unwind enough weft from a stick shuttle for the next pick causes pull-marks in the selvedge.

Tiny loops at the edge of the work are a good fault at first — they show that you are not pulling the weft too hard. These loops also occur if the bobbin of a boat shuttle unwinds too fast. Try putting some crumpled tissue paper under the bobbin to increase friction. A bobbin which unwinds too slowly, or jerkily, can be the cause of small pull-marks and streaks in the work. Once the weaver has become accustomed to the shuttle, and to the width of the particular warp, the weft should automatically touch the selvedge thread snugly and require no particular attention.

Experienced weavers notice that while both selvedges are good, one is just a fraction better than the other. If the poorer selvedge is always on the same side of the cloth, the probable cause is that the weaver is better at handling the shuttle with one hand than with the other; but, if the poor selvedge is sometimes on the right and sometimes on the left, the twist of the yarn (whether $\overleftarrow{s}$ or $\overrightarrow{z}$) may be a contributing factor.

Specialised forms of weaving, such as rug-weaving, require specialised techniques in selvedge management.

The general instructions given so far are for table looms, but there is no reason why your first weaving cannot be done on a treadle loom. Begin with two treadles only at first, one tied to lamms numbers one and three, and the other to two and four.

Open the first shed, pass the shuttle, beat, open the next shed while the beater is still at the fell of the work, push the beater back, pass the shuttle,

and so on. (More details of weaving with a treadle loom are given in Chapter 15.)

Shuttles

As the shuttle itself is not always blameless in the production of poor selvedges perhaps this is the best place for a brief discussion of shuttles (fig 89).

The shuttle most often used with the rigid-heddle and table loom is the stick shuttle. It is poked through the open shed, sufficient weft having been first unwound from it. The notches at each end are inclined to snag the warp (and any unwary passer-by) unless it is used with care. Although it is useful with the small shed of table looms it should be discarded in favour of some other type if possible, and should seldom, if ever, be used with treadle looms.

A small rug shuttle can be slid through the shed on table looms. Larger rug shuttles can be thrown or skidded through the shed on treadle looms. Although the yarn must still be unwound for the next pick, the rug shuttle is an improvement on the stick shuttle and is very useful for bulky weft.

Boat shuttles and throw shuttles are fitted with a central wire spindle on which a small bobbin is placed. The bobbin unwinds as the shuttle runs rapidly through the shed, so no time is wasted unwinding weft. The weaving process becomes more rhythmical, and after the initial learning period the selvedges improve.

Throw shuttles made to take very large bobbins should be avoided: what you save in time spent changing bobbins should be weighed against the probable effect on your weaving. The longest satisfactory length of bobbin is 10 cm (4 in). Longer bobbins in handthrown shuttles (of the type normally used in handweaving) do not unroll evenly because of the length of each traverse, and this gives rise to a tugging sensation in the weft. Bobbins must be a loose fit on the spindle, and there should be about 2 cm (¾ in) space at each end of the bobbin to allow the end-play needed for smooth unwinding.

If the bobbin (whether wood, plastic, or paper) jams at the end of the aperture provided for it, place a wooden bead on each end of the spindle. The yarn pays off best if it is led from underneath the bobbin and then out through the slot in the side of the shuttle.

Individual weavers have their own preferences concerning the size and weight of boat shuttles, but 33 to 38 cm (13 to 15 in) in length, and 170 to 225 g (6 to 8 oz) in weight seem to be generally favoured. The wider the cloth to be woven, the heavier the shuttle used. Whatever its size, be sure that the shuttle is comfortable in the hand and very smoothly finished. There are some dreadful shuttles on the market, so clumsy and rough that they are virtually unusable.

At least a dozen bobbins will be needed, and some means of winding them. Winders, both hand operated and electric, are made for the purpose, or you may be able to fabricate one from some workshop or household article. Some spinning wheels can be converted to wind bobbins by substituting a fixed tapering spindle for the bobbin and flyer unit, or by fitting a tapered spindle in the orifice.

Plastic and wooden bobbins are convenient, and the flanges at each end allow slightly more yarn to be wound on each bobbin than on the paper type. The paper type are quieter in use.

To make a paper quill to be used as a bobbin, cut an oval of strong brown paper about 8 x 10 cm (3 x 4 in) and wind it tightly around the winder spindle, beginning with the narrow side of the oval. Secure the final round with sticky tape. Trim the ends of the quill with scissors if necessary. Each quill may be used many times.

The bobbin, of whatever type, is pushed on to the spindle of the winder until it is a firm fit, and two or three turns of yarn are wound around by hand so that the yarn grips.

The traditional method of winding bobbins is to build up a small hump at each end and then to fill in the centre by guiding the yarn back and forth. The yarn is tensioned firmly with the fingers of the left hand while the right hand turns the winder (fig 106). There are sound reasons for making these humps, but nevertheless many workers with handspun wool have not found the method entirely satisfactory. They prefer to dispense with the humps and to wind the bobbin from end to end, making sure that each layer is slightly shorter than the last. The result resembles a cigar-like tapered oval.

Bobbins should not be made so large that they touch the sides or the bottom of the bobbin aperture. If you use paper quills, take care to keep the yarn well away from the ends of the quill, otherwise it is inclined to slide off and tangle around the spindle.

The boat shuttle is placed on the palm of the hand and supported with the fingers (especially the forefinger and thumb), near the end of the open shed. A flick of the wrist propels it through the shed. It slides along the shuttle race and is kept on an even course partly by the race, and

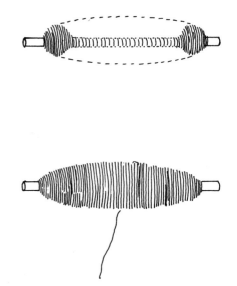

Fig 106. A paper quill wound in the traditional way, showing (*upper*) beginning the bobbin by building up humps, (*lower*) the finished bobbin

partly by the support given by the lower layer of warp threads. It is caught with the other hand, and a thumb or finger is placed on the bobbin to stop it unwinding further. The hand holding the shuttle is simultaneously moved back toward the selvedge, thus relaxing tension on the weft, and the pick is beaten.

Rhythm is more important than speed, and shuttling too fast can cause the work to waist, especially if the sett of the warp is not quite close enough. This causes the weaver to resort to using a stretcher to hold the work out to the proper width, and time is lost in moving the stretcher every few minutes. Don't be discouraged if the first metre (yard) or two woven with a boat shuttle displays very untidy selvedges: a little practice soon overcomes this problem.

Some yarns, such as mohair, are too fuzzy to run off a bobbin well. For these use a rug shuttle or a small ski shuttle. They are much slower to use but slide through the shed easily provided they are not overfilled.

Although a small throw shuttle can be used with some table looms there is usually insufficient shed for a true throwing action — it is more a matter of pushing, or sliding.

The Weaver and The Loom
Weaving should be a pleasure, but it certainly won't be if the weaver feels at odds with the loom.

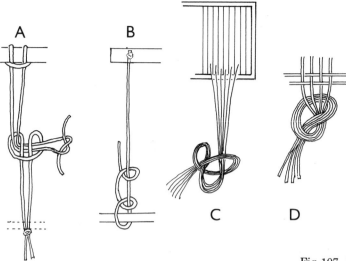

The essence of pleasurable weaving is a relaxed, easy style, and an understanding of how the loom works, so that it will do the bidding of the weaver.

All too often a loom described as 'cranky' has nothing the matter with it. The weaver has simply not taken the trouble to understand it, and this lack of understanding no doubt accounts for the number of looms to be found, covered in dust, in barns, basements, and spare rooms.

The first step in loom management is to learn the names of the principal parts of a loom. It is surprising how many weavers cannot describe their loom when asking for advice about it, cannot remember whether it has a rising or a sinking action, and cannot distinguish between lamms and treadles.

The next step is to realise that because the moving parts of a loom are actually performing a task, those parts need maintenance. Cords may stretch or wear out, pulleys and axles may become stiff from lack of lubrication, split-pins may fall out, and bolts and wedges may work loose. The timber of the loom itself needs to be protected from the warping and cracking which can be the result of general neglect or excessive sun.

The third step is to observe the loom in use and understand how and why it works, so that if something does go wrong you are better able to identify the cause of the trouble.

Rigid-heddle and table looms give very little trouble provided they were well designed in the first place. The lifting cords may need adjusting to obtain a clean shed, and springs may need replacing from time to time.

A treadle loom normally arrives unassembled, with a leaflet of instructions (sometimes very skimpy) for putting it together. If it is a loom with cords, chains, or wires prepared to the correct length by the maker, the chances are that it will be in working order as soon as it is assembled and will need no further adjustment.

The success of fixed-length ties depends a good deal on the design of the loom, those with front-hung treadles probably giving the best results. Even so, the weaver needs to know how and when to make adjustments. Unusual tie-ups may disturb a fixed-length system which was perfectly satisfactory for standard tie-ups. Similarly a loom made for a dry climate or a centrally-heated house may need adjustment when transferred to a damp humid situation. The handweaver's loom is not a precision machine: it is a folk tool, and it needs the human touch.

To prepare a treadle loom for use (and it is not the maker's job to teach the purchaser how to use the loom) it must be set up so that all the shafts hang level, with the heddle-eyes at the correct height in relation to the reed. Tie a strong cord to the breast beam, pass it through the reed and heddle-eye, and then tie it to the back beam. Check the warp-line for the type of loom by referring to figs 84 and 87. Raise or lower the heddle shafts, or alter the height of the beater, until the warp-line is correct.

All the cords used for tying the shafts, lamms and treadles must be readily adjustable for height and length. The most popular knots for the purpose are the snitch knot, used with double cords, and the two half-hitches, useful with single cords (fig 107).

Peg the jacks of the *countermarch* loom with the locking pins provided, so that the jacks cannot move while the shafts are levelled. Use the carpenter's level to check that each shaft hangs perfectly level — adjust the cords from the outer tips of the jacks to the shafts if necessary. All the shafts should hang at the same height. Tie the Y-shaped bridle cords from the inner ends of the jacks to the rising lamms. (The rising lamms are the lower set, or the longer set if both sets are on the same axle.) Tie the cords from the centre of the lower rail of each shaft to the sinking lamms — all the lamms should be horizontal.

For the *counterbalanced* loom, use the carpenter's level to check the upper roller, and then the secondary rollers. Pulleys, if used, must be checked by measurement.

When the rollers are level, fix them in some way so that they cannot move while the shafts are being levelled: it is impossible to adjust the shafts properly unless the rollers on which they are suspended are immobilised. Adjust the length of the cords carrying each pair of shafts over the secondary rollers, and hang all shafts at the same height. Tie the shafts to the lamms. The lamms should be horizontal, or tilted slightly upward.

For the *jack* loom, ensure that the shafts are level — adjust the cords from the outer tip of the jacks to the shafts if necessary. Hang each shaft slightly lower than the previous one so that there is a slope of perhaps 2 cm (¾ in) from front to back. (On some of the more sophisticated looms the shafts run in guides, and the whole centre castle is tilted slightly back from the vertical to achieve the same effect.) As with other looms, the lamms are horizontal, or nearly so. The bridle cords from the inner tips of the jacks are connected to the lamms.

This preliminary levelling of shafts, rollers and lamms is essential but, apart from routine checking from time to time, it is done only the first time the loom is set up.

The major adjustments on a treadle loom take place between the treadles and lamms. Both treadles and lamms are levers, and because the efficiency of a lever alters according to the distance from the pivot point (axle), the tying-up is not quite as straightforward as one might wish.

The treadles must usually be tied progressively higher the further they are away from the pivot point of the lamms. If the lamms are pivoted on the left side of the loom, the treadles should rise towards the right side of the loom; a total of 8 cm (3 in) is the usual difference in height.

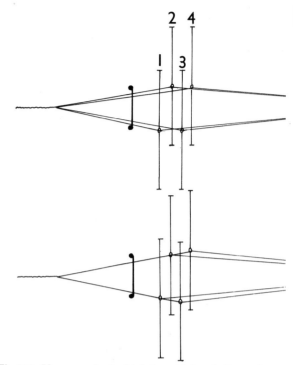

Fig 108. *Upper*, a shed which is not 'clean': the ends on shaft 3 are above the level of those on shaft 1, and the ends on shaft 4 are hanging below the level of those on shaft 2 in the upper layer of the warp. *Lower*, a clean shed. Note the differential height of the heddle-eyes needed to achieve it

Rear-hung treadles, viewed from the side of the loom, should hang more-or-less horizontal; but short treadles, such as those found on looms which are rather short from front to back, may need to rise towards the front of the loom to obtain sufficient leverage. Furthermore, to obtain a good clean shed the shafts nearer the back of the loom must rise or fall more than those nearer the reed; therefore the cords between treadles and lamms must be progressively shortened from shaft one to shaft four, with number four the shortest.

Front-hung treadles are simpler when it comes to this last adjustment; they usually slope uphill, and this slope has the effect of cancelling out the leverage problem found with rear-hung treadles. The cords need little, if any, differential tightness.

The final adjustments to the loom are made after a warp is on it. Weave a heading to steady the warp, then examine the shed, using each treadle in turn. If the shed is not as clean as it should be, press each shaft in turn with the fingers to find out which shaft carries the warp ends spoiling the shed (fig 108). Tighten or loosen the cords to the treadles accordingly.

If the preliminary levelling of the whole loom has been well done, the treadle-to-lamm tie is the only one which needs altering, so don't complicate the issue by fiddling with every cord in sight.

Note. Countermarch looms need enough weight suspended on the rising action to balance the weight on the sinking action; a minimum of four treadles should therefore be tied up, even if they are not all wanted for the particular weave. If the whole warp sinks in the reed when the locking-pins are taken out, more weight is needed on the rising lamms; if the warp rises, more weight is needed on the sinking lamms.

The first time these treadle-to-lamm adjustments are made, the weaver spends a good deal of time under the loom, every muscle protesting. But take heart: experience is a great teacher and the next tie-up takes only a few minutes. (The tie-up varies according to the pattern to be woven.)

Minor troubles with the shed often seem to disappear as soon as enough work has been done to permit the cloth to pass over the breast beam, so don't be too pernickety at first.

If, during the weaving, a hitherto acceptable shed suddenly becomes poor, it is almost certain that a knot has come undone, that a quick-release hook has fouled around some part of the loom or that a lamm has worked its way off its axle.

Occasionally a beginner complains that the loom has been set up as directed but that when a treadle is depressed nothing happens — the loom feels locked up. If this happens make sure you have removed the locking pins from the jacks, and that there is nothing preventing movement in rollers, pulleys or lamms. Another fruitful line of investigation is to follow the path of each cord to see if it is twisted around another one, or tangled around a lamm, or tied to two shafts by mistake. One weaver found an unusual cause of the trouble — she had threaded all the warp ends through heddle-eyes on all four shafts!

Reeds and spare steel heddles rust easily; store any not in use by wrapping them up in plenty of brown paper to keep out the air.

If the loom shows a tendency to move across the floor, anchor it by placing a pad of foam rubber or foam plastic (3 cm or 1¼ in thick) under each leg: this is astonishingly effective.

14 Finishing the Cloth

WITH THE EXCEPTION of floor rugs, tapestries and wall hangings, almost anything you weave must be washed before it is ready for use. This has very little to do with cleanliness: the washing is for the purpose of closing up the rather open texture of the cloth (fulling), for eliminating any marks caused by the reed, and for improving the 'hand' (feel) of the cloth.

The difference made by washing is quite remarkable. Fabrics for clothing will, of course, need to be washed so that they do not shrink after making up.

Wool has the ability to puff up and expand during wet finishing, thus filling in minute gaps in the weave. The scales of the wool fibre also mesh together in the process, and the cloth is less likely to fray when cut and sewn, and more likely to retain its shape. This ability to 'full' is one of the factors that makes wool the ideal fibre for clothing fabrics. Wet-finishing causes the cloth to lose about 10 per cent in length and width, and this loss must be allowed for in the initial calculations.

The cloth appears shoddy and disappointing when first cut from the loom and released from tension. The washing method transforms it from a mere interlacement of yarns to an integrated textile. The difference between fulled and unfulled cloth is shown in fig 109.

How much fulling? The answer to this question depends in part on the type of article intended: a fine stole does not require the same treatment as a wool skirtlength. The weaver must decide what is needed and then try to achieve that effect. Some fleeces and yarns full much more readily than others; woollen-spun yarn fulls better than the worsted type. A cloth that is to be brushed needs thorough fulling if it is to withstand the action of the machine.

It is good policy to weave a little extra to use as samples for fulling purposes. Experiment until the most satisfactory treatment has been found.

The ends of the piece to be fulled may be machine stitched to prevent fraying, although this should not be necessary with well woven cloth. Remedy any imperfections in the weaving with a darning needle and matching yarn, copying the weave exactly. If there are any knots, untie them and darn in the ends.

Soft water is essential for fulling, so if you live in a hard-water area use a water softener. Dissolve

Fig 109a. Cloth after being cut from the loom; note the reed marks

Fig 109b. The same cloth after wet finishing; note that the reed marks have disappeared and that the cloth is better integrated

142

plenty of pure soapflakes in a quantity of hot water (52°C, 125°F). Immerse the cloth and leave it to soak for twenty minutes to loosen residual dirt and dressing in the yarn. At the end of this time the suds will be flat and lifeless and a fresh lot must be made. Lift the cloth out of the tub or bath while doing this as the pounding effect of running water can cause an unpleasant fuzziness on the surface.

For the second wash use barely enough suds to cover. Press the cloth up and down with the hands, or tramp it with bare feet, so that the suds are forced through the weave. Do not twist, and do not rub the cloth against itself. Rearrange its position in the tub from time to time so that all parts are equally treated.

This process will take anything from a few minutes to an hour or more, depending on the size of the piece, the nature of the yarns, and the intended end-use. It is impossible to give specific instructions — examine the cloth frequently by holding it up to the light to see if the yarns have meshed together. Scratch it with the thumbnail; if the threads still move past each other readily, continue the fulling. Some weavers detect a change in the character of the fabric, which they describe as slippery, almost slimy.

If you are in doubt about the extent of fulling, stop. The process is irreversible and too much fulling felts the cloth. You can always wash it again another day if you are not satisfied with the first treatment.

An automatic washing machine may be used — provided you try a sample first, and provided you have the courage to put the whole length in! Be particularly careful if any handspun wool has been used. Run the machine for only a minute at a time, and rearrange the position of the cloth in the machine after each minute of washing.

Rinse several times in warm water, spin for a minute or two in the machine to remove excess water, or roll briefly in towels or blankets. Do not wring or twist the cloth and do not leave it lying about wet.

It should now be carefully rolled, without creases or distortion, keeping warp and weft straight, on a large slatted wooden roller. (If you have any doubts about the cleanliness of the roller, cover it with cotton cloth before use. New timber often exudes sap or resin and these can cause staining.) A strong cardboard tube can be used but is not so efficient.

Any wrinkles or distortion rolled in at this stage are permanent. Smooth the cloth both forward and sideways with the hands to make a firm neat roll, but don't overdo the sideways movement as this seems to cause a frilly edge. Foam plastic attached to the top and edge of the table used for the rolling process gives a drag to the cloth which is helpful in achieving a firm result.

Leave the roll in a shady place to dry, rewinding from the other end each day if it is a long length. If you think it needs to be pressed, do so before the cloth is quite dry and use plenty of steam. Commercial steaming is worth trying, as texture can all too easily be spoilt by a heavy hand with an iron.

Linen and cotton pieces should be soaked overnight in cold water, then washed vigorously in hot soapy water. Grasp the fabric in both hands and pull it back and forth on the bias as if straightening a sheet from the clothesline. Work over the whole piece in this way, and pummel it up and down in the tub. This treatment improves the hand of the fabric and eliminates any reed-marks resulting from the grouping of threads in the dents.

Rinse well, drip for a few minutes, then wind it on to a roller for an hour or two. While the cloth is still quite wet commence ironing with a hot iron and continue until it is bone dry. This initial setting and polishing with a hot iron gives linen its typical crisp hand.

Other fibres, or mixtures of fibres, may need variations in the washing process. Rugs, wallhangings and tapestries may need pressing or steaming.

15 Projects For New Weavers

The following twenty projects have been designed for new weavers, and the first ten may be woven on small table looms. They cover the basic weave structures which form the foundation of weaving: plain weave and the standard twills.*

A working knowledge of these weaves is as essential for the weaver as knit and purl are for the knitter. Twill, curiously enough, is often avoided by beginners, but as the majority of pattern weaves, so tempting to new weavers, are derived from twill it is essential to be familiar with this weave before attempting patterns.

Without this understanding of basic structure the weaver is forced to rely entirely on printed directions, cannot develop or vary the pattern and certainly will not be able to do any original designing.

READING THE DRAFTS

As explained in Chapter 12 the threading draft takes the form of a diagram on squared paper. The sequence given is repeated for the whole width of the warp, including the selvedges, unless a separate draft is shown for these.

A simple draft is given in fig 110. At A is the threading draft, already explained. At B is the tie-up draft (the reason for this term will become clear when you use a treadle loom). This part of the draft contains crosses or circles written between the same pair of lines as one or other of the shafts. Crosses indicate that the particular instructions were written for a sinking shed, and circles indicate that they were written for a rising shed.

At C is a set of vertical columns showing the order in which the shafts are to be used. Look at the first mark in these columns. Run your eye upward to the marks in the tie-up draft directly above. If the tie-up draft shows marks against shafts 1 and 3, then you should use shafts 1 and 3 for that pick.

The marks in the treadling draft may vary in style to indicate the type of yarn to be used for that pick. For instance, a thick yarn may be indicated by a heavy dot, and a fine yarn by a light dot. Various symbols may also be used in the threading draft to show various textures or colours of yarn in the warp.

There are fourteen combinations in which the four shafts can be used in weaving.

* Satin is also one of the basic structures but it cannot be woven on a loom with only four shafts.

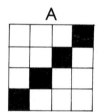

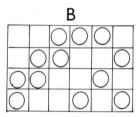

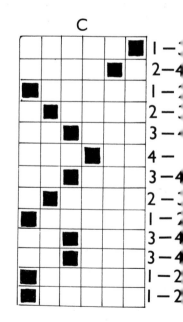

Fig 110.

(Mathematically there are sixteen, but because no shed is produced when all four shafts are raised or all four lowered, these are of no use to the weaver.) The fourteen combinations are:

1 and 3 together
2 and 4 together
1 alone
2 alone
3 alone
4 alone
1 and 2 together
2 and 3 together
3 and 4 together
4 and 1 together
1 and 2 and 3 together
2 and 3 and 4 together
3 and 4 and 1 together
4 and 1 and 2 together

Very few pieces of weaving use more than six of these combinations. Four-shaft looms are usually provided with six treadles, and each treadle can be tied to one, two or three shafts as required for the particular weave. If the loom has only four treadles, each will be tied to a single shaft and the weaver will have to depress one, two or three treadles at a time. (This is called a direct tie.) In the same way, the user of a table loom must lift one, two or three of the levers at a time.

Learn to read drafts at a glance as soon as possible, otherwise weaving instructions will remain something of a mystery. (They are not nearly so difficult as knitting directions.) In fig 110 the numbers of the shafts to be used have been written alongside the treadling draft to assist you in the learning process; this is not done in normal drafts.

If a rising-shed loom is used to weave a pattern written for a sinking shed, the pattern (unless completely reversible) will weave face-down. If you prefer to have the right side of the work face-up, the conversion is quite simple: simply fill in the blank spaces in the tie-up draft with circles, and read the circles instead of the crosses.

Several slightly different methods of annotation are used for weaving drafts, but once the general principle is understood you should have no difficulty in following any of them. The method given in this book is the one most often used by handweavers.

The order in which the treadles are tied is largely a matter of convenience. There are several standard ties, but feel free to alter the tie to suit particular circumstances. If you prefer the plain weave treadles in the centre, by all means put them there.

It is usually recommended that the feet be used alternately, but if it suits you to do otherwise, or to use only one foot, do not fear that you have broken the rules. Do what you find most comfortable.

Note. Where a warp length is suggested in the following table loom projects it *includes* the appropriate loom allowance — 20 cm (18 in) plus contraction allowance. Double this allowance if a treadle loom is used.

Fig 111. Two cushions woven with natural black, white and grey wool ★

TEN PROJECTS FOR THE TABLE LOOM

1. *Two Cushion Covers (plain weave, fig 111)*

Size: 42 x 42 cm (16½ x 16½ in) finished.

Warp yarn: 125 g (4 oz) of black 2-ply wool, or 180 g (6½ oz) of 3-ply. The 2-ply measures approximately 3840 m per 0.5 kg (3840 yds per lb); the 3-ply measures approximately 2400 m per 0.5 kg (2400 yds per lb).

Warp length: 3 m (3 yds).

Sett: 10 or 12.

Width in reed: 45 cm (18 in).

Weft: 175 g (6 oz) altogether of natural black, grey and white handspun singles wool, approximately 1200 m per 0.5 kg (1200 yds per lb). Very small quantities of dyed orange fleece, and black grey and white fleece, unspun, are also required.

Threading and weaving details are given in fig 112.

Weave a 2 cm (¾ in) heading in black, then weave:

16 picks black
6 picks grey
2 picks white
4 picks black
1 pick grey ⎱
1 pick white ⎰ x 4 times
10 picks grey
2 picks black
1 pick white
2 picks black
1 pick white

Repeat this sequence until the work measures 40 cm (19 in) from the beginning, then weave a further 40 cm (19 in) in plain black for the back of the cushion. Finish with 2 cm (¾ in) in black.

Note. Start all the shuttles from the right-hand side of the loom. In this way all the colour changes occur at the right-hand selvedge leaving the left selvedge tidy for inserting the filling and sewing up. It will be noticed that in the sequence '1 grey, 1 white x 4 times' the selvedge thread is not always caught in by the weft.

As the cushion is to be seamed up this is not of great importance, but it can be overcome by correct placement of the shuttles. When the shuttles come from the left side of the loom, place the one first used near the breast beam, and the second near the fell. When the shuttles come from the right of the loom place the first near the fell and the second near the breast beam. This has the effect of twisting the two weft yarns around each

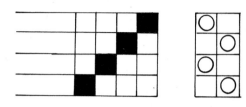

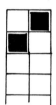

Fig 112. Draft for plainweave. This draft is also used for projects 2, 3, 4, 9, 10, 11, 12, 13, 14 and 15

other and the selvedge is neater.

Before commencing the second cushion, weave 2.5 cm (1 in) with any scrap yarn to separate the first cushion from the second.

Begin with 2.5 cm (1 in) in black, then weave 5 picks in grey. With the shed for the fifth pick still open, take a small rolag of black fleece, draw it out until it is almost long enough to span the width of the warp, and twist it lightly. Lay this soft fleece alongside the last grey pick, beat, and change the shed.

Follow with 5 picks of grey, lay in a piece of grey fleece; 5 picks grey, lay in white fleece; 5 picks grey, lay in dyed orange fleece. Continue with:

5 picks grey
4 picks black
1 pick white
4 picks black

Repeat the entire sequence until the work measures 40 cm (19 in), then weave 40 cm (19 in) in grey. Finish with 2.5 cm (1 in) in black.

After washing and pressing, seam up the covers (by hand or machine) using the initial and final headings as the seam allowance. Seam up the right-hand selvedge, but leave the left open. Make a calico liner a little bigger all around than the cushion and fill it with dacron stuffing. Insert the liner, turn in the open side of the cover and slip-stitch by hand.

2. Primitive jacket (plain weave, fig 113)

Selvedges were not important for the cushion covers, but for this jacket they should be tidy because it will be stitched up with the selvedges edge to edge and in full view.

Size: to fit 85-95 cm bust (34-38 in). The length from the shoulder is 72 cm (27 in) plus fringe.

Warp: 200 g (7 oz) of dark green 4-ply wool and a little light green. The yarn is 1600 m per 0.5 kg (1600 yds per lb).

Warp length: 4.75 m (5¼ yds).

Sett: 12 (10 may be used on the rigid-heddle loom).

Width in reed: 30 cm (12 in).

Weft: approximately 200 g (7 oz) of handspun wool (1100 m per 0.5 kg or 1100 yds per lb). The weft used in the sample was Romney 52's plant-dyed olive green and spring green. The two colours were carded together with a drum carder before spinning.

In making the warp wind the first 6 ends with dark green. Wind the next 10 ends in dark green and light green alternately, either warping with both yarns at once (as in Chapter 16) or cutting and joining the colours at the end of each half portee. Continue making the warp with dark green until 15 ends remain to be warped, then warp 10 in light and dark green alternately, and finish with 5 dark green.

Use the threading and weaving draft given for the cushions (fig 112).

Work in plain weave for 155 cm (60 in) for the left side, and a similar piece for the right side — these pieces will form both front and back. Weave two pieces each 50 cm (20 in) long for the sleeves. The beginning and end of each section should be hemstitched on the loom, leaving approximately 2.5 cm (1 in) unwoven between sections for fringes. Wash and press the work.

To make up the jacket, place the two selvedges which will form the centre back seam on a flat surface and stitch them together by hand, edge to edge, to within 15 cm (6 in) of the shoulder line. Sew the sleeves to the garment with a similar flat seam. Join the under-sleeve seams with backstitch — the fringe may be concealed inside the sleeve or left exposed, as you choose. Slip stitch the side seams, leaving vents 12 cm (5 in) at the hipline.

This type of garment, made from rectangular pieces, does not fit the body in the same way that a shaped garment does, but is very useful as a casual cover-up over sweaters and slacks for either men or women, and folds flat for packing.

Fig 113. Primitive jacket; this can be woven on a simple loom 30cm (12in) wide ★

3. Hudson Bay jacket (plain weave, fig 114)

This jacket is an adaptation of the garment made from a trading-post blanket by Hudson Bay settlers. It can be woven on small looms (50 cm or 20 in wide), including rigid-heddle looms.

All construction lines consist of selvedges sewn together by hand, so there is no problem with neatening the inside. The remaining edges (centre front and sleeve hems) are hemstitched on the loom to form tiny fringes.

The jacket may be made longer, to fit a taller person, by making the warp wider in the loom and allowing extra length in the warping. The part of the warp which is wasted when the width is reduced for weaving the hood can be utilised to weave pockets, or may be used for sewing up and making toggle cords. Study fig 115 for the layout of the pieces which make up the garment.

Fig 114. Hudson Bay jacket, designed to be woven on small looms ★

Hood

Centre back

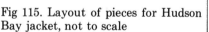

Body

Yoke and Sleeves

Fig 115. Layout of pieces for Hudson Bay jacket, not to scale

Size: to fit 85-95 cm bust (34-38 in). The length from the shoulder to hem is 72 cm (27 in).

Warp: 280 g (10 oz) of machine-knitting 2-ply worsted used double or 4-ply used single. The yarn for the sample was cornflower blue.

Warp length: 3.5 m (4 yds).

Sett: 12.

Width in reed: 50 cm (20 in).

Weft: 225 g (8 oz) of handspun singles wool, approximately 1600 m per 0.5 kg (1600 yds per lb). For the sample a pale grey fleece was dyed tones of green and blue with synthetic dyes; it was carded before spinning.

Use the plain weave draft as given for the previous projects in fig 112.

The beginning and end of each section should be hemstitched on the loom.

Sleeves and yoke (woven as one piece): weave 42 cm (16½ in) — this is the length from the bottom of the sleeve to the beginning of the neck opening. To weave the neck slit, mark the centre thread of the warp and work with two shuttles, one for the left-hand side and one for the right, until the slit is 13 cm (5 in) long.

Continue with the left shuttle as before but weave 4 picks with scrap yarn on the right side to mark the front yoke opening. Hemstitch both sides of this scrap weaving. Resume, using the blue weft on the right side, and weave with two shuttles as before until the neck slit measures a total of 26 cm (10 in). Then, with a single shuttle, weave across the full width of the warp until a further 42 cm (16½ in) has been woven.

For the body of the garment weave 115 cm (46 in), or the bust measurement plus 20 cm (8 in). (Garments without shaping need to be very easy fitting.) After finishing the body section weave in a smooth stick the width of the warp and a few picks of scrap weaving to secure it.

Reduce the width of the warp to 38 cm (15 in) by cutting away surplus warp threads — draw the cut ends back through the reed and heddles and let them hang from the cross-sticks. (They may be rethreaded later for pockets if desired.) Weave 58 cm (23 in) for the hood.

To make up: wash and dry the entire length. Separate the sections, and cut between the two rows of hemstitching marking the front yoke opening. Sew one selvedge of the hood to the neck slit, matching the front edges, easing it to fit if necessary. Fold the remaining hood selvedge in half and slipstitch it together for the top. Mark the halfway point of the piece woven for the body and pin it to the centre back yoke. Match the fringed edges to the yoke opening. Sew the body to the yoke with a 1 cm (½ in) seam, using backstitch. A similar seam forms the undersleeve join. Turn up a small hem at the hipline if you wish and fasten the fronts with toggles and cords.

Many variations are possible on this theme. If the sett is closer the jacket can be woven in a twill — this gives a more flexible fabric. A weft stripe woven near the beginning and end of the body piece and on either side of the yoke opening will give a vertical stripe up the centre fronts.

A warp stripe, placed about 2.5 cm (1 in) in from the right selvedge during warp-making will give a horizontal stripe across the yoke and down the sleeves. The stripe on the body section may be used either at hip level or at yoke level, depending on which edge is joined to the yoke. A fully striped warp will give horizontal stripes around the body — not usually considered flattering except for the tall and slender.

4. Place Mats (plain weave, fig 116)

Size: 45 x 30 cm (18 x 12 in).
Warp: Knitting cotton, such as Gem or Aquarius or something of equivalent size (1600 to 2000 m per 0.5 kg; 1600 to 2000 yds per lb). For 8 mats approximately 225 g (8 oz) will be needed in white, and 50 g (2 oz) in ecru.
Warp length: 5 m (5¾ yds) for 8 mats.
Sett: 12 or 14.
Width in reed: 32 cm (13 in).
Weft: 400 g (14 oz) of heavy slub linen in white. This yarn is 750 m per 0.5 kg (750 yds per lb) and under the old count system was known as 2½ lea.

Make the first 10 cm (4 in) of the warp with white cotton, then alternate 2.5 cm (1 in) ecru stripes with similar size white stripes until 3 ecru stripes have been warped. Finish with 10 cm (4 in) in white.
Use the same draft as in fig 112.

Fig 116. Cotton and linen place mat, quick and easy to weave but still retaining an air of traditional formality

Weave 4 cm (1½ in) for the hem of the first mat, and then weave in 2 picks of ordinary string for a hem marker. Weave a further 47 cm (19 in), repeat the 2 string picks, and finish with 4 cm (1½ in) for the other hem. Weave in another marker to separate each mat from the next.

When all 8 mats have been woven, wash and finish the fabric and cut the mats apart. Withdraw the string markers, turn up the hems and hemstitch them in place with a finer crochet cotton. There is a lot of initial shrinkage in these mats but the finished size should be as given above.

5. Mohair and wool stole (hopsack, fig 117)

Draft: Use the draft in fig 118; note the selvedge threading.
Size: 50 x 190 cm (20 x 78 in) plus fringes.
Warp: 125 g (5 oz) 3-ply knitting wool or similar soft yarn.
Warp length: 2.5 m (2¾ yds).
Sett: 12.
Width in reed: 52.5 cm (21 in).
Weft: 225 g (8 oz) of brushed mohair or hand-spun mohair.

Use two shuttles for the weaving, starting both from the same side of the loom, and note that 2 picks are laid in each shed.

After an initial heading with scrap yarn leave 10 cm (4 in) unwoven for the fringe. Overcast or hemstitch this edge when a few picks have been woven. Weave 200 cm (80 in), beating lightly and carefully to balance the weave. Hemstitch or overcast the end, then cut the stole from the loom, leaving 10 cm (4 in) for fringe. To give the fringes

Fig 117. Mohair and wool loosely woven in hopsack weave make a comfortable, airy stole

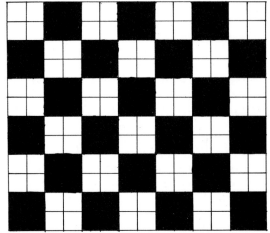

Fig 119a. Weaver's diagram of hopsack, a variation of plain weave

Fig 119b. Hopsack woven with white warp and black weft to show the structure plainly

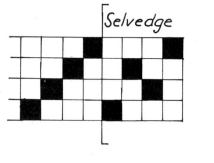

Selvedge

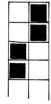

Fig 118.

the same fluffy appearance as the stole, cut 20 cm (8 in) lengths of mohair and hook them into the overcast edges with a crochet hook. Wash the stole gently in warm soapy water.

Hopsack, sometimes called basket weave, is a variation of plain weave. The structure is shown in fig 119.

6. Ruana (2/2 twill, fig 120)

This is an all-purpose cover-up garment, called a poncho in some areas and a ruana in others. It consists of two rectangles seamed together.

In the sample, the centre front and back seams are sewn up, leaving a slit for a head-opening. If the front is left open the right-hand side of the garment can be tossed over the left shoulder, Peruvian fashion.

This garment can be any length from waist to ankle and the warp is planned accordingly. All sorts of oddments of yarn can be used (provided they do not vary too greatly in size) as informal stripes suit this style very well.

Twill was chosen for the weaving as it gives a more softly draping quality than does plain weave. The handspun weft was spun evenly so that there would be no bumps to disturb the diagonal line of the twill.

Size: the sample garment measures 90 cm (36 in) from the shoulder, plus fringes.

Warp: 375 g (13 oz) of Polwarth 2-ply, approximately 1900 m per 0.5 kg (1900 yds per lb). The yarn was dyed shades of yellow, yellow-green and green, using yellow and black synthetic dyes as in Chapter 9. The warp was made up as uneven stripes.

Warp length: 4.5 m (5 yds).

Sett: 14, for a soft twill.

Width in reed: 53 cm (21 in).

Weft: 375 g (13 oz) of handspun Perendale, Cheviot, or similar fleece dyed yellow. The draft for twill is given in fig 121.

Weave in 2/2 twill, taking care to keep the angle of weave at a steady 45° — use a set-square to check the angle until you can work by eye alone. Weave 200 cm (80 in), leave as much as desired for the hem fringes, then weave a further 200 cm (80 in).

After washing and light fulling cut the cloth through the centre fringe area. Stitch the two pieces together with a centre front and back seam, allowing a long slit for the head opening.

Note. The selvedges in twill sometimes give trouble with the outside thread failing to catch in. The solution is quite simple: finish the 4-pick sequence, cut the weft, and start the next sequence with the shuttle coming from the *same* direction as it did for the last pick. Once the correct side to start from has been established, no further cutting and re-starting is needed.

If a selvedge thread subsequently fails to weave in, it means either that a mistake has been made in

Fig 120. The ruana, of South and Central American origin, is an all purpose unisex cover-up. Like the old Highland plaid it can also be used as a blanket at night

★

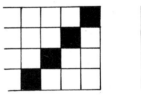

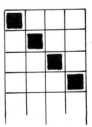

Fig 121. Draft for 2/2 twill, used for projects 6 and 16

Fig 122a. Weaver's diagram of broken twill

Fig 122b. Broken twill woven with white warp and black weft

the treadling or that a new shuttle has been inadvertently started from the wrong side.

With the threading given the twill will slope to the right when treadled 1-2, 2-3, 3-4, 4-1. If treadled in reverse order (4-1, 3-4, 2-3, 1-2) the slope will be to the left. A twill may be reversed at intervals to give a zig-zag effect in the warp direction, but after each reverse it may be necessary to cut and restart the shuttle, as above.

Not all weavers admire the diagonal line of the twill. For those who find it too rigid and uncompromising the broken twill (fig 122) is suggested. The order of treadling is different, thus breaking the line, but the construction has the same virtues as the straight version. Broken twill is also useful when using weft which is too uneven to do justice to the straight twill. The treadling sequence is: 1-2, 2-3, 4-1, 3-4.

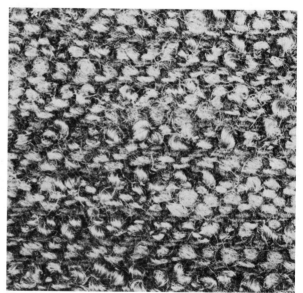

Fig 123. Textured fabric for chair seats ★

7. Chair seat fabric (1/3 twill, fig 123)

In 1/3 twill the weft passes over the three warp ends and under one; on the reverse side the weft passes over one and under three. Most of the weft shows on the surface of the fabric, thereby making the best use of any fancy or handspun yarn. It makes a rather thick fabric in most cases, possibly too thick for clothing.

The sample fabric is intended for upholstering dining chair seats. Make the warp the width to suit your chairs.

The draft for 1/3 twill is shown in fig 124.

Warp: Dark brown singles wool, 2500 m per 0.5 kg
      (2500 yds per lb).
Sett: 18.
Weft: Olive green singles wool, the same size as the
      warp yarn, heavy blue millspun loop wool,
      and an unevenly spun blue-green handspun
      singles about twice as thick as the warp yarn.
The weft is used in the following order:
   2 blue-green
   2 olive
   2 blue loop
   2 olive
   2 blue-green
   2 blue loop
   2 olive

Start all the shuttles from the same side of the
loom. In order to keep the selvedges reasonably
tidy, place each shuttle in order of use on the fell
of the cloth and pick up the next to be used from
nearer the breast beam.
   The structure of 1/3 twill is shown in fig 125.

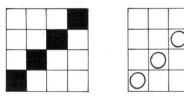

Fig 124.

8. Fabric for casual jacket (plain weave with 1/3 twill, fig 126)

The 1/3 twill makes a rather thick fabric but, if
several picks of plain weave are inserted between
the twill picks, the cloth is lighter. The twill picks
stand out prominently, rather like saddlestitching. To make the most of this effect the yarn used
for the twill picks should be softer and bulkier
than the yarn used for the warp and plain weave.
This is a good way of using oddments of hand-
dyed yarn.
   If the background plain weave is woven as a
balanced cloth there is no reason why the jacket
cannot be cut so that the twill picks form a vertical stripe on the body.

Fig 125a. Weaver's diagram of 1/3 twill. Note that the
weft passes over three warp ends, then under one, in
twill progression, thus showing more weft than warp on
the face. On the reverse side the structure is 3/1 twill;
the warp passes over one and under three, thus showing
more warp than weft

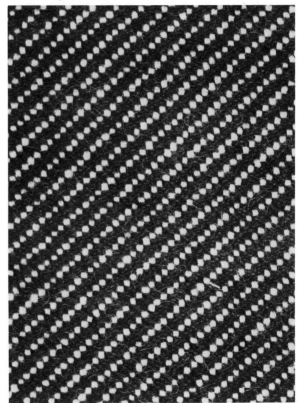

Fig 125b. 1/3 twill woven with white warp and black
weft

Fig 125c. The reverse side (Fig 125b), showing the 3/1 twill formation

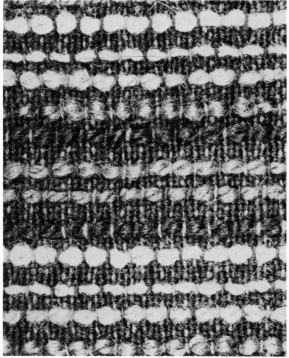

Fig 126. 1/3 twill lifts, in combination with plain weave, have been used to produce a saddle-stitching effect

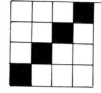

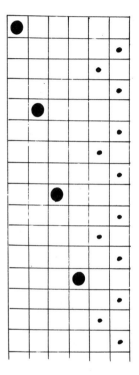

Fig 127.

Handwoven cloth, if well woven and finished, is not difficult or different to sew, but unless you are an experienced dressmaker use a very simple style. Buy or draft the pattern before deciding on the best width to weave.

Follow the draft given in fig 127.

Warp: Singles wool, 2500 m per 0.5 kg (2500 yds per lb).

Sett: 16.

Weft: Plied wool to match the warp in colour and size, and oddments of handspun wool for the twill picks, used in random colour order.

9. Tote bag (weft-faced plain weave, fig 128)

Plain weave is often referred to as 'tabby'. Strictly speaking, plain weave is only tabby when it is a perfectly balanced weave.

This bag is plain weave but it is not tabby because the weft covers the warp entirely. The warp, usually plain white cotton, is spaced far enough apart to make it possible for the weft to be beaten down over it. If the warp is too widely sett the work becomes sleazy and the weft, instead of being quite firmly packed, is inclined to slide up and down the warp.

Weft-faced work can be done on the 10 or 12 dent rigid-heddle looms if the reed is half sett: thread a hole and slot, miss a hole and slot, and so on. It may be necessary to beat the work with a fork instead of the heddle-reed.

Read through the instructions, noting the remarks about selvedges, sleying, laying in the weft, and the technique of beating.

Warp: approximately 50 g (2 oz) of cotton yarn at 1125 m per 0.5 kg (1125 yds per lb) or a finer yarn, such as Donaghy's 16/6s cotton, used double. Household string is often waxed or sized and is not altogether suitable.

Warp length: 1.25 m (1½ yds). This length allows for a little practice at the beginning.

Sett: 5 (use a 10 dent reed).

Width in reed: 30 cm (12 in). Make the warp with an uneven number of ends and allow 10 extra for selvedges.

Weft: 2-ply carpet wool at 800 m per 0.5 kg (800 yds per lb) used double on the shuttle. Approximately 280 g (10 oz) was used for the sample bag.

Threading and sleying: contrary to the usual practice the first and last heddles contain 3 threads and the second-to-last heddle on each side contains 2 threads. The remainder are threaded with a single end only. Use the draft in fig 112.

When sleying, put the triple end in the first dent, the double end in the next, and a single end in the third dent. Then skip a dent, thread the next with a single end, and continue threading alternate dents until the other selvedge is reached. Use a single end, followed by a double and a triple in the last three dents. The selvedges are thus strengthened by being made of thicker threads, closely sleyed.

Take particular care over the initial heading because the tension must be perfect and the work must weave at exactly the same width as it is in the reed. Any waisting will cause endless problems

Fig 128. A sturdy shoulder bag woven of carpet wool in weft-faced plain weave ★

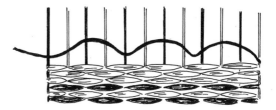

Fig 129. 'Waving' the weft is essential in weft-facing weaving if the weft is to cover the warp satisfactorily

with the tension, and it will not be possible to use the beater effectively. The warp tension must be very tight.

The weft yarn, used double, must be laid in with sufficient slack to allow it to cover the warp. The weft is laid in in the usual way, then formed into undulating waves (fig 129) with the fingers to allow this slack.

Hold the weft at the selvedge (yes!) while making the waves, to ensure a snug fit around the outermost end. When the waves are neatly formed, *change the shed* and beat.

Changing the shed before beating distributes the extra slack evenly across the whole width of the warp and makes it easier to cover the warp yarn. If this technique is not used, small bubbles of weft are inclined to form at the base of the waves. The beater does not need to be used with force; if the warp tension is tight enough, a good pull forward, pressing heavily rather than banging, is all that is needed.

Where weft joins occur, allow tails of about

15 cm (6 in) of both the old and the new weft to lie on the surface of the work. Later, when a few more picks have been woven, thread each tail in a packing needle and work it down alongside the adjacent warp end, concealing it under the well-packed weft, for about 2 cm (¾ in). Clip the remaining yarn off short. Weft-direction darns are not satisfactory — they work loose and come up to the surface.

Using an odd number of warp ends simplifies the task of keeping the selvedges tidy in those areas where alternate picks of two colours are used. Start both shuttles from the right.

The first shuttle (A), in the 1-3 shed, weaves across as far as the second-to-last end. In the next shed (2-4) shuttle B weaves right across. For the next pick (1-3) shuttle A returns to the right side of the loom without having wrapped around the last warp end.

The yarn from the B shuttle must now be wrapped around the outermost end to compensate for the shortfall of the other. Push the shuttle down between the last two ends, bring it out to the side of the work, then push it down between the same pair again. Once this wrapping has been done the shuttle is ready to be returned to the right side in the 2-4 shed.

Note. It is the thread that weaves right across which does the extra wrapping; the one that falls short makes a small vertical rise on the back of the work. If this compensation is not made, not only will the selvedges be untidy but the work will tend to slope downhill at the edges and rise to a hump in the centre.

In the sample bag four colours were used: very dark olive, beige, white and green.

Work in olive for 15 cm (6 in), then weave a colour pattern band as follows:

2 beige
6 olive
2 beige
12 olive
1 olive } x 8 times
1 green
8 green
1 green } x 8 times
1 white
12 olive
1 green } x 8 times
1 white
8 green
1 green } x twice
1 white
9 green

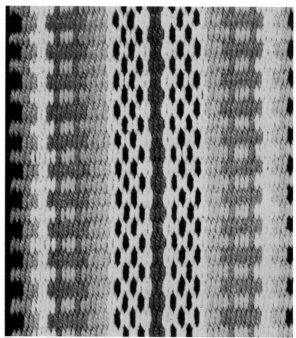

Fig 130. Warp-faced plain weave braids can be woven on the inkle loom or the conventional loom. (*Weaver: Sarah Ward.*) ★

1 white } x twice
1 green
9 green
1 white } x 8 times
1 green
14 olive
2 beige } x 3 times
6 olive

Continue in plain olive until the work measures 76 cm (30 in) from the beginning. There is little loss in length in weft-faced weaving.

As soon as the work is cut from the loom (leaving at least 8 cm or 3 in fringes), remove any scrap weaving at the beginning and end and tie the warp ends to each other in pairs to prevent ravelling. Press the bag and sew up the sides neatly, edge to edge. Turn in a hem of 2.5 cm (1 in) at the top and catch it down invisibly. Insert a suitable lining, slipstitching it to the hem.

The shoulder-strap is made of carpet wool and may be twisted, plaited or braided. Thirty to forty strands are needed for a reasonably thick cord.

10. Braid (plain weave, warp-faced, fig 130)
Warp-faced braids are useful as belts, straps and decorative trims. They are often woven on inkle looms and for most purposes are not more than 10 cm (4 in) wide. Wider pieces can be woven, but the

increased width is more difficult to weave.

The four-shaft loom is threaded for plain weave in the usual way, but the reed is discarded. It is not so easy to do warp-faced work on the rigid-heddle loom because the heddle-reed must be retained (to form the two sheds), yet its use prevents the work from being easily drawn in to conceal the weft. Working very close to the breast beam is a possible solution.

The easiest warp is cotton; the fuzziness of wool makes the shed rather difficult to open at such a close sett. No extra ends are added for selvedges. The weft is usually identical to the warp in size, but may be a little thicker. The weft colour should match the outside threads of the warp.

A belt shuttle, made for the purpose, should be used if it is available; a suitable substitute is a stick shuttle with one edge planed and sanded to a paper-knife slimness. Alternatively, an ordinary shuttle may be used to carry the weft and a separate knife-edge implement used to beat it in. It is quicker and easier to use a shuttle which is both weft-carrier and beater.

Because the reed has been discarded it is not available to keep the warp at the proper width. Tie the warp to the cloth stick at approximately the planned width of the braid. Weave in plain weave; draw the weft straight across with no allowance for slack, and press each pick into place with the edge of the shuttle. Draw the work in over successive picks until the warp is at a width which prevents the weft from showing. Put in a contrasting marker at this point and take the measurements from the marker. There is a good deal of warp take-up — allow twenty per cent.

The only finishing required is to darn the weft yarn in at the beginning and end and to plait or braid the warp fringes.

The arrangement of the warp colours forms the pattern. In the braid illustrated the warp arrangement is:

5 black
1 ochre } x twice
1 black
4 ochre
1 yellow
1 ochre
5 yellow
1 red
1 yellow
3 red
1 orange } x 3 times
1 red
2 red
1 ochre
1 red
6 ochre
3 yellow
1 brown } x twice
2 yellow
1 brown
3 yellow
2 red
1 red (centre thread; repeat in reverse to the top).

There are a total of 119 ends. The yarn used was Strutt's No 8 cotton (2240 m per 0.5 kg or 2240 yds per lb). The sett is approximately 42, finishing at a width of 7 cm (2¾ in). The weft was the same in black.

If the rigid-heddle loom is used, thread the first and last ends through a hole. On an inkle loom, thread the first and last ends through a leash. On the four-shaft loom thread the heddles 1 2 3 4 as usual, ending 2 3 4 (read from the right).

If you look at the braid from a side view you will realise that the patterns formed by the warp colours are of the same type as those resulting from weft colour changes in weft-faced weaving. Armed with this knowledge, and a little experience, you will soon be able to compose your own designs.

TEN PROJECTS FOR THE TREADLE LOOM

These projects, like those for the table loom, are simple to weave and the warps are easy to make. This simplicity is deliberate; it is best to get to know the quirks of a loom, and to feel on friendly terms with it, before attempting something more ambitious.

There is nothing difficult about weaving on a treadle loom. However, all the actions involved in the weaving — throwing the shuttle, using the beater, treadling and changing the shed — should be done with a smooth, relaxed motion. The treadles, in particular, should be used with a steady rhythm so that the sheds open and close without any suggestion of jerking. This can be easier to accomplish on a counterbalanced or countermarch loom than on a jack loom, which is inclined to close the shed rather suddenly. It helps if you control the speed at which the treadle rises with your foot so that the shed does not slam shut.

Actions that are excessively slow will make the weaving slow, but deliberately forcing the pace can have a bad effect.

In wool weaving, beating is done on an open shed. In practical terms this means changing the shed at the moment the reed touches the fell of the cloth and not an instant before. For handspun warps you may be even more cautious and delay changing the shed until the pick has been beaten. Then, with the reed still at rest against the fell, treadle and open the next shed and push the beater back. The rule is: *never move the reed on a closed shed.*

Using the beater when the shed is closed means that the warp is at its closest possible sett and friction will be at its greatest. Don't be tempted to beat a second time unless a particularly firm cloth, such as might be needed for upholstery, is wanted. Wool cloth is rather light and open-looking on the loom; one which is firm may have an uncomfortable resemblance to cardboard by the time it has been washed and fulled.

The warp tension should be sufficient to give a clean shed but not so taut that it will subject the yarn to undue strain. The depth of the shed should be sufficient only to allow the shuttle to be thrown with ease — no more than one and a half times the depth of the shuttle. A shed which is very deep merely strains the warp.

Avoid working up very close to the reed, as this too strains the warp. Move the warp forward

Fig 131. A rag rug has nostalgic charm and is fully washable

frequently, because if this is not done the same part of the yarn is moved up and down in the reed many times and may weaken and break from this abrasion. Remember, too, that the chief cause of horizontal streaks in the cloth is infrequent winding-on.

If the cross-sticks are not needed during the weaving, take them out, as they too can be a cause of needless friction. It is quite simple to put them back later — just open each plain weave shed in turn and insert the sticks. If you decide to keep the sticks in the warp, tie them as suggested on page 172 so that they can be moved back individually rather than as a pair.

Rocking each one on edge makes moving it back through the warp easier than trying to slide it on the flat. If the motion of the weaving process causes the sticks to work forward toward the heddle shafts, secure them to the back of the loom with elastic bands which can be slipped on and off easily.

11. Rag rug (unbalanced plain weave, fig 131)
Recycle your cast-off dresses or other household fabrics as a bedroom or bathroom mat.

Warp: Approximately 250 g (8 oz) of knitting cotton or cotton yarn of similar type, in several colours, made up as a striped warp.

Sett: 12. (The warp gives stability to the rag weft and a lesser sett results in a sleazy product.)

Weft: Strips of cotton cloth (old sheets, curtains, dresses, shirts and so on) 2 cm (¾ in) wide, preferably cut on the straight, and sewn together into usable lengths by hand or machine. About 1350 g (3 lbs) will be needed for a rug measuring 180 x 90 cm (6 x 3 ft) although the weight varies according to the fabric used. A bathmat measuring 90 x 60 cm (3 x 2 ft) takes about 500 g (1 lb). Nylon selvedge strips, available from some craft supply shops, may also be used.

Leave 10 cm (4 in) unwoven for the fringe at the beginning, then weave 2 cm (¾ in) with the warp yarn used double. This forms a firm edge for the rug. Be careful to keep this heading the same width as the warp in the reed because otherwise the mat will not lie flat.

Sort the rag strips into colour groups and weave in stripes. It is not necessary to make the strips lie flat in the shed — let them lie just as they come from the shuttle — change the shed and beat. Because the rags are a variable commodity it is permissible to finger the selvedges to neaten them in this case. When one length of rag runs out, taper the end with scissors and taper the beginning of the next strip so that the overlap is not too bulky.

Finish the rug with 2 cm (¾ in) in doubled warp yarn, as at the beginning. Allow 10 cm (4 in) for the fringe when cutting the work from the loom. Knot the fringe in groups of four with overhand knots, or plait or braid them in small sections.

Rag rugs can be washed by hand or in the washing machine.

A popular variation on this theme is the finger-twist fleece rug. Although the general principle is the same, considerable practice and skill are needed to produce a really good rug — they are by no means as quick and easy as they look. The warp yarn used is stronger, especially if the sett is wider (often 4 to 6). Unspun fleece, washed and finger-twisted into lengths, is used as weft. Methods differ, both in the preparation of the fleece and in the weaving itself, but the result is a warm, attractive, hand-washable floor covering.

If this type of work appeals to you (and it often seems that every weaver has a burning ambition to make a fleece rug) weave a small mat first to learn the technique and overcome any problems.

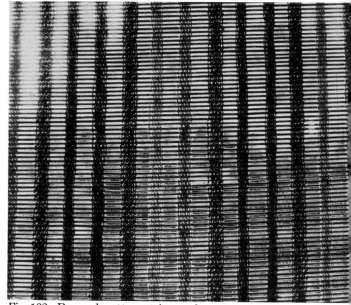

Fig 132. Re-used rattan strips make attractive sunblinds which shield the glare and yet allow air to circulate

12. Rattan blinds (unbalanced plain weave, fig 132)

Another recycling project. The cotton yarn used in the rattan blinds imported from the Far East often perishes after a few years and defies mending. The rattan strips are usually still in good order, apart from a little dust and dry mildew. They weave up well on a new warp.

Naturally, the width of the blind is limited by the width of the loom. Salvage the rods from the top and bottom of the blind, and the pulleys. The pulley cords will probably have to be replaced.

Warp: Cotton or other suitable yarn, various thicknesses, types and colours. Make the warp with 8-end stripes of each colour.

Sett: 8. Raddle the warp at this sett — do not take any account of the fact that the warp will be sleyed irregularly.

Weft: Salvaged rattan strips. This rigid weft causes more take-up than usual in the warp — allow at least 20 per cent extra.

Use an 8-dent reed. Sley the warp stripes at 4 per dent for two dents, then leave 6 empty dents. Any thicker yarns can be sleyed 2 or 3 per dent in 3 dents. Leave the first and last 2 cm (¾ in) of the reed empty to allow room for the protruding ends of the rattan. The striped bands are closely sett and will weave almost warp-faced.

Weave an initial heading with scrap yarn to test the tension, then weave in plain weave, using the rattan strips as the weft. At intervals trim the ends of the rattan neatly, with heavy scissors, about 2 cm (¾ in) beyond the first and last warp bands.

As soon as the weaving is cut from the loom, knot the warp yarns together in pairs to prevent ravelling. Do not cut the warp ends off short — they can be used to tie the blinds to the top and bottom rods.

13. Upholstery fabric (plain weave, fig 133)

Warp: Black 2-ply wool, tan 2-ply wool, both approximately 1500 m per 0.5 kg (1500 yds per lb), and green bouclé wool similar in size or a little heavier.

Weft: Black singles wool, 2000 m per 0.5 kg (2000 yds per lb).

Sett: 14.

The first 8 ends of the warp are black and brown alternately, the second 8 ends are black and green alternately. Make the warp with two cops of yarn (see Chapter 16).

Weave in plain weave with a firm beat, or two sharp blows.

14. Skirt fabric (plain weave, fig 134)

Warp: Dark red singles wool, lighter red singles wool (both 2500 m per 0.5 kg, 2500 yds per lb), one end of each alternately.

Weft: Plied wool of a similar size to the warp yarn in dark red.

Sett: 16.

In the threading take each pair of threads from the cross-sticks in turn, according to the order in the cross; it does not matter whether the dark end or the light end is threaded first from each pair. In some places in the warp two dark ends may lie side by side, or two light ends; in other places the ends may alternate from dark to light. In this way a pleasant striated effect is achieved.

An alternative treadling, giving a tiny textured effect, is 1-2, 1-3, 2-4, 3-4.

See also the coat fabric woven on the same warp, project 20.

Fig 133 Upholstery fabrics with stripes in the warp are quick to weave with a one-colour weft ★

Fig 134. A skirt fabric which cuts and sews well

15. Fabric for loose-cushion upholstery (plain weave, fig 135)

This fabric is intended for the type of easy chair with loose cushions on the back and seat. It may not be firm enough for tight upholstery. Measure the cushions first to ascertain the best width to weave.

Warp: Black worsted and white worsted, fairly well twisted, both 8000 m per 0.5 kg (8000 yds per lb.) Cotton yarn may be substituted for the worsted. The warp is made with two cops of yarn and threaded with black and white alternating.
Sett: 20.
Weft: Brown millspun bouclé, well twisted, white handspun singles wool, and brown 2-ply rayon. The bouclé and the white wool are wound together on the shuttle.

Work in plain weave, with a firm beat, using two picks of brown-white followed by one of rayon. This is not a balanced weave — there are only 14 picks of weft to 20 of warp, and the warp yarn is much finer than the weft.

16. Fabric for a sports coat (2/2 twill, fig 136)

Warp: Singles wool yarn (2500 m per 0.5 kg, 2500 yds per lb) in black, olive green and mid-blue. The warp is made in stripes of 8 black, 2 olive, 8 black, 2 blue.
Sett: 20 (2 per dent in a 10 dent reed).
Weft: Olive green wool as used in the warp.

Several lengths can be woven on the one warp and yet, with a change of weft colour, appear quite different. A blue-grey weft gives a blue tone to the cloth, a coffee brown weft gives a warm brown tone, and a black weft gives a darker all-over effect. If the warp order is repeated in the weft colours the cloth will weave as conventional checks.

Different colours can be used as the weft stripes, for a more subtle check, but they should be of the same general value (brightness or intensity) as the warp colours, even though they come from a different part of the colour wheel. For instance, black might be paired with a very dark brown, light grey with oatmeal, or bright blue with violet.

Cloth 70 cm (27 in) wide is regarded as the most economical to weave for a man's jacket. Buy the pattern first, or unpick a discarded jacket, to be sure of weaving the right length and width.

Twill is the traditional serviceable weave for

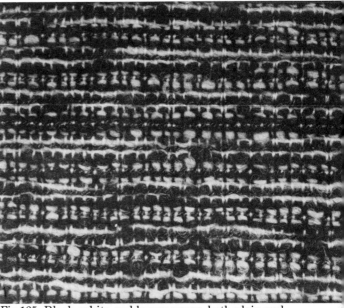

Fig 135. Black, white and brown yarns, both plain and textured, make an understated upholstery fabric

Fig 136. Sports coat fabric for the conservative man. Most Irish and Scottish tweeds are woven in twill, often with very interesting colour arrangements in warp and weft

garments of this kind, but plain weave and hopsack are also used. Fancy patterns do not appeal to most men.

Other useful drafts for tweed type fabrics are Wheat, Bird's Eye, Seed, Herringbone, Small Goose Eye and Pebble. The best source book for drafts is Marguerite P. Davison's *Handweaver's Pattern Book*.

17. Curtains (fig 137)

Warp: Natural cotton, such as Coats's tobacco cotton, 2800 m per 0.5 kg (2800 yds per lb).

Sett: 18 (use a 10 dent reed, and note the unusual sleying).

Weft: Natural and white slub linen/cotton mixture, or any linen, cotton or synthetic slub yarn of a size reasonably similar to the warp yarn.

Thread block A of the draft 9 times (18 ends), then thread block B 3 times (18 ends). Repeat as often as necessary, ending with block A. If the curtains are to be sewn together, reduce the first and last A blocks to 10 ends. Note that 5 times as many heddles are needed on shafts 1 and 4 as on shafts 2 and 3.

When sleying note that the A block is sleyed 2 per dent in 9 dents of the reed. The B block is sleyed 3 per dent, then miss a dent, over the next 11 dents, as in fig 138.

This draft is just about foolproof. The result is attractive even if the plain warp cotton is used as the weft also, and the little square holes hold their shape almost as well as if the slub yarn is used.

Slub yarn containing linen or jute is often rather stiff. If it appears to be strong enough, use it as the warp, and the plain cotton as the weft — the curtains will fall into folds more readily.

18. Floor cushions (canvas weave, fig 139)

Warp: 'Berber' carpet wool (500 m per 0.5 kg, 500 yds per lb), and a cotton or well-twisted wool to tone, about a quarter the size of the carpet wool. The thick yarn is threaded on shafts 1 and 4, and the fine yarn on shafts 2 and 3, as shown in fig 140.

Sett: 12. Use a 9 dent reed, sleying the fine yarns 2 per dent and the thick yarn 1 per dent.

Weft: The same yarns as in the warp, used in the order indicated in the treadling draft. Wind two shuttles of thick wool because two picks are laid in the same shed.

This is a thick, firm fabric. Experiments with other yarns and setts should produce good upholstery fabrics.

19. Fabric with supplementary warp pattern (fig 141)

Fancy yarn is expensive to buy and time-consuming to spin. The draft in fig 142 is very useful when only a modest quantity of a special yarn is available.

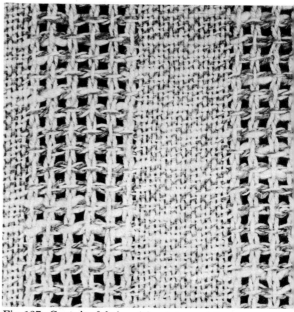

Fig 137. Curtain fabric with plain and lacy areas arranged as vertical stripes

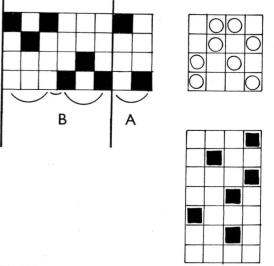

Fig 138.

The background yarn is arranged as plain weave on shafts 1 and 2. The extra yarn is threaded on shafts 3 and 4 and may be arranged to occur as often or as seldom as desired. The weight and sett of the yarns will dictate the end use for the cloth.

As will be seen from a study of the treadling draft, the fancy yarn is woven in at intervals, but between these 'tie-down' points it floats over the surface of the cloth in a warpwise direction. This makes a welcome change from the usual horizontal effect.

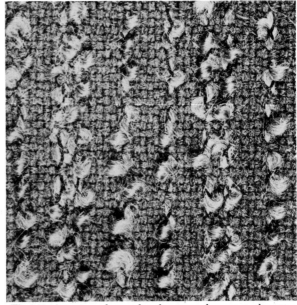

Fig 139. Deep texture gives the impression of softness but this floor cushion fabric is thick and firm

Fig 141. A textured yarn has been used as a supplementary warp forming 'floats' in the warpwise direction. This idea is capable of many interesting interpretations

★

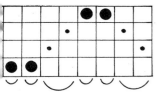

Sley as shown

Fig 140.

Sley as shown

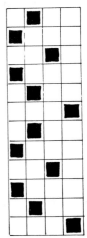

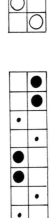

Fig 142.

Fig 143. Textured coat fabric, not so heavy as it might appear, woven on the same warp as the skirt fabric in Fig 134.

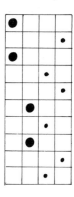

Fig 144.

Use a reed which is coarse enough to allow the fancy thread to be dented with one or two of the background ends — this prevents gaps in the plain weave behind the warp floats.

A long length of cloth woven in this way may suffer from tension problems (because the fancy thread is woven-in less often than the supporting yarns) and the use of two warp rollers may be called for.

20. Coat fabric (fig 143)

This coat fabric is woven on the same warp as the skirt length in project 14.

Weft: Yarn the same as the skirt weft for the plain weave picks, and a thick slubby handspun yarn of the same colour. The treadling is shown in fig 144.

The fabric is not as coarse and heavy as it might appear at first glance. Most of the handspun weft shows on the right side of the cloth; the underside is comparatively smooth and close. If the sett is 16 there should be 14 to 16 picks of weft in every 2.5 cm (1 in) of weaving.

16 Weaver's Fancy

ONCE you have mastered the basic skills of weaving you will be well equipped to follow your own creative impulses, searching all the while for some means of making your work different from mass-produced goods.

The handweaver can make use of yarns more varied in type and tension than the power loom is able to handle at speed. Random effects beyond the capability of a programmed loom can be woven, and finger techniques (impractical or impossible in factory production) are used.

You can experiment with special dyeing such as tie-dyeing, and thus relate the colour effects to the dimensions of the finished piece. You can create yarns especially for the project in hand — the use of mixed fibres is an interesting field, and the use of $\overleftarrow{s}$ and $\overrightarrow{z}$ twist as design elements is well worth exploring.

Handweavers have an opportunity to relate the design of the weaving to the finished size of the article being made — cushions, curtains and bedcovers need not appear as if cut from a length of cloth. The scale of the design can be large, to suit large areas, or small, to fit small areas.

It is impossible in a book of this size to do more than cover the groundwork of weaving. However, a knowledge of how to make a warp, dress a loom, and execute simple weaves, provides the best possible foundation on which to build. Those who become interested in one of the more specialised forms, such as rugs, tapestries, wall hangings or three-dimensional work, will find that the Booklist in Appendix C points the way to further information on these, and to other types of loom.

POSTSCRIPT FOR THE RIGID-HEDDLE LOOM

Over half of the projects in Chapter 15 are in plain weave, although not all of them are at a sett suitable for this loom. The owners of such looms may therefore feel restricted, may look with envy at the greater opportunity for 'fancy' work on the four-shaft loom, and may wonder what can be done to give their weaving more variety.

Great interest can be given to plain weave by the use of contrasting colours. Some dark-light arrangements appear at first glance to be in some more complex weave — it is hard to believe that they are 'only' in plain weave. An excellent small book illustrating the use of light and dark colours is Vera Miles's *Weaving Patterns for the Two-way Loom* (Dryad Press). All the designs are executed in black and white, but the same ideas can be applied to yarns in two shades of one colour, or two different textures, or two degrees of lustrousness.

A spaced-and-crowded plain weave such as is often seen in sheer curtains can be woven by threading some sections of the heddle-reed more densely than others. This can be done by using two threads per space in the denser sections, by leaving out alternate holes and slots in the lighter sections, or by leaving parts of the heddle-reed empty. Open spaces are inclined to crowd together when the work is taken from the loom but this tendency can be reduced if a bouclé yarn is used for either warp or weft or for both. Commercially, an automatic version of leno (see page 166) is used to hold these spaces open, thus making such work practical with smooth yarns.

There are scores of finger-manipulated techniques possible on a plain weave foundation. A small selection follows.

Four Lace Weaves
These weaves require a plain-weave foundation with the warp so arranged that the extreme right-hand thread is in the 'up' position when the shed is opened ready for weaving to begin from the right. The first thread in a heddle-reed must therefore be in a hole, and the first thread in a four-shaft loom on shaft 1 or 3. Discard a thread if necessary.

1. Leno

Weave several picks of plain weave ending with the shuttle passing from left to right. Open the next shed. Take a smooth flat stick, similar to a warp stick but tapered at one end and, beginning at the right, pick up the first thread from the lower layer of the warp with the point of the stick. Move the hand slightly back toward the right, then pass the point of the stick *over* the first thread in the upper layer. (If the selvedge threads are the double ones used in heddle-reeds, count each pair as one thread.)

Point the stick downward and pick up the next thread from the lower layer, bring it up again and pass it over the next thread from the upper layer. Proceed thus all across the warp (fig 145). The warp tension may need to be slackened a little during the pick-up process. You may find it helpful to hold the upper layer aside with the left hand while picking up the next lower thread.

When the whole row has been completed, slide the stick up to the reed, and turn it on edge. Pass the shuttle right to left through the shed thus created between the stick and the fell of the cloth. Remove the stick, and beat.

Open the next shed, pass the shuttle, and beat with enough force to match the size of the gap left by the twisted leno shed. Weave several plain weave picks before working the leno twist again.

This and other lace weaves improve in appearance when the work is cut from the loom and the tension relaxes. Do not beat too lightly or the work will be sleazy.

2. Mexican lace (fig 146)

Similar to leno, but *two* threads are picked up from the lower layer initially. The stick is then passed over one, under one, as before.

3. Double Mexican lace (fig 146)

Similar to Mexican lace, but *three* lower threads are picked up initially and the stick is then passed over *two*, under *two*.

4. Brooks bouquet

Open the shed for plain weave, with the shuttle waiting on the right. Pass the shuttle through the shed until it has passed under six raised warp ends. (The number is arbitrary — choose any grouping which suits your design.)

Bring the shuttle to the surface. Take it back over the last three raised warp ends, then under them, and pull the weft tight enough to form the 'bouquet'. Go forward under the next nine threads, warp three, and so on. Beat gently.

Change the shed, and weave several picks of

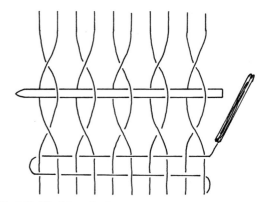

Fig 145. Working the leno twist with the aid of a pick-up stick

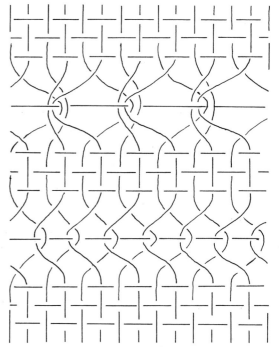

Fig 146. *Upper*, double Mexican lace. *Lower*, Mexican lace

plain weave before making another row of bouquets. This technique looks best in fine cotton or linen, not too closely woven.

Four Surface-Interest Techniques

1. Saddlestitching

An effect similar to the 'saddlestitching' in project 8 can be worked on a rigid-heddle loom by the use of an extra stick *behind* the heddle-reed. The stick is darned over and under selected warp ends behind the heddle-reed when it is in the down position. The stick is then pushed close to the heddle-reed and turned on edge. A thick weft is passed through the new shed thus formed in front of the heddle. Slide the stick to the back of the loom, flat, and leave it there until it is needed again. Several rows of plain weave are worked after each pattern row, using the finer background yarn.

2. Clasped wefts

Pass a shuttle through the shed, right to left, and link it around another yarn at the left of the loom, as shown in fig 147.

Put the shuttle back into the same shed, and use it to pull the second yarn as far into the shed as desired. Close the shed and beat. In the next shed the clasped yarns may be drawn across to the same place as before, or to some different place, according to the design planned. These wefts will, of course, lie double in the shed. This means that either the initial sett should be wider to allow for the double wefts or that a finer yarn should be chosen for weft.

3. Inlay (fig 148)

Wind a small cardboard shuttle with a few metres (yards) of a yarn somewhat thicker than that used for the background cloth. Weave one pick of plain weave with the background yarn.

Leave the shed open and insert the pattern yarn in the same shed, placing it only in the area you wish it to cover. Bring the remainder of this yarn up through the warp and let it lie on the cloth. The beginning tail of yarn may be tucked into the shed (for reversible work), left on the surface (if this is to be the wrong side), or taken through to the underside (if that is to be the wrong side).

Most weavers prefer the upper surface to be the right side and accept the little loops which appear where the weft turns back in the other direction as part of the design.

Change the shed, and weave one pick with the background yarn. Change the shed again, weave another background pick and leave the shed open. Insert the inlay yarn in the pattern area (fig 148).

A little experimentation will show that with forethought and the use of several small inlay shuttles, quite complex designs can be woven. Some weavers use an inlay with every pick of background weft; some use a twill lifting instead of plain weave. There are many variations.

4. Boutonné (pulled-up loops)

On a plain weave foundation open a shed and weave. Beat, and reopen the shed, and pick up small loops of the weft yarn with a knitting needle, commencing at the right side of the work if the

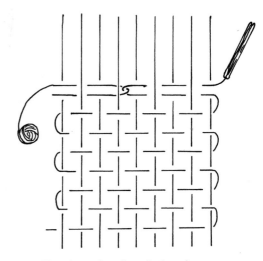

Fig 147. The clasped-weft technique is an easy means of interlocking two weft colours to form a design

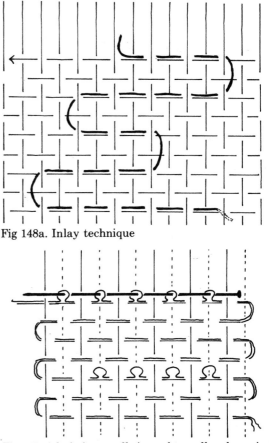

Fig 148a. Inlay technique

Fig 149. A knitting needle is used to pull up loops in the boutonné technique. A fairly well twisted weft makes the best loops

Fig 148b. A thick bouclé cotton has been laid in to form a simple motif

Fig 150. This beautiful example of boutonné work was handwoven from New Zealand crossbred wool

shuttle has just passed from right to left (fig 149). Loops may be picked up between every pair of raised warp ends, or between every second or third.

When the loops have all been picked up evenly, close the shed and beat; withdraw the needle and beat again. Weave one or more plain picks before working another looped pick.

As with inlay, there are many variations in working methods. If two colours are used in each shed it is possible to pull up loops of colour A in one area and loops of colour B in another. The use of two wefts per pick, one remaining unlooped, gives a firmer cloth. By combining the boutonné technique with the inlay method separate shuttles can be used for individual motif areas.

POSTSCRIPT FOR THE FOUR-SHAFT LOOM

Almost every weaver is initially attracted to the idea of throwing a shuttle back and forth through the warp. This, surely, is what weaving is all about?

But after a year or so the weaver begins to realise that the most interesting part of weaving is the designing and planning that is done beforehand, and that the actual weaving (which has been unkindly described as 'shuttle-shoving') has taken its rightful place as but one part of the whole process. However, the task of warp-making and dressing the loom intervenes before the design can be confirmed on the loom.

Weavers are always interested to learn of anything that will relieve the comparative tedium of these intermediate steps, provided that the quality of the work does not suffer.

Many ingenious warping aids have been invented, most of them excellent, but before rushing off to buy the latest thing you should stop and consider whether the amount and type of weaving to be done really warrants the purchase. It is very easy to become obsessed with equipment, and very doubtful whether a lot of extra equipment does anything for the average weaver other than to clutter up the house.

Even with no more sophisticated warping equipment than a board (which makes an excellent warp, possibly the best), there are several ways of making a warp more speedily. Two are listed below.

Warping with Two Threads

A warp may be made with two cops of yarn at once, thus almost halving the time taken. Place both cops of yarn on the floor near the feet — the yarn feeds off best directly from the top of cops — standing them on large nails hammered into a piece of heavy timber if they show any tendency to fall over. Balls of yarn should be placed in bowls or cartons.

Tie both yarns to the first peg of the board. Then make the warp in the usual way, but *keep the forefinger between the two yarns at all times*. The threads in the cross will be in pairs, two over and two under, instead of the usual one over, one under, formation. Do not split these pairs in raddling.

When threading, thread a pair from under the cross-sticks, followed by a pair from over the sticks. As long as the *pairs* are taken in order it does not matter which thread of each pair is taken first, unless some particular colour sequence is required.

Warping with two balls at once is a very useful technique when a warp consisting of one end of yarn A, followed by one end of B, is needed, as otherwise the yarn must be cut and joined at the end of every half portee.

It is not wise to make a warp with more than two yarns at a time unless a paddle or similar device is used; the correct order for threading is difficult to maintain and there is too much risk of the yarns twisting together and becoming unweavable.

Weavers who prefer mixed warps (those involving many different yarns) may do well to convert

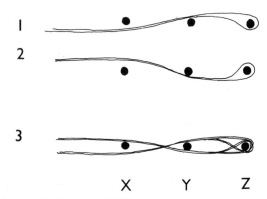

Fig 151. Making a raddling cross

to sectional or semi-sectional warping, both of which are clearly described in Harriet Tidball's *Weaver's Book*. A good account of the use of a paddle is given in Shirley Held's *Weaving: a Handbook for Fibrecraftsmen*.

Making a Raddling Cross

The cross at the X-Y end of the board can be made in a slightly different way so that the groups for the raddle are already counted out, ready to be placed in the appropriate dents. Suppose each raddle group is to consist of 10 ends: take the yarn around the board as shown at (1) in fig 151 until 10 ends have been warped. Take the next 10 ends around the pegs as shown at (2) in fig 151. Continue making groups in this way until the warp has been completed.

The appearance of the warp is shown at (3) in fig 151. Note that the cross appears between X and Y as usual: ignore the rather confused looking false cross between Y and Z. When this method is used the counting tie is best made exactly where the cross occurs.

Raddling takes only a few moments, but note that the raddling cross cannot be used for threading because there is no way of ascertaining the correct threading order within each group. The second cross (at B-C), which is made in the usual way, must be picked up on cross-sticks for the purpose of threading.

OTHER TIME-SAVING TECHNIQUES

The raddle itself should be conveniently placed on the loom, and it saves time if some regular means of attaching it is provided. This can take the form of fitted brackets or hooks, or some arrangement of wires or cords to suspend the raddle from the top of the loom.

A fixed raddle sounds attractive but, in fact, a raddle which is capable of floating a little is better — a thread temporarily tangled in a floating raddle is more likely to be detected before it breaks, while one caught on a fixed raddle may snap before it is either seen or felt.

Threading can be done more quickly if the cross-sticks are held steady at a good working height and distance from the shafts. This may be accomplished by making some permanent holding arrangement with hooks or wires.

The shafts of a counterbalanced loom are inclined to slide up and down while the threading is being done. An efficient way of holding them steady is to use fingers (sometimes called castles) suspended from the top of the loom. The fingers are made of timber, and the notches should be designed to fit the heddle sticks or frames of the particular loom (fig 152). Fingers are also useful with other looms to hold the shafts apart so that one can make a clear distinction between each shaft when threading.

The weaver often wishes for a third hand, and fig 153 illustrates a means of freeing both hands for the task of selecting the correct thread from the cross and drawing it through the eye of a heddle. A thick, soft cord is attached to the breast beam, or to some other part of the loom, or even to the weaver's belt, and is formed into a lark's-head loop. A group of threads is passed through this loop and held at tension with the tightening of the loop. Naturally, the group of threads must be to the left of the heddles waiting to be threaded. As each warp end is selected for threading it can quite easily be pulled out of the group secured by the cord.

Two heddles are sometimes discovered to be crossed over one another on the shaft after threading has been completed. Instead of re-threading, cut one of them away, using scissors for string heddles, or wire-cutters for steel, and replace it with a temporary string heddle. The size and height of the eye of the existing heddles should be matched, and it may be found helpful to use a suitable knitting needle as a gauge in tying

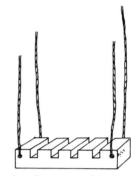

Fig 152. Wooden fingers used to support the shafts

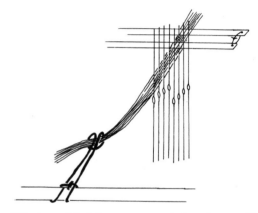

Fig 153. A cord holding a group of threads acts like a third hand

the eye. The reef knot (square knot) is usually used (fig 154).

Quick Samples

As samples are so necessary when trying anything new it is desirable to find some way of getting a sample warp on the loom as quickly and easily as possible, perhaps taking some short cuts which would not be recommended for a full warp. The following method will be found useful.

Take a strong piece of cardboard about 50 x 25 cm (20 x 10 in). Wind the warp yarn around the card lengthwise, each round lying neatly beside the previous round, until enough for a warp not less than 15 cm (6 in) wide has been wound. A cross is not needed.

Secure the threads in the order in which they were wound with masking tape, one strip on top of the yarn, one strip underneath, about halfway up the card. Cut through the yarns at the bottom of the card.

Support a reed on a table, using either special reed holders, or stacks of books, or clamp it to the edge of the table. Draw the cut ends of the yarns through the dents of the reed, keeping to the order as secured by the sticky tape. Place the reed in the beater, with the sleyed ends facing toward the heddles.

Stand at the back of the loom, and thread the ends from the reed through the heddles. Tie the warp in small groups to the back apron stick. Remove the sticky tape. Wind the warp on the roller — only a turn or two will be needed. Tie the other end of the warp to the front apron stick, and begin sampling.

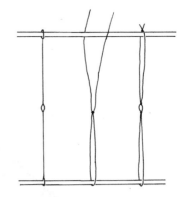

Fig 154. Trying a string heddle on the loom

WEAVING ON PAPER

A good deal of experimental work can be done on paper if the weaver learns the technique of plotting the structure of the weave on squared paper. The steps in making a graphic representation of a weave (a 'draw-down') are shown in fig 155. Use paper with 3 mm (⅛ in) squares.

In the first pick, shafts 1 and 3 are operated, so a mark is placed on the first line of squared paper directly under each place in the draft where a 1 or a 3 occurs. Small arrows have been drawn to make this plain in the diagram. The second pick calls for shafts 2 and 4 to be used: mark the 2's and 4's on the second line of squares. The third pick calls for the 1's and 3's to be marked. In the fourth pick shafts 1 and 2 are used, and the 1's and 2's are marked in the appropriate squares. Each pick is marked in the same way until enough has been 'woven' to see the way in which the weave intersects. On the right hand side of the diagram only pencilled marks are shown; on the left side the squares have been blacked-in in the usual way, leaving the squares representing exposed warp as white.

Note that this diagram has been worked out for a sinking shed. That is, when shafts 1 and 2 are operated the ends threaded on them are lowered and are therefore covered over by the weft. A rising shed reverses the situation: 1 and 2 rise, and the remaining ends are covered by the weft.

Although the sinking method is more direct, the rising method shows the loom-controlled movement of the warp ends better. Because of its directness the sinking method is used by hand-weavers, but the rising method is favoured in industry.

To work out a diagram showing the interaction of various colours in the warp and the weft, proceed as follows:

1. Make a new drawing showing the colours of the warp yarns in the threading draft and the colours of the weft yarns in the treadling draft.
2. Make a draw-down of the actual weave, using pencil marks only.
3. Taking each *vertical* line of squares under the threading draft in turn, mark the *blank* squares with the colour of the warp yarn shown for that column.
4. Taking each pick in turn, mark the *pencilled* squares with the colour of that pick of weft.

The draft used in the example is Rosepath. It is a traditional variation of twill, although it is often used in the 'overshot' manner. Note that because each warp end is drawn through the eye of a heddle on 'odd' and 'even' shafts alternately, it is still possible to weave plain weave. Most drafts are written in this way, thus enabling the weaver to use one (or more) plain weave picks after each pattern pick to give the cloth extra stability.

The use of one pick of plain weave after each pattern pick is an essential feature of traditional overshot weaving, but these plain weave ('tabby binder') picks are not shown on the draw-down because they have a confusing effect. An overshot draft may be headed with the instruction 'Use tabby', but for the most part the weaver is expected to know to do so.

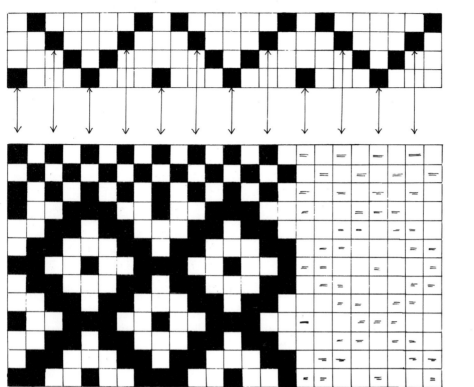
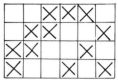
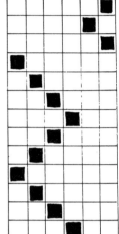

Fig 155. Making a 'draw-down

17 Handspun Warp and Weft

WEAVING with handspun yarn is a subject about which the novice can find, for the most part, only passing references, yet with the current worldwide revival of interest in handspinning some practical guidelines are called for. Nothing special in the way of weaving equipment is required but, if much handspun work is to be done, the loom and accessories should be chosen with this in mind.

A handspun warp is trickier to use than a mill-spun warp and there are times when the weaver wishes it were possible to resist the challenge and be satisfied with the rustic pleasures of knitting and crochet instead.

It is a real accomplishment to be able to spin the yarn and weave it into cloth. The craftsman can choose the fleece, dye it any colour, spin a yarn to suit the requirements, weave it the way he or she wants, and finish it in the way planned from the beginning. The finished article cannot be repeated or copied exactly, and may well be something the machine either cannot or will not make. Tremendous satisfaction is to be gained in the process.

However, unless the finished product has something to recommend it apart from the immense number of hours which went into the making of it, the general public may not be very impressed. The public preference is for work which looks aggressively hand-made, and the greatest challenge facing the spinner-weaver who hopes to sell craftwork is to produce something which combines this desire for the primitive with his or her own knowledge of what represents sound construction and fitness for purpose.

SPINNING THE YARN

Warp needs more twist than weft, singles yarns more than plied yarns, but how much is more?

Many traditional spinning wheels were made with two flyer whorls, one giving a ratio of about 7:1, and the other a ratio of about 11:1. Tradition has it that the lower ratio was used for weft, and the higher ratio for warp, the rate of treadling and the rate of drawing remaining constant.

Every fleece has its own characteristics, and every yarn is spun with a purpose in mind, so it is probable that no general rule can be given. Each spinner will have to make individual decisions on the basis of experiments and sampling. A 'short' fleece may need more twist than a 'long' fleece to produce the same strength; a fine fleece needs different handling from a strong one. Too much twist can produce a hard cloth, but too little contributes to warp breakages, fluffing during weaving, and 'pilling' afterwards.

A handy test for a singles yarn is to break a piece in a quiet room: if it breaks with an audible snap it is strong enough for warp — and may even be overtwisted. If it pulls apart without snapping it is too weak. Experiments will be needed to find the least amount of twist needed to cause a snap *with that particular fleece.*

Singles yarns intended for warp are usually woollen spun. A woollen singles is believed to be stronger than its worsted counterpart because the arrangement of the fibres within the yarn is more resistant to fraying. A woollen cloth is typically rough-surfaced and warm to the hand, while worsted is inclined to be smooth and hard. (Queen Victoria noticed that hard worsted kilts cut the legs of her Scottish troops and asked for woollen cloth to be used instead.) The smooth worsted cloth of industry is invariably woven of plied yarn; the finishing of a true worsted is beyond the resources of the home weaver.

Plied yarns need only enough extra twist to withstand the friction of the heddles and reed. Fancy yarns often include a strongly spun binder thread, and this binder gives sufficient strength to the yarn for it to be used for warp even if the other component is soft and weak. However, soft yarns can shed so much fluff that the heddles and reed become clogged with loose fibre. This must be cleared away before work can continue.

It goes without saying that warp yarns of any kind need to be spun with extra care. Weak places

173

are undesirable, but an irregular yarn is suitable provided both the thick and thin places have the required strength.

For the weft yarn, extra strength (as such) is not necessary, but for a tweed-type fabric the amount of twist in the weft should be similar to that in the warp to achieve the tweedy look. The fulling of a cloth with a well-twisted warp and a very soft weft can be a problem, and for this reason hand-washing should be tried first.

The making of samples, washed and fulled, is essential before any large project is undertaken. Samples should be made with a rather light beat (even on a table loom) because it is impossible to match a heavy beat on a full-width warp. The samples should be at least 15 cm (6 in) square as this is the smallest possible piece from which the hand of the fabric can be judged.

When the handspun singles warp yarn is washed after spinning it becomes quite kinky, and while it is drying it should be weighted, as described in the spinning section, to reduce this tendency. If much warp spinning is done it is worth while to fabricate some kind of reel to wind it on for drying. Yarn which is *almost* dry can be wound into cones with a cone winder, but to be on the safe side it should be rewound every day till completely dry in case residual dampness causes mildew.

Be careful about using two different fleece types in either warp or weft. They may shrink at different rates, causing a seersucker or crepe effect if you are lucky, or a complete failure if you are not. For the same reason, if two different yarns are spun (one thick, one thin, for instance) take care that each has a comparable amount of elasticity. Wool is very accommodating, but don't expect too much of it — make a sample first.

The fleece chosen should be appropriate for the article to be woven, taking into account its tactile qualities. No matter how finely it is spun and woven, a shawl made from a strong fleece will never be soft and comforting. Knitters are fussy about fleece, and weavers should be equally fussy. However, some types which would never be acceptable to a knitter can be used appropriately in weaving. Strong fleeces can be used for rugs, wall-hangings and selected fabrics such as heavy tweeds. Fleeces with kemps (hairlike fibres) have a place in tweed and upholstery. Stained fleeces may be over-dyed interestingly.

The ability to full varies from breed to breed, fleece to fleece. Many weavers favour Cheviot, Perendale and Down wool types, and feel that some of the long-wools do not always full so successfully. Your own preferences can be established only by experimenting with the types available.

Making the warp

Handspun warps, especially if they are to be sized, are best made in sections no more than 30 cm (12 in) wide for ease of handling. Remember to make *two* crosses, one at each end of the warp. Handspun warps, even the best of them, are not as smooth as millspun warps and will almost certainly resist being rolled on through the crosssticks. The sticks will therefore have to be taken out; the warp is rolled on through the raddle only.

When about 65 cm (27 in) remains to be wound, pick up the second cross for the purpose of threading. Place one of the cross-sticks in the part of the cross nearest the warp roller, and tie a cord from end to end so that if dropped it cannot fall out of the cross. Push this stick to the rear of the loom. Put the second stick in the part of the cross nearest the breast beam and tie a cord from end to end in the same way. Cut the ties securing the cross.

This stick will be rather more difficult to work back toward the rear of the loom, so proceed as follows: tie a weight, such as a heavy book, to the loop at the end of the warp so that the warp hangs down from the breast beam under tension. Both hands will then be free to work the stick back.

Grasp a section of the upper layer of the cross just in front of the stick and at the same time push down firmly with the other hand on the lower layer of the cross until the threads separate. Repeat this action across the width of the warp until the cross is free of all adhesions, and then push the stick to the rear of the loom. Tie both sticks together in the usual way.

This method is much easier than trying to push the sticks back as a pair. A little pre-planning of the placement of the cross on the warping board will ensure that the distance the sticks must be moved is minimal.

If only one cross is made, the sticks must be worked down the entire length of the warp during beaming, to the detriment both of the warp and the weaver's temper.

The sectional method of warping is also suitable if the tensioner does not cause too much abrasion.

A fairly common method of dressing a loom is to thread the warp from front to back through reed and heddles, then to tie it to the warp stick and wind it on. This is not desirable with wool, much less with handspun wool, as the friction of the extra journey through heddles and reed is damaging.

Even less to be recommended is the practice of threading the warp ends through the heddles and reed from the back of the loom *before* beaming. The yarn is then dragged through to the front of the loom and is finally wound back on to the warp roller. It is a marvel any warp survives such treatment.

To be on the safe side, a handspun warp should be made a little longer than usual to allow for any surprises by way of unexpected contraction. If the cords from the warp roller are long enough to allow the warp stick to come right up close behind the heddles, very little yarn is wasted.

Sizing the Warp

It was the practice in times past to size the warp — that is, to treat it with a substance which coated the surface of the yarn to reduce fuzziness and make it easier to weave. For some reason this practice does not seem to have been generally adopted by handweavers, yet, as it was universal in the days when all yarn was handspun, it must have been considered of value. Many early industrial patents were concerned with contrivances for sizing yarns in factory conditions, for smoothing away any excess of size, and for drying the warp rapidly enough to meet the demands of the new machines.

Sizing was continued among artisan weavers until the end of the nineteenth century, as is shown by paintings and drawings done at the time. Several Van Gogh sketches show a bowl of paste and the brush for applying it standing behind the loom. It was apparently the practice with these old looms to lift the warp roller out of its notch and to support it temporarily on brackets built out from the back of the loom for the purpose. The exposed length of warp was brushed with size and allowed to dry.

The paste-it-on-the-loom system is rather messy for the handweaver of today; sizing the whole warp chain before beaming commences is recommended.

A suitable product is glue size (from hardware stores); or, if this is not available, the rather more costly kitchen gelatine. Soften six 5-ml teaspoons of the granules in a little cold water, allow them to swell, then dissolve with one litre (35 fluid ounces) of very hot water. While the water is still hot immerse the warp chain in the solution and leave it long enough for good penetration. Run the warp chain through the hands to remove the excess size,

and hang it outdoors to dry, tying it between two verandah posts or poles if possible. Shaking the warp while it is drying encourages the warp strands to separate from each other.

When the warp is dry it feels as if it is starched — but the size washes out quite easily during the finishing.

Cellulose or starch wallpaper paste has also been suggested as a size, but experiment first to see how well it washes out.

Weavers who use the sectional warping method will have to adapt the procedure, perhaps by sizing the yarn before it is wound on to warp spools.

Millspun singles, if dyed for use as warp, also benefit from sizing because dyeing removes the spinning oil used in industry, and the yarn is then kinky and difficult to use.

Suggestions for Weaving

Plain weave is a long-time favourite with handweavers although, like stocking stitch in knitting, it shows up every imperfection. Unless it is enlivened by colour, interesting dyeing, texture, or some other point of interest, it is just what the name says — plain. If the weaver uses only the natural sheep colours there is a real danger of the product being what one observer described as 'good, strong, institutional cloth'. Even such a simple variation in threading as 11, 2, 3, 4; 1, 22, 3, 4; 1, 2, 33, 4; 1, 2, 3, 44 can help to remove the cloth from the flannel class.

Fancy yarns often lose most of their effect in the close interlacements of plain weave. The twills, and their endless variations, give these yarns the breathing space they need. A 3-shaft point twill (threaded 2, 3, 2, 1) allows most of the textured yarn to show on the face of the cloth. The plain weave in this case is to be found on shaft 2 followed by shafts 1-3. A 'float' of weft over three warp ends is obtained by using shafts 1-2 or 2-3. A 4-shaft point twill (2, 3, 4, 3, 2, 1) with a thick thread placed in the warp to coincide with the two points is also a very useful draft. Three-end floats (1-2 or 3-4) give an opportunity for using a thick or fancy yarn in the weft. The treadlings should be worked out for a rising or sinking shed to suit the action of the loom. The 3-shaft draft can be used on counterbalanced looms if the empty fourth shaft is tied to the treadles to balance the action.

Small overshot drafts, such as Rosepath (really a point twill), Thousand Flowers, Weaver's Fancy, and so on, can be used as a basis for texture work by combining the use of plain weave with pattern picks in a way that does not produce an identifiable motif.

Generally speaking, if pattern is the interesting element in a textile it does not need the assistance of texture; if texture is the interesting element the introduction of pattern may be an intrusion.

Yarns spun with slubs, loops or snarls, are useful in texture work; but, as with so many things in life, 'less is more'. A fabric woven entirely with fancy yarn is often less effective than one woven with a combination of plain and fancy yarns. The eye is able to rest on the plain yarn, and the excitement caused by the special yarn is greater. The interplay between rough and smooth is further emphasised by the way in which light falls on the fabric, creating tiny shadows and highlights. Yarn spun with regularly occurring slubs (or other texture effects) can have the disconcerting effect of creating a texture pattern, so deliberately irregular spinning is desirable.

Do not feel obliged to work entirely with handspun yarn. Valuable lessons can be learned by incorporating handspun yarn in a warp made largely of millspun yarn. The proportion of handspun yarn can be increased with each project as you gain confidence (fig 156).

Figs 156a, b and c. Three simple experiments with handspun and millspun wool

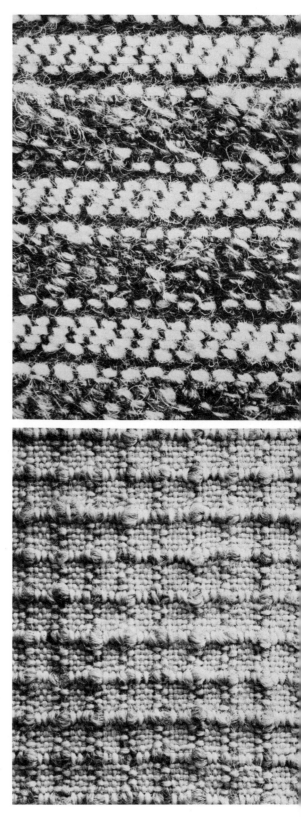

A first attempt at weaving with an all handspun warp should not be too ambitious. Start with something small, such as a scarf, a stole, or a cushion cover. A small article can act as a testing ground for the spinning and save the weaver from the disappointing experience of spending many hours spinning unsuitable yarn. A second project might be larger, perhaps using a plied yarn or a thick singles. After two or three practice pieces the weaver will be in a better position to decide on the type of work preferred and to spin accordingly.

Most sheep are white, and perhaps it is worth mentioning that, contrary to popular belief, a white warp is neither versatile nor particularly attractive. A white or near-white warp has the effect of dimming even bright colours. The eye is drawn to the lightest colour first, and the warp yarn can therefore give the appearance of a series of small seeds or flecks. The all-over effect is dusty.

This can be proved by making a warp consisting of broad black and white stripes (10 cm or 4 in wide) and weaving with weft stripes of similar size and colour, first in plain weave and then in the twills. The dusty effect of the warp is very noticeable in the plain weave areas where the dark weft crosses the light warp. The 2/2 twill areas are enlivened by the crisp diagonal line, but the broken twill is inclined to suffer in the same way as plain weave.

Weavers are often advised to weave a sample colour blanket using a warp made in broad stripes of the spectrum colours (as indicated by the colour wheel) and to weave it with the same colour stripes in the weft. A more valuable exercise might be to use three variations of each weft colour — pale, medium and full tones. It will be observed that the weft colour needs to be of the same intensity as the warp to avoid the seed effect, regardless of the actual hue.

Most of the projects in Chapter 15 are variations on very simple themes, and can be adapted easily for use with handspun warps. In the long run however, every weaver must meet the challenge of how best to use the yarn to retain or enhance its distinctive character.

Problems in Finishing

A fabric woven in plain weave with singles handspun warp and weft often shows a curious surface effect after the wet finishing. Diagonal lines, slanting to left or right, appear on the surface as if a bird had left footprints on the cloth (fig 157). No amount of pressing removes these crowfeet. They occur only in plain weave. This effect can also show up in samples made with millspun singles, and occasionally even with well-twisted plied yarns.

Various suggestions have been made concerning cause and remedy. Fabrics woven in factories do not show these crowfeet, probably because the factory has much more sophisticated means of wet-finishing the cloth than the handweaver has at her disposal. Steaming the cloth before it is washed has been suggested, or drying the cloth under tension on a tenter frame. The use of opposite twists ($\overline{s}$ or $\overline{z}$) in warp and weft has also been advised, but an examination of factory-woven fabrics reveals that these often have the same twist in both warp and weft.

In an effort to find out more about the cause a series of samples was woven, using yarn with various degrees of twist. All the yarn was spun from the same fleece. A single set of samples is not sufficient to prove anything, but it was noticed that where both warp and weft were well-twisted the crowfoot effect showed up very plainly; the same warp crossed with a softer twisted weft did not show these marks.

A sample with well-twisted warp and weft was held up to a window; both warp and weft were distorted and no longer lay in perfectly straight vertical and horizontal lines. A sample with a softer twisted weft did not show this distortion. A set of samples woven with the same selection of yarns, but in twill, showed no crowfeet or distortion.

It seems likely that the effect may be caused by overtwist. Plain weave evidently does not give the yarn enough space to relax its tensions, while twill does. A possible solution is to reduce the amount of twist, particularly in the weft, as the amount of twist in the warp cannot be reduced without danger of rendering it too weak for use.

Another effect, known as rivering, sometimes occurs. The warp is deflected from the vertical and crowds together in places. This is caused by the use of a heavy weft on a fine (usually millspun) warp. The difference in size between the two yarns is too great; the warp plays an insufficient part in gripping the two elements of the weave, and acts only as a weft-hanger.

Fig 157a. Plain weave, handspun singles warp and weft, before washing

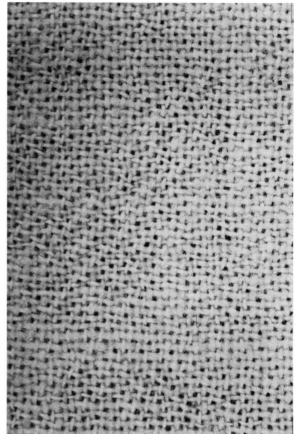

Fig 157b. The same fabric after washing. Note that the reed marks have disappeared but that the 'crowfoot' effect has appeared. Another piece of the same fabric was steam pressed *before* being washed but the crowfeet still appeared when the fabric was subsequently washed

Appendix A

YARN COUNTS (OLD SYSTEM)

IN THE OLD SYSTEM of yarn counts, now super-
seded by Tex, each fibre (cotton, linen, wool,
worsted) had a different base number from which
the yardage per pound was calculated. These differences apparently arose from the fact that in
earlier times communications between various
fibre-spinning areas were very poor.

The number for cotton was 840. A number 1
single̵ ⸻ ⸻ was spun to a thickness giving 840
yards ⸻ ⸻⸻
as fin
poun
numb

Wl
geth
rally
pour
cula
to fi
cott

Wool was measured in different ways in different areas, but a very common count was the York-
shire 'skein' of 256 yards per pound. In this system
1's wool had 256 yards per pound, 10's had 2560,
and so on, again divided by the ply number —
although wool is frequently used as a singles yarn.

The count for worsted-spun wool was based on
a 'hank' of 560 yards per pound. Thus, number 1
worsted had 560 yards per pound. Worsted is
almost always plied for extra strength, so the
ıre calculated was divided by the ply number.
r some obscure reason the ply number for wor-
d was given first, not second as for cotton —
l6ˢ worsted but 16/2ˢ cotton.

It will be seen from the above brief résumé that
2/20 (or 20/2) yarn varied greatly in length de-
nding on whether it was measured as cotton,
ɔol, linen or worsted:

2/20 cotton	8400 yards per pound
20/2 linen	3000 yards per pound
20/2 wool	2560 yards per pound
20/2 worsted	5600 yards per pound

There are obvious advantages to a system such
as Tex, where the calculation is the same for all
fibres. Take note however that fibre of a certain
size cannot necessarily be substituted for a different fibre, even of the same size, because each fibre
has its own behaviour-characteristics on the
loom; a change of sett may be necessary.

Appendix B

THE SHEEP OF GREAT BRITAIN
British Wool Characteristics

(By courtesy of the British Wool Marketing Board and the National Sheep Association.)

Breed	Fineness (Bradford Count)	Average fleece weight (lb) (kg)	Average length of Staple (in) (cm)	Demi or Lustre	Main Uses
BEULAH SPECKLED FACE	44-48	3-4 1¼-2	3-4 8-10	Flat	Tweed carpets.
BLACKFACE	Coarse	4-7 1¾-3	8-12 20-30	Demi	Carpets, rugs, tweeds, mattresses.
BLACK WELSH MOUNTAIN	48-54	3 1¼-1½	3-4 8-10	Demi	Speciality or black and brown yarns.
BLUE FACE LEICESTER	48-50	5 2¼	5-6 13-15	Demi-Lustre	Furnishing fabrics, moquette, bunting.
BORDER LEICESTER	44-48	6-10 2¾-4½	8-10 15-25	Demi-Lustre	Hosiery, knitting yarns, paper felts, bunting.
BRITISH OLDENBURG	48-56	9 4	5-7 13-18	Demi-Lustre	Moquettes, hosiery.
CHEVIOT	48-56	4-5 2-2½	4 10	Demi	Tweeds, high-class hosiery.
CLUN FOREST	56-58	5-7 2¼-3	4 8-10	Demi	Hosiery and knitting yarns and felts.
COLBRED	48-54	5-7 2¼-3	4-7 10-18	Demi-Lustre	Knitting hosiery.
COTSWOLD	46-48	12½ 5½	7-10 18-25	Lustre	Bunting.
DALES-BRED	32-40	4 2	8 20	Demi	Carpet wools.
DARTMOOR	36-40	15-18 7-9	10-12 25-30	Lustre	Carpet wools, bunting and low-quality yarns and mechanical cloths.
DERBYSHIRE GRITSTONE	50-56	5 2¼	6-8 15-20	Demi	Hosiery, rug wool, woollen trade.
DEVON CLOSEWOOL	46-50	5-7 2¼-3	3-4 8-10	Demi-Lustre	Hosiery, fabrics, tweeds.

Breed	Count	Bulk	Weight	Type	Uses
DEVON LONGWOOLLED	32-36	14 / 6½	12 / 30	Lustre	Carpets, bunting and low-quality yarns and mechanical cloths.
DORSET DOWN	56-58	5-7 / 2¼-3	2-3 / 5-8	Demi	Speciality and white knitting yarns, paper felts and tweeds.
DORSET HORN	54-58	5-7 / 2¼-3	3-4 / 8-10	Demi	,, ,,
EXMOOR HORN	48-56	5-7 / 2¼-3	3-4 / 8-10	Demi-Lustre	Hosiery, knitting yarns, felts.
HAMPSHIRE DOWN	56-58	5-6 / 2¼-2½	2-4 / 5-10	Demi	High-class hosiery, knitting yarns, felts, etc.
HERDWICK	28-32	3-4½ / 1½-2	5 / 15	Demi	Carpets, belting, and low, strong quality yarns, mechanical cloths.
JACOB	44-56	4-6 / 2-2½	3-6 / 8-15	Demi-Lustre	Dyeing blends woollens, worsted.
KERRY HILL	54-56	5 / 2¼	4 / 10	Demi	Hosiery and knitting yarns and felts.
LEICESTER	40-46	11-13 / 5-6	8-10 / 20-25	Lustre	Lustre yarns and linings.
LINCOLN LONGWOOL	36-40	11-14 / 5-6½	12-16 / 30-40	Lustre	Lustre yarns, linings, mechanical cloths buntings.
LLANWENOG	56-58	5 / 2¼	3 / 8	Demi-Grey Down	Hosiery, handknitting, tweeds.
LONK	44-50	5-6 / 2¼-3	4-6 / 15	Demi	Various carpet and hosiery.
MANX	44-48	4-6 / 2-2½	3-5 / 8-13	Demi-Lustre	Woollen, special dyeing blends.
NORTH COUNTRY CHEVIOT	50-56	4-5 / 1½-2½	3-4 / 8-10	Demi	Tweeds, hosiery and knitting yarns.
ORKNEY NATIVE	50-56	3-5 / 1½-2¼	1½-3 / 4-8	Demi Flat	Hosiery, woollens.
OXFORD DOWN	54-56	8-10 / 3½-4½	4-5 / 10-13	Demi	Hosiery and knitting yarns and felts.
RADNOR	48-56	4-5 / 2-2½	2-6 / 5-15		Tweeds, flannels.
ROMNEY	48-54	8-10 / 4-4½	6-8 / 15-20	Demi	Hosiery and knitting yarns, paper felts.
ROUGH FELL	Very coarse	5 / 2¼	8 / 20	Demi	Carpets, rugs, mattresses.
RYELAND	56-58	6-8 / 2¾-3½	3-4 / 8-10	Demi	Hosiery and knitting yarns and felts.

SHETLAND	56-60	2-3 1-1½	4 10		Speciality Shetland yarns.
SHROPSHIRE	54-56	6-8 2¾-4	4 1 0	Demi	Hosiery, knitting yarns, paper felts, mechanical cloths.
SOAY	44-50	3-5 1½-2¼	2-6 5-15	Demi Flat	Woollens.
SOUTH DEVON	36-40	12-16 5½-7¼	8-12 20-30	Lustre	Bunting, low-quality yarns, press cloths.
SOUTHDOWN	56-60	4-6 2-2¾	2-3 5-8	Demi	Speciality felts.
SOUTH WALES MOUNTAIN	40-50	3 1¼-1½	3-4 8-10	Demi	Carpets.
ST KILDA	48-50	3-5 1½-2¼	2-6 5-15	Demi Flat	Woollens.
SUFFOLK	54-58	5-7 2½-3	3½ 8	Demi	Hosiery and knitting yarns and tweeds.
SWALEDALE	28-40	4 2	6-10 15-25	Demi	Carpets, tweeds.
TEESWATER	40-48	12-15 5½-7	8-12 20-30		Carpets, tweeds, bunting.
WELSH MOUNTAIN	36-50	3 1¼-1½	2-4 5-10	Demi	Carpets, tweeds, flannels, blankets, rugs.
WENSLEYDALE	44-48	10-16 4½-7	8-12 20-30	Lustre	Lustre yarns and linings.
WHITE FACE DARTMOOR	36-40	12-16 5½-7	10-12 25-30	Lustre	Bunting, low-quality yarns, press cloths, etc.
WILTSHIRE HORN	50-56		½	Demi	Hosiery and knitting yarns.

Cross Breeds

MASSAM EWE	44-46-48	5-7 2¼-3	6-7 15-18	Demi-Lustre	Carpet yarn, squeeze cloths.
SCOTTISH GREYFACE	32-40 46-48	6-8 2¾-3½	6-12 15-30	Demi Slight Lustre	Carpet, mattress, tweeds, woollens.
SCOTTISH HALFBRED	48-54	6-8 2¾-3½	5-7 13-18	Demi-Lustre	Hosiery, moquette, woollens, tweeds.
ROMNEY HALFBRED	56-58	6 2¾	2-4 5-10	Demi	Paper felts, hosiery, handknitting, woollens.
WELSH HALFBRED	48-54	6-7 2¾-3	5-6 13-15	Demi	Hosiery, handknitting.

THE SHEEP OF SOUTH AFRICA

(By courtesy of the South African Wool Board)

Breed	Quality or count	Microns	Staple length	Percentage of annual wool clip
Merino (Also Döhne Merino, Letele, Walrich, Kaffrarian poll.)	70s/74s 58s/60s 56s	19 to 27	75 to 90mm (12 months growth)	70%
Cross-bred (South African Mutton, Merino, Corriedale, British breeds, and crosses between these and Merino.)	Variable	Variable	45 to 75mm (12 months growth)	9%
Coarse and coloured wool (Mutton breeds, Dorper and crosses between Dorper and other breeds.)	Variable	Variable	Variable	7%
Karakul (grey to black.)	Carpet type	Carpet type	50 to 75mm (6 months growth)	7%
Wool from Lesotho, the Transkei and Ciskei (Merino and cross-bred.)	Variable	Variable	Variable	6%

THE SHEEP OF AUSTRALIA

The Australian Wool Corporation suggests the following wool usages:

Breed	Characteristics	Craft use
Merino	Soft handle, fine (60s/80s up), often short. Frequently coloured.	Knitting — fine shawls, babywear, light sweaters. Fine-weaving.
Corriedale	Soft handle, medium fineness (50s/56s), good staple length.	Good sweater yarn. Knitted caps, mittens, etc.
Cheviot	Crisp handle, medium staple length, medium fineness (56s/60s).	Knitted sweaters, caps, etc.
Lincoln	Harsh handle, very long staple, lustrous, coarse wool (32s/36s).	Floor rugs, wall hangings, etc.
Romney Marsh	Medium soft handle, medium fine (46s/50s), long staple, lustrous.	Hardwearing garments — sweaters, socks, caps, scarves, etc. Good for weaving into dress fabrics, rugs.
Border Leicester	Crisp handle, long staple, fairly coarse (40s/46s).	Rugs, wall hangings, work sweaters.
Border Leicester cross	Soft handle, good staple length, medium fine (46s/56s).	Good knitting yarn — baby clothes, shawls, sweaters, scarves, etc. Excellent for weaving.
Perendale	Crisp handle, long staple, fairly coarse (50s/60s).	Rugs, wall hangings, hard wearing sweaters.
Suffolk	Soft handle, medium fine (58s/60s), short staple.	Usually carded for spinning. Caps, scarves, etc.
Southdown	Soft handle, medium fine (58s/60s), short staple.	Knitted garments etc.
English Leicester	Crisp handle, fairly coarse (40s/46s), long staple, lustrous.	Rugs, wall hangings, weaving into garments.

Australian wool for handspinning

(by courtesy of the South Australian Ministry of Agriculture and Fisheries)

Breed	Wool description	Fibre diameter – count – crimp relationship			Staple length (cm) (12 months growth)	Comments	Uses
		Quality or count	Microns	Crimps per 25 mm			
Merino	**Superfine**	70s and higher	19 and finer	14 to 15 and higher	5 to 7	Difficult to spin. Generally too short, parts and dyes poorly and felts easily.	Not recommended for beginners.
	Fine	64s	21 to 22	12 to 13	7.5 to 10	Spin slowly with little tension in order to preserve softness and firmness. Ply firmly.	All fine knitting and crochet: hair pin lace, babywear, shawls, light jumpers and cardigans.
	Medium	60s	23 to 24	10 to 11	8 to 11	Usually very good spinning. Dye evenly and well.	Weaves: lace stoles and evening fabrics. Suitable for weft.
							Not suitable for heavy knitwear, because constant washing causes matting and shrinkage.
	Strong	58s	25 to 26	7 to 9	9 to 12		Heavier knitted and crocheted outerwear.
	Extra-strong	56s to 50s	27 to 30	5 to 6 and lower	10 to 12		
Comeback Polwarth Cormo Zenith Polmo	**Comeback**	60s to 58s	23 to 26	7 to 11	10 to 15	Generally longer staple length, and easier to spin than Merino of similar quality. Shrinkage much less than Merino. Dye evenly and well.	Knitting and crochet: very suitable for babywear and adult lacy knitwear, light to medium weight jumpers and cardigans. Weaves: suitable for light fabrics requiring good draping qualities, particularly lace weaves.

Breed	Classification	Quality count				Spinning notes	Uses
Cross-bred Corriedale	**Fine crossbred**	56s to 54s	27 to 29	4 to 6	10 to 15	Easy to comb and spin. Spin finer than required but do not overspin. Good breed for looms, and elasticity of yarn overcomes tension problems. Dyes well.	Knitting and crochet: finer qualities suitable for baby-wear, lacy summer weight, lacy blouses, medium to heavy cardigans and jumpers. Weaves: finer qualities suitable for stoles, lightweight tweed. Stronger qualities suitable for rugs, wall hangings, carpets.
	Medium cross-bred	50s to 48s	30 to 33	2 to 3	12 to 17		
English long wool 1. Border Leicester 2. Lincoln 2. Cheviot 4. English Leicester 5. Romney Marsh 6. Perendale	**Strong cross-bred**	46s to 44s	34 to 36	1 to 2	14 to 20	Dye extremely well. Beware of kemp in the Cheviot. Spin with firm tension.	Knitting and crochet: finer qualities suitable for heavy skiwear and hard wearing outer garments, pram covers, blankets, berets. Weaving: rugs, carpets, wall hangings, heavy tweed fabric, bags.
	Extra-strong cross-bred	40s and lower	37 and higher	less than 1	18 to 25		
Short wools or downs 1. Dorset 2. Ryeland 3. South Suffolk 4. Shropshire 5. Hampshire 6. Dorset Down 7. Southdown 8. Suffolk Merino × Downs		64s to 50s	21 to 30	4 to 12	5 to 9	Usually too short, spongy and parts poorly. Crimp and staples usually poorly defined.	Not suitable for beginners. If longer than 7.5cm, with practice can be spun readily. Useful where elasticity in the yarn is required. Knitting and crochet: blankets, rug hooking, shawls, light jumpers and cardigans. Weave: uncrushable fabric e. g. tweed

THE SHEEP OF THE UNITED STATES OF AMERICA
(By courtesy of the American Sheep Producers' Council)

Comparison of Grades

Over a period of many years, man's attempt to describe wool precisely in terms of words and numbers has evolved through several phases.

Oldest of the systems is called the blood system. Evolving from the blood system was the count system which is a somewhat more technical classification of wool. Third, and most accurate, is the micron system.

The blood system was originally derived from the fine wool Merino and Rambouillet sheep. Their wool was called FINE. If a sheep was one-half Rambouillet or Merino and one-half another breed, usually an English mutton-type breed, the resultant fibres were almost always coarser or larger in cross section diameter than the pureblood. These wools were called one-half blood. The same principle applies for the three-eighths blood and quarter blood wools which describe the amount of fine wool breeding behind the particular sheep that produced the wool.

The numerical count system is a more technical classification of wool in terms of fibre diameter. This count refers to the number of 'hanks' of yarn, each 560 yards long, which can be spun from one pound of wool top. Thus, a 64's wool would yield 35,840 yards (560 yards times 64) or 107,520 feet of yarn. This is equal to 20.4 miles of yarn that could be spun from one pound of 64's top.

The micron count system is a substantially more technical and accurate measurement of the average diameter of wool fibre in a given lot of wool. The micron (1/25,000 of an inch) is used as the actual average diameter measurement. An 80's wool which averages 18.1 microns is less than one half the average diameter of a Common and Braid 36's which has an average diameter of 39.7 microns.

The micron system was largely developed at the Denver Wool Laboratory, USDA, under the direction of Mr Elroy M. Pohle. There is a growing effort to institute the use of the micron system in the technical description of wools for tariff classification. Eventually this system may become the standard for describing wools in the United States.

Breeds of Sheep and Grades of Wool

Fine wool breeds
American, or Delaine-Merino	64's to 80's
Rambouillet	62's to 70's

Crossbreed wool breeds
Corriedale	50's to 60's
Columbia	50's to 60's
Panama	50's to 58's
Romeldale	58's to 60's
Targhee	58's to 60's

Medium wool breeds
Southdown	56's to 60's
Shropshire	48's to 56's
Hampshire	48's to 56's
Suffolk	48's to 56's
Oxford	46's to 50's
Dorset	48's to 56's
Cheviot	48's to 56's

Long wool breeds
Lincoln	36's to 46's
Cotswold	36's to 40's
Romney	40's to 48's

While these are commonly accepted limits for breeds of sheep and grades of wool, individuals of any of these breeds might yield a wool outside these count limitations.

Border Leicester, Cotswold, Lincoln and Romney
The so-called 'long wool' breeds, with coarse wool grading from 36's to as high as 48's in the case of the Border Leicester and the Romney. These sheep are extremely big-bodied and grow much longer wool than other breeds. They may sometimes produce a staple (wool fibre length) up to 10 inches long in a season. The coarseness of the wool makes it less desirable than that of certain other breeds, yet for certain areas, such as those with extremely high rainfall, these breeds have many advantages.

Cheviot
A medium-woolled, white-face producer developed in France. Wool grades mostly at 48's to 56's. The Cheviot is a combined lamb and wool producer, though not extensively used in the United States.

Columbia
One of the few breeds developed in the United States. Stabilised from a cross of a Rambouillet ram with a Lincoln ewe. Wool ranges from 50's to 60's but largely groups in the 56's. This breed was developed in an effort to combine the wool-producing qualities of the Rambouillet and the range-producing qualities of the Lincoln.

Corriedale
Wool grades from 50's to 60's. A white-face New Zealand breed that is a good combination wool and lamb producer. This breed has been declining in number in range country as demands for larger-bodied sheep increase.

Delaine
Another wool breed developed from the basic Merino, somewhat smoother-bodied, otherwise very much like the Merino.

Dorset
The Dorset breed was developed in England. The Dorset is a medium-sized sheep with a very white, strong, close fleece of wool. It's a good meat producer and its wool is in the high medium grade.

Hampshire, Shropshire, Suffolk and Oxford
All these breeds are of the meat or lamb producing type, and originated in England. All have brown or black heads, noses, feet and legs. They are medium wool producers. Wool grades from 48's to 58's with some in the 60's. Because black fibres tend to show up in the wool, it is usually discounted. Wool production per fleece is much lighter than in the fine-wool breeds. These sheep and crosses of them with other breeds, are

the best lamb producers. Most of these breeds, with the exception of Suffolk and Hampshires, are raised in smaller farm flocks.

Merino
Produces very fine diameter wool. Originated in Spain, the Merino tends to be small-bodied with many long loose folds of skin. Wool sometimes grades in as high as 80's. Strictly a wool producer, as the lamb carcase is narrow and leggy.

Montadale
This sheep was developed from a cross between a Cheviot and Columbia, and is a relatively new breed. Its characteristics include a small head with the face and legs devoid of wool.

Navajo
Producer of extremely coarse wool. Used almost exclusively by the Navajo Indians in the production of Navajo blankets and rugs. This wool amounts to less than 5 per cent of total U.S. wool production.

Panama
Another United States breed developed by using the reverse cross that resulted in the Columbia. Wool has been held somewhat finer than in the Columbia, but the body development has not been as large.

Rambouillet
Developed in France and Spain from the basic Merino breed. Larger bodied, slightly coarser wool, grading from 62's to 70's, more desirable carcase, but not as good from the standpoint of lamb production as many other breeds. This breed is used extensively in the range country.

Southdown
Southdowns are the oldest English breed and were first brought to America in large numbers in 1880. They produce excellent carcases and are used primarily in the Midwest and East in the farm flock States.

Targhee
The Targhee was developed by the United States Sheep Experiment Station at Boise, Idaho, and is a cross between a Rambouillet and a long-wool producing breed. It produces high quality apparel-type wool and the sheep are adapted to rugged ranch conditions in the West.

Appendix C

BOOKLIST

Spinning
BAINES, PATRICIA. *Spinning Wheels, Spinners and Spinning*, Batsford, London, 1977.
DAVENPORT, ELSIE. *Your Handspinning*, Sylvan Press, London, 1953.
FANNIN, ALLEN. *Handspinning: Art and Technique*, van Nostrand Reinhold, New York, 1970.
HORNE, BEVERLEY. *Fleece in Your Hands*, New Zealand Spinning, Weaving and Woolcrafts Society 1974, (revised edn Interweave Press, Colorado, 1979).
LINDER, OLIVE & HARRY. *Handspinning Cotton*, Cotton Squares, Arizona, 1977.
SIMMONS, PAULA. *Spinning and Weaving with Wool*, Pacific Search Press, Seattle, 1977.
TEAL, PETER. *Hand Woolcombing and Spinning*, Blandford Press, Poole, 1976.
THOMPSON, G. B. *Spinning Wheels*, Ulster Museum catalogue, Belfast, 1963.

Sheep
EASTWOOD, MARSHALL & WICKHAM. *Sheep Breeds in New Zealand*, Ministry of Agriculture and Fisheries, Wellington, NZ, 1978.
McDOUGALL, D. S. A. *British Sheep*, National Sheep Assn., Berkhamstead, 1976.

Knitting and Woolcrafts
DUNCAN, MOLLY. *Creative Crafts with Wool and Flax*, Reed, Wellington, NZ, 1971.
MON TRICOT (ED.). *Knitting Dictionary of Stitches, Knitters Basic Book 1, Knitters Basic Book 2*, Mon Tricot, Paris.
THOMAS, MARY. *Mary Thomas's Knitting Book*, Hodder & Stoughton, London, 1938. (Reprinted by Dover, New York.)
THOMPSON, GLADYS. *Patterns for Guernseys, Jerseys and Arans*, Batsford, London, 1960. (Reprinted by Dover, New York).
TURNER, DOROTHEA. *Ways into Woolcraft*, published by the author, Wellington, NZ, 1978.

Colour and Dyeing
BROOKLYN BOTANIC GARDEN. *Natural Plant Dyeing, Dye Plants and Dyeing*, Brooklyn Botanic Gardens, New York, 1964.
DUNCAN, MOLLY. *Exploring Colour and Design for Handweavers*, Reed, Wellington, NZ, 1978.
DYER, ANN. *Dyes from Natural Sources*, G. Bell & Sons, London, 1976.
GRAE, IDA. *Nature's Colours*, Macmillan, New York, 1974.
HICKETHIER, ALFRED. *Colour Matching and Mixing*, Batsford, London, 1970.
HUTCHINSON, AMY. *Plant Dyeing*, Daily Telegraph, Napier,

NZ, 1941 (distributed by New Zealand Spinning Weaving and Woolcraft Society).

LLOYD, JOYCE. *Dyes from Plants of Australia and New Zealand*, Reed, Wellington, NZ, 1971.

THURSTON, VIOLETTA. *The Use of Vegetable Dyes*, Dryad Press, Leicester (revised edition, 1967).

Plant Identification

ALVIN, K. L. & KERSHAW, K. A. *Observer's Book of Lichens*, Frederick Warne, London, 1976.

BRETAUDEAU, J. *Trees: a Little Guide in Colour*, Paul Hamlyn, London.

FITTER, R. & A. *Wild Flowers of Britain and Northern Europe*, Collins, Glasgow, 1974.

GREY-WILSON, C. *Alpine Flowers of Britain and Europe*, Collins, London, 1979.

MARTIN, W. & CHILDS. J. *New Zealand Lichens*, Reed, Wellington, NZ, 1972.

PARHAM, B. E. V. & HEALY, A. J. *Common Weeds in New Zealand*, Government Printer, Wellington, NZ, 1976.

POOLE, A. L. & ADAMS, NANCY. *Trees and Shrubs of New Zealand*, Government Printer, Wellington, NZ, 1962.

Weaving

Of general interest:

BLACK, MARY. *New Key to Weaving*, Bruce Publishing Co, Milwaukee, 1949.

CHETWYND, HILARY. *Simple Weaving*, Studio Vista, London, 1969.

DAVISON, MARGUERITE P. *A Handweaver's Pattern Book*, M. P. Davison, Swarthmore, 1949.

HALSEY, M. & YOUNGMARK, L. *Foundations of Weaving*, David & Charles, Newton Abbott, 1975.

HELD, SHIRLEY. *Weaving: a Handbook for Fibre Craftsmen*, Holt, Rinehart, Winston, New York, 1973.

LARSEN, J. L. & THORPE, A. S. *Elements of Weaving*, Doubleday, New York, 1967.

MILES, VERA. *Weaving Patterns for the Two-way Loom*, Dryad Press, Leicester, 3rd edn, 1971.

MILLEN, ROGER. *Weave Your Own Tweeds*, M. P. Davison, Swarthmore, 1948.

PLATH, IONA. *Handweaving*, Scribner, New York, 1964.

SIMPSON, L. & WEIR, M. *The Weaver's Craft*, Dryad Press, Leicester, 1932.

STRAUB, MARIANNE. *Handweaving and Cloth Design*, Pelham, London, 1977.

TIDBALL, HARRIET. *The Weaver's Book*, Macmillan, New York, 1962.

WILSON, JEAN. *Weaving You Can Wear*, van Nostrand Reinhold, New York, 1973.

ZNAMEROWSKI, NELL. *Step by Step Weaving*, Golden Press, New York, 1967.

Of more specialised interest:

ALBERS, ANNI. *On Weaving*, Wesleyan University Press, Conn., 1965, and Studio Vista, 1974.

ATWATER, MARY. *Byways in Handweaving*, Macmillan, New York, 1954.

BEUTLICH, TADEK. *The Technique of Woven Tapestry*, Batsford, London, 1971.

BURNHAM, DOROTHY. *Cut My Cote*, Royal Ontario Museum, Toronto, 1973.

COLLINGWOOD, PETER. *The Technique of Rug Weaving*, Faber & Faber, London, 1968.

CYRUS, ULLA. *A Manual of Swedish Handweaving*, Branford, Mass., 1956.

d'HARCOURT, RAOUL. *Textiles of Ancient Peru*, University of Washington Press, 1962.

FREY, BERTA. *Designing and Drafting for Handweavers*, Collier Macmillan, New York, 1958.

HOFFMAN, MARTA. *The Warpweighted Loom*, University of Oslo Press, 1964.

HOOPER, LUTHER. *Handloom Weaving*, John Hogg, London, 1910.

KLEIN, BERNAT. *Eye for Colour*, Collins, London, 1965.

LARSEN, J. L. & CONSTANTINE, M. *Beyond Craft: the Art Fabric*, van Nostrand Reinhold, New York, 1973.

PENDLETON, MARY. *Navajo and Hopi Weaving*, Collier Macmillan, New York, 1974.

TABER, B. & ANDERSON, M. *Backstrap Weaving*, Watson-Guptill, New York, 1975.

TOVEY, JOHN. *The Technique of Weaving*, Batsford, London, 1965.

Periodicals

The Australian Handweaver and Spinner. Handweavers and Spinners Guild of Australia.

Shuttle Spindle and Dyepot. Handweavers Guild of America.

The Weaver's Journal. Association of Guilds of Weavers, Spinners and Dyers, United Kingdom.

The Web. New Zealand Spinning Weaving and Woolcrafts Society.

Appendix D

GLOSSARY OF WEAVING TERMS

Angel sticks (lary sticks)
Pair of sticks placed from front to back of the loom to support raddle, reed etc., while dressing the loom.

Apron
Canvas tacked to warp roller or cloth roller. (Cords are often used instead of canvas.)

Apron stick
Stick to which warp yarn is attached; secured by canvas or cords to warp or cloth rollers.

Back beam (back bar, warp bar, warp beam, slabstock)
Timber bar similar to breast beam but at the rear of the loom.

Beaming
Action of winding warp on to the warp roller.

Beater (batten, sley)
Swinging frame housing reed with which the weft is beaten into place.

Block
A unit of pattern.

Breast beam
Timber bar at front of loom over which cloth passes on its journey to the cloth roller.

Castle (cape)
Superstructure of loom housing and supporting the shafts.

Choke ties
Tight ties around the warp to keep it orderly during beaming.

Cloth roller (cloth beam)
Roller, at the front of the loom, on which the cloth is wound up as weaving progresses.

Cop (cone, cheese)
Factory-prepared packages of yarn, of cylindrical or conical shapes.

Cross (figure of eight, lease)
A crossing-over of yarn during warpmaking to keep the portees in order.

Cross-sticks (figure-of-eight sticks, lease-rods, shed-sticks)
Pair of sticks used to secure and identify the cross after the warp has been made.

Dent
Space between teeth of reed or raddle.

Draft
Diagram indicating threading, tie-up and treadling sequence. Also used as synonym for 'pattern'.

Draw
In phrases such as 'straight draw' this refers to the action of drawing the warp ends through the eyes of the heddles.

Draw-down
Graphic representation of the interlacement of the weave; usually on squared paper.

Dressing the loom
All processes preparatory to weaving, but often used of beaming-threading-sleying.

End
Correct name for a warp thread.

Entry, entering
In phrases such as 'straight entry' this means the threading of yarns through the eyes of heddles. See also 'Draw'.

Fell
The edge of the weaving where the last pick was beaten into place.

Fingers (castles)
Wooden supports for holding the shafts steady during threading.

Fulling (milling)
Term used by handweavers to describe wet-finishing of cloth, especially woollen cloth.

Heddle (heald, yeald)
Strings or wires with central eyes by means of which warp ends are raised or lowered. (Strictly, heddles are of string and healds are of wire.)

Heddle-box
Timber structure containing shafts on a table loom.

Heddle-reed
Wooden or metal plate perforated with holes and slots, used to make the shed on some simple looms.

Heddle shaft (harness)
Collection of heddles supported in a framework of some kind. In the US 'harness' is the usual term; in older English terminology 'harness' meant a set of four shafts.

Jack (jack-lever, couper)
Pivoted levers used to raise or lower the shafts.

Knee-beam
Timber bar found on some treadle looms to keep cloth away from the weaver's knees.

Lamm (march)
Lever connecting treadles to shafts or treadles to jacks.

Overshot
Popular form of pattern weaving derived from twill. A thicker pattern weft 'shoots' or floats over the background, producing a brocade-like motif.

Paddle
Hand-held plate (timber, metal or plastic) perforated with holes; used to keep yarns separated when making a warp with several threads at a time.

Pawl
Metal or wooden tongue which engages in the teeth of a ratchet.

Pick (shot)
One row of weft.

Portee
One return journey around warping-board or mill; the portee may consist of two or more ends, depending on the number of cops used simultaneously. (From French *porter*, to carry.)

Raddle (spreader)
Coarse comb used to spread the warp to the correct width during beaming.

Ratchet
Toothed disc used in conjunction with a pawl to secure tension on rollers.

Reed
Kind of comb, closed both top and bottom; used to space out warp ends and to beat the weft. Formerly made of strips of reed, now of metal strips.

Rigid-heddle
Alternative name for heddle-reed.
Rising shed
The shafts rise when the loom is operated.
Sett
Number of warp ends and weft picks in a square unit of cloth. (In Scotland, the colour order of the warp for a tartan.)
Shaft
See Heddle-shaft.
Shed
Space created between the upper and lower layers of the warp.
Shedding
Action of making a shed.
Shuttle race
Timber support for the shuttle attached to, or part of, beater.
Singles
Yarn that is not plied.
Sinking shed
The shafts sink when the loom is operated.
Sizing
Coating the warp with a substance to make it more manageable.
Sleying
Drawing the warp ends through the dents of the reed.

Tabby
Word sometimes used instead of 'plain weave'.
Take-up
Loss of length caused by the interlacing of warp and weft.
Tenter-frame (stenter)
Contrivance, seldom seen outside industry, for drying cloth under tension.
Tie-up (chain draft)
Order in which treadles are tied to the lamms, or the diagram giving instructions for this.
Treadle (pedal)
Foot-operated lever for raising or lowering shafts.
Treadle loom (pedal loom, floor loom, foot loom)
Loom operated by treadles.
Warp
The lengthwise elements in a piece of weaving.
Warp (warp chain)
The yarn made up as a warp ready for beaming and which may have been crocheted into a chain.
Warp roller (warp beam)
Roller at back of loom which holds unwoven warp.
Warp sticks
Wooden slats used as packing on the warp roller.
Weft
The transverse elements in a piece of weaving. (Woof is obsolete.)

Appendix E

ADDRESSES OF NEW ZEALAND SUPPLIERS, ETC.

Note: The authors have personal experience of New Zealand suppliers only. Readers in other countries are advised to refer to their local craft organisations for information and addresses.

Associations
The New Zealand Spinning Weaving and Woolcrafts Society, Inc. Private Bag, Havelock North, can put you in touch with the nearest spinners' and weavers' organisation.

Dyes
CIBA, manufactured by CIBA-Geigy (NZ) Ltd, available through weavers' guilds.
Panhue, distributed by Elizabeth Simm, 47 Baddeley Avenue, Auckland 5. Also available through craft supply shops.

Equipment and Supplies
Ashford Handcrafts Ltd, Box 180, Ashburton (spinning wheels).
Creative Woolcraft Supplies, Box 39, Waikanae (craft equipment, books, supplies).
Fred's Shed Ltd, 47a Martin Street, Monaco, Nelson (looms).

Charles Fuller, R D Mangapai, Northland (looms).
Heritage Looms, Box 33889, Takapuna; workshop at 5 Cleveland Road, Parnell, Auckland (jack looms).
Pipy Craft Ltd, 228 Wellington Street, Howick (spinning wheels, carders, flick carders, looms, etc).
John Rappard, Box 1121 Dunedin (Little Peggy spinning wheel).
Sleeping Beauty Craft Products, Box 1512, Auckland (spinning wheels, looms, carding machines, etc).
Sunflower Looms, Valley Farm, Sunshine Bay, Eastbourne, Wellington (looms).
David Thorp, Loburn, R D 2 Rangiora (looms).
The Wheel and the Loom, 146 Manukau Road, Epsom, Auckland (spinning wheels, looms, fleece, books, etc).
Woodspin Industries NZ Ltd, Box 9637, Wellington (Nagy wheel).

Fleece
Michael Hastie, Te Mahanga Road, R D 11, Hastings (local and overseas mail orders for individually packed fleeces).
Woolstores, especially those in Canterbury, Hawke's Bay, Marlborough, Napier, Otago and Southland.

Index

Figures refer to page numbers; those in **bold type** refer to illustrations and their captions.